A Pocket Full Of Mischief

By
Paul J. Ankorne

A Pocket Full of Mischief
First Edition
Published by DreamStar Books, November 2004

Lasyard House
Underhill Street
Bridgnorth
Shropshire
WV16 4BB
Tel: 0870 777 3339
e-mail: info@dreamstarbooks.com

Set in 'Garamond'

Printed and bound in Great Britain by Antony Rowe Ltd

About the author

Paul J. Ankorne was born in 1936 in London. He became an orphan at the age of 3½ yearsin late 1939, at the outbreak of the Second World War and taken into care for the next 13 years, at Ashford Residential School, ran by the LCC. (London County Council.)

At the age of 13 he won an art scholarship to Wandsworth College of Art in London for 3 years.

On his 16th birthday, he was thrown out of Ashford to make his own way without any assistance and was lucky enough to get a part as Scenery Artist at Lime Grove TV Studios until he was called up by the British Army, just before his 18th birthday. He did 3 years active service with the Rifle Brigade in Kenya and Malaya before being demobbed in Singapore in 1957, the only release allowed that year by Far Eastern Command, to make his own way back to the UK.

Paul decided to make his way overland from Singapore to India, via Malaya, Thailand and Burma, into India, which includes 'Forbidden Journey' in Northern Burma to Assam. (India.) Once there, he took up a number of jobs to earn a crust ending up as a tea planter in Northern Assam for 3 years, before returning to the UK in 1961.

After readjustment, which was painful, he tried a number of different career moves, from Salesman to The Police, and eventually Social Work, until his eventual retirement on the Island of Bute, off the West Coast of Scotland, where he now lives.

Married, (now divorced,) with four adult children all living in Scotland. Paul has designed and built his own home and although now fully retired, enjoys doing art and is undertaking to write a trilogy with this, his first book, 'A Pocket Full of Mischief', now in print. He is well into his second book, 'Mischief in Long Trousers', which is all about the adventurous side of a very full life.

.

Dedicated to Bobby

CONTENTS   Page

PART ONE
3 To 8 Years Old

CHAPTER ONE

It was a miserable, late November afternoon in 1939. Britain had already declared war with Germany, with the signs of desolation, littering the streets of London all around. I sat feeling devastated, squashed into the back seat of the little black Ford saloon car, as it sped along the highway. The car with its occupants, was heading away from London, in a light drizzle of rain.

The weather was typically English for the time of year with a heavy damp fog hanging in a grey sky, like a dirty net curtain. As the drizzle became a constant downpour, the single windscreen wiper was fighting at full speed to keep the deluge of water clear of the split windscreen. I knew nothing about our proposed destination, to where we were all going, nor the reason why.

As the rain got even heavier, loud splashing noises thrown up by the tyres rushing through puddles became even more audible. The big burly driver sitting alone up front was having difficulty with visibility seeing through the split window ahead.

The scene both outside and in was depressive in the extreme. Sitting beside me on the back seat was a big woman called Mrs Rumple stuffing her fat jowls with sweets called mischiefs. She took up so much room she was sitting more on top of me than beside me.

This world I was leaving behind me, as I sat on the back seat feeling very confused and very frightened and in my pathetic state, I wondered why my own little world was tumbling down about my ears.

In spite of the rotunda frame occupying almost all of the back seat beside me I was trembling in fear not understanding anything that was happening. I was just three and a half years old, slightly built and small in stature for my age, and very frightened.

To an outside observer I could be seen clinging desperately to the arm of the fat lady sitting beside me. Mrs Rumple was a L.C.C.

Welfare Officer who was in the process of discharging her duty as escort. She was big, and I mean big, she spread herself over the back seat like a beached whale. A lady in her mid forties, wearing a pinkish blouse and her business suit, hat, shoes and handbag all in black. A sever mass of tight black curly hair spilled out below the brim of her hat but somehow didn't belong to her. Her fat round cherubic face was caked in thick pink make-up with her very shocking red lipstick mouth designed to devour little boys as easy as demolishing a large fresh cream cake. Her hanging jowls constantly on the move munching sweet after sweet while humming like a bee collecting pollen from flower to flower. Her constant hum was getting on my wick, sounding like a single engined aircraft, droning above our heads.

The name Rumple, I thought, was perfect, as if God himself had handed it to her personally. At this time I was too lost in my own bewildered thoughts, just about the same time as the last of the daylight began to fade. We were now going through a small village called Ashford, as the driver turned to my chaperone to inform her we would soon be there. Where, I wondered.

Upon Rumple's ample lap was a small brown dirty paper parcel with my name tag attached. The car slowed then turned off the road coming to an abrupt halt as the driver wound down his window. He spoke briefly to a man in uniform who looked like a copper, I'm going to prison I thought, as I felt a trickle of piss run down my leg. As we paused for a few moments at the entrance in front of a pair of huge impressive gates, I could see a grey ribbon of driveway stretching ahead into the institution. The driver took a right fork along the drive and within a few minutes parked outside the entrance of a large collection of buildings.

My escort looked at me sharply as if I was about to do a runner as she squeezed out of her side of the car. Mrs Rumple instructed me to cross the back seat to her where she awaited for me to block any escape route.

The Councils' little black car had finally unloaded its cargo. The sixteen mile trip from London to Ashford had taken just over an hour to complete its journey, although to one so small it seemed an eternity.

"I haven't got all day" fatty shouted at me as if she was my prison warder. It was obvious this fat woman of few words had suddenly found her voice and was anxious to be rid of me, so she could return to more important matters. With impatience she pulled me from the car into the pouring rain outside. I felt her podgy sweaty hand enclose around my small mitt as she dragged me through puddles towards a closed door. With me in one firmly held hand and my grubby brown parcel jammed under her armpit, she pushed open the door as I tripped over the step into the floor inside.

Another squirt of piss ran down the inside of my leg. Still dragging me along a stone clad corridor to get to another door where she knocked before entering with me in tow. Fatty was determined to give me no chance to abscond. The bright lights of the matrons' office made me squint, as fatty deposited my brown paper parcel onto the large office desk in front of us.

Miss Richards surveyed the pathetic bundle of wretchedness in front of her, noticing the wet patch in front of my shorts. Miss Richards, the matron, signed some official piece of paper denoting she was now responsible for me, like taking delivery of a registered letter from the postman.

Fatty departed in a hurry.

The matron came from behind her desk, leant over me, cooing in my ear like an expectant female dove. "Let's have a look at you, my darling," she cooed. "You are very small," she said. She bustled about the floor like a practised ballerina fussing over me like one of her own.

"Do you need a wee wee?" she asked looking down at my shorts.

Dropping my head even lower afraid to answer her I continued to study her office floor.

She gently raised my head upwards with her hand under my chin so she could look me eye to eye. "No Miss" I said.

Miss Richards, the matron, was a plumpish kindly figure of a woman of medium height and homely proportions. She had vivid blue kind eyes, topped with hair of pure silver that suited her comfortable figure of authority. She was also well rehearsed in dealing with little children, but with a manner that belied her skills.

When she stood directly in front of you she seemed like a giant especially to any three year old.

"Paul, darling" she oozed, "I'm sure you will get to love your new home once you have settled in."

Was she going to be my new mummy? I wondered, with her talking about home and such. It seemed like a very large strange place to be called home, I thought. So this was to be my abode for the next thirteen years and I instinctively knew I wasn't going to like it!

"Come with me darling", the matron still laying it on thickly as she offered her hand, which I refused. I followed her from her office as she walked passed several doors to a door on its own at the end of a narrow passageway.

I suddenly remembered my brown paper parcel on her desk and hesitated as if I should return.

Miss Richards opened the single door then waited for me to step through. I suddenly backed up wanting to return to the remnants of my past, sitting on the matron's desk.

She took hold of my hand as we both stood still with this vast view of a thousand kids all sitting at tables in this place called the Grand Dining Hall. The panoramic view that attacked all my senses also took my breath away and with my spare hand I pinched the end of my dick to stem the flow of more urine.

I didn't know what I expected but the Dining room was bigger than a football field, which made me gasp with awe. There were eight rows of a dozen tables, each table seating some ten kids. The children varied in age groups from toddlers to teenagers. The first half of this huge Hall was full of boys and the other half nearest the kitchen area was full of girls.

We had entered this place alongside a full size theatre stage, which was directly opposite the kitchens at the far end. I was soon to learn that although there were almost an equal number of girls and boys, never the twain would mix.

Both east and west sides of this Grand Hall were the largest pair of huge arch top doors which led respectively to each of the different sex accommodation areas.

The strangest sight of all was the sea of hybrid faces all full of intense purpose, bent over their plates with such concentration as if perhaps they were fed only once a day. Not a word was spoken and save for the clinking of cutlery and china the atmosphere was unnerving. The concentration on so many faces with the sole intent of cleaning their plates of every morsel of food was hypnotic as well as abnormal. What was this place, this institution of misery I was to be part of and which I had no say in the matter?

I was taken to an empty chair and told to sit as the matron left me, bustling away like a friendly hippo on ice-skates.

The rest of the boys at the table ignored me, they only had eyes for the food on their plates. I felt even more alone as I stared blankly at my empty space on the table in front of me. I presumed a plate of food would soon be set before me and, although I was hungry, I didn't feel like eating anyway. I think just being among hoards of kids inside such a gigantic building I found it to be intimidating, an alien environment. A plate of food was eventually placed before me but I made no attempt to eat. I sat there looking at it strangely, not recognising what kind of food it was.

To be sitting in a room so full of kids where no one was allowed to utter a word was depressive, as well as unnatural.

I could feel the welling of tears surging upwards, pushing their way through my eyes in a steady stream accompanied by sobbing. The sudden total silence, followed by the pitch of a high shrill whistle blast startled me making me almost fall off my chair.

In one movement, like a single body, everybody stood up behind their chairs. Not sure what to do I just sat there as I knew, to do otherwise on legs of jelly, was unwise.

I was to learn later, most commands at Ashford were done by this system of whistles, like some military organisational exercise.

I looked at my plate, now cold, feeling sick and conspicuous, fully aware that I was the only one in this huge den of iniquity still sitting down. With my head bowed like an ostrich taking cover, I stared into the damp patch in the front of my shorts. Then I became aware that, table by table, the boys and girls marched out of the Dining room in order, and in total silence.

Within minutes the entire Hall was empty, save for the kitchen staff, which was exclusively female.

I sat on my own in the comfort of knowing that I was at least free from two thousand eyes staring at me. Now alone, I could feel the tension flow from my body and as I stopped sobbing I began to relax. What am I supposed to do next, I wondered?

Looking about me without restraint, getting bolder by the second, I noticed a gangly urchin come back through the big arch doorway, coming towards my table.

His gait was like a monkey with a pronounced spring in his step as he pranced towards me. He stopped within a few feet of me, abruptly giving me a winning smile that went from ear to ear.

Bobby had big brown deep eyes you could have bathed in, topped with a bush of dark brown unkempt hair that was so unruly it had a life of its own. He was just five and a half years old, with attitude. Bob was also a good six inches taller than me and moved with a confident swagger, almost cocky in style. His arms, which hung loosely either side of his lean body, were too long in proportion to the rest of his frame. He looked down on me wearing that winning smile across his dial, like an infectious rash.

"Hi" said Bob, "I'm going to be your big boy and look after you." I looked up at him as if he was talking gibberish, not having a clue what the hell he was talking about, not understanding the Ashford jargon. He could see I was confused, so changing tack he asked me what my name was, doing his best to get at least one word out of me. So I gave him one!

"Paul" I said.

"Paul what?" said Bob with encouragement.

"Just Paul" I said being more talkative.

Bob started to chatter to himself doing his very best to break the ice, then soon decided a different tack might be better.

"Right" said the voice of authority "follow me Paul," Bob ordered. So I got out of my chair, took hold of his hand as he gently led me out of the Grand Dining room.

"You must be tired" said Bob "so I'll get you showered and help you into your bed, next to my own" said Bob.

Bob was now firmly in charge and I felt completely at ease in his competent care. Hand in hand we walked down the long quarter mile flagstone corridor, to the dayroom and showers.

The shower room was noisy, full of boisterous boys of every age group. A good one hundred feet long, it ran the full length adjoining the day room, capable of showering between eighty to a hundred boys at any one time. The merriment of boys' behaviour was in complete contrast to my very first vision of the Dining Hall. The culture shock made me cling to Bob like a baby suckling its mother's breasts. At one end only, there were six slipper baths that only boys of fourteen or over were permitted to use. Bob undressed himself, and then stripped me also to the buff. He took me into a newly vacated shower then, with a well soaped flannel, covered my body in suds.

He then did likewise to himself before shampooing both our heads, then held me with himself under the shower head to rinse us off. He towelled me off till I shone like a new pin, before drying himself off. He then stood me on the bench seat, turned his back on me while I climbed onto his back, as he gave me a piggyback up the stone stairs to the first floor dormitory.

As we came onto the landing, I whispered in Bob's ear "I need a wee wee".

Bob took me into the night toilets and indicated an empty cubicle. "No" I said "you must come in with me" I said nervously, "Okay" said Bob "but you hold your own dick, okay".

Still completely naked, he then put me into bed and went to fetch me a night shirt. Once he resettled me, he sat on my bedside talking away and reassuring me he was in the next bed, if anytime I needed him.

Like the dayroom downstairs, each dorm was about one hundred feet long by twenty feet wide. Forty beds in all, with twenty each side. Every other bed was in front of an eight foot high arch topped window, which because of the war raging outside, was totally blacked out to prevent any internal light being seen from outside. All the beds were spaced apart with military precision and each bed had a single bedside locker, just like the barracks on any army base.

Each bed was allowed a single pillow and bed making was similar to hospital beds, including the box mitred corners.

There was a single swing door at each end with a blue night light over the door. There was also a letterbox size glass window in each door, at adult eye level, set into the door. The floorboards running longitudinal were highly polished each day, as part of house cleaning routines, done every morning by the boys themselves before breakfast.

Bob was casually telling me all of this as he sat on my bed holding me in his arms.

As I began to feel drowsy, I looked up into his big brown eyes, like deep water ponds inviting you in for a swim, and fell over into the land of nod and deep sleep.

I decided I liked Bob, I liked him very much, I dreamed.

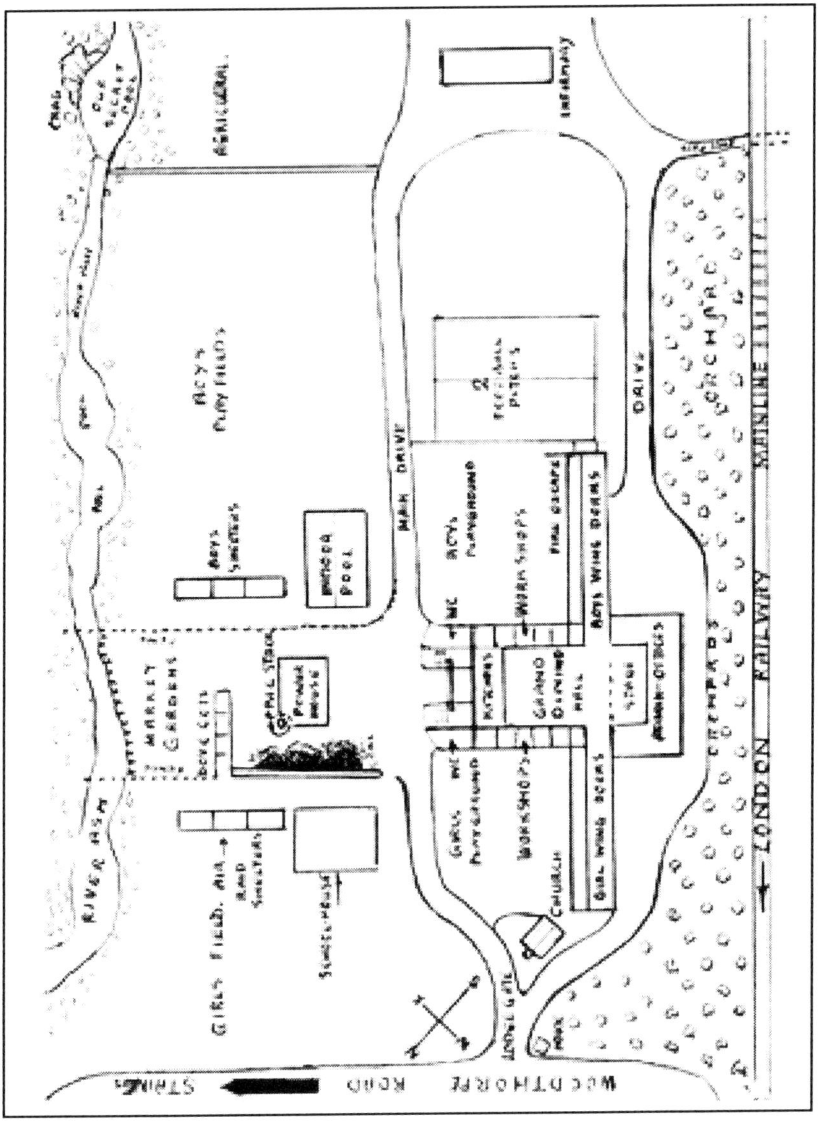
LONDON RAILWAY
ORCHARDS
ORCHARD
MAIN DRIVE
DRIVE
BOYS PLAY FIELDS
MARKET GARDENS
GRAND DINING HALL
WORKSHOPS
CHURCH
INFIRMARY
AGRICULTURAL
ROAD

CHAPTER TWO
The Regime

Ashford Residential School, Woodthorpe Road, Ashford in the county of Middlesex, is an Orphanage owned and run by the London County Council. (L.C.C.) This orphanage was the largest in the country, if not the whole of Europe. This institution provided employment to a good proportion of the population within the village of Ashford and outlying districts.

The entire estate was more than five hundred acres in size with a profusion of buildings, mainly built before the turn of the last century. The Victorian structures were very large and imposing on the eye, with prison or army like accommodation blocks in one continuous long edifice mass. The huge central block of the Grand Dining Hall with all its offices for administration attached, separated the girls and boys accommodation.

There was also an array of trade departments, a church, heated swimming pool, infirmary or hospital and a power house to generate all electricity required at Ashford. The power house also had the tallest chimney within a twenty five miles radius. On the top of this very high steeple-like structure was a lightning conductor for the whole of Ashford and the surrounding districts. This chimney was known affectionately as "the big stack" in Ashford jargon. Very awe inspiring, it was too! The entire estate complex, which also had orchards, market garden produce, along with agriculture, was designed to make the whole, totally self sufficient.

On the schools southern boundary was Woodthorpe Road and the 117 bus route going to Hounslow in one direction with Staines in the other. On its eastern boundary was the mainline railway going north to London.

The River Ash ran along its western flanks with agricultural farmland to the north of the infirmary.

I soon learnt the importance of the River Ash, which was to play such a vital role in endless hours of recreational play and many adventures in my future years to come.

In these early troubled war years nobody ever thought of absconding because, simply put, there was nowhere else to run.

The Ashford regime was draconian in extreme. The strictness, with all its rules and regulations, showed no mercy to any boy who flouted any of its rigid doctrine. With adopted Victorian values in its religious concepts, and especially in ethos on children's' behaviour, was carved in stone.

The discipline of punishments was both unforgiving and relentless to any boy who attempted any breaches of its rules. Corporal punishment was a bye word dished out daily for all kinds of misdemeanours, minor or otherwise. For example any trait of individuality that was often misconstrued or seen as a threat to the smooth running of this mighty machine was severely dealt with.

In fairness the efficient operation of successfully running such a large organisation of a thousand children brought its own difficulties.

The very fabric of Ashford as an institution could only be run as a military model, because to attempt a family orientation type model would have been impossible. There was no room for deviation with this number of children in care, and I use the term very loosely. Beside the usual forms of chastisement of belt, cane and even the cat o' nine tails when felt necessary, was very much a daily occurrence.

There were other forms of punishments commonly used such as extra household cleaning duties to occupy your leisure hours. Boisterous behaviour of any kind was generally discouraged for obvious reasons, as it was seen as not being conducive, or constructive towards acceptable behaviour.

The Ashford regime was none negotiable.

Boys being just that, would go to any length to flaunt or at least try to bend as many rules, they thought they could get away with. Life wouldn't be much fun otherwise.

The one system above all else that worked very well was what boys call 'big boy carers' or 'buddy boys', who would take on their responsibilities with pride. A smaller boy designated by staff to a big boys' charge. This may well have been designed to specifically help out staff shortages especially in times of war. Whatever the reason, it was a superb system which in the main worked very well indeed, as I well know from my own formative years of first hand experience.

This personal care on a one to one basis was in fact the backbone of Ashford, where all juniors had a big boy to show them the ropes, take care of their personal hygiene and most important, to protect them from bullies or sexual predators.

Not, on any occasion, did I ever see sexual abuse between any member of staff and a child. Child beating or mental abuse yes, but sexual, no. However, there were times of boys between themselves giving, and on rare occasions, forced sexual activities. There is not a boy's school anywhere, that doesn't have its share of homosexuality.

In this respect, Ashford was no exception, even if it was a very small minority.

I was most fortunate to have been given Bobby, who was two years my senior, as my big boy and protector. Keeping me out of trouble however, was a challenge he failed miserably at.

He failed, I think, because we were two peas from the same pod, but we did become inseparable as well as best friends. He did his very best to become angelic in his behaviour, hoping I too would copy, but this was doomed from the off.

His laid back easiness and attitude in all his dealings with me, gave me so many opportunities to take advantage of his gentle nature, winning him over became a walk in the park.

With a total of only four housemasters in control of our lives on a daily basis, there was no surprise this old tanker of a ship sprung a leak from time to time. These four housemasters were divided into two distinct teams of pairs.

One team comprised of Mr Walton and Mr Hammond, who worked in close harmony together. Mr Walton was the most senior ov all four masters and was also a strict disciplinarian. Ex-navy, in his mid fifties, he was the fittest man I knew, being a superb gymnast and a breath-taking swimmer, in charge of swimming within the school. Walton had an Adonis like physique to die for. He was also the strictest, about five feet ten inches in stature. The respect he commanded was of a hard, but very fair man. His counterpart couldn't be more different, as Mr Hammond was a good six footer with fair hair, to Walton's dark hair and had brown eyes and spoke with a distinct southern accent. He was seen as a gentle giant that loathed using physical punishment, which belied his boy handling skills that could often be very subtle.

The other team, or pair, was Mr Sims and Mr Gibb. Sims was ex-army and liked to think of himself as sergeant major material. Small in stature, about five foot seven inches tall with a fattish body and cocky gait. He was the pits. His love or worship for the cause was legendary and I don't believe a day went by where some young child didn't get a thrashing, deserved or otherwise.

He was a bully and a coward who got all his kicks by beating little boys.

I took an instant dislike to the man, nicknamed Hitler, because he wore a similar moustache on his otherwise feminine upper lip. He didn't care for me either, as he demonstrated on numerous occasions.

His sidekick was Mr Gibbs, an ex-RAF bomber pilot who had been invalided out of the services prior to the start of the Second War. Another six-footer, like Hammond, also with fair hair and also the most junior of the four, in his mid thirties. He very rarely resorted to physical forms of discipline and like Hammond preferred a more gentle approach. However Sims never let Gibbs forget who was in charge on their team.

With only a total of four masters in control of almost five hundred boys, things were difficult enough at any time, but when you consider only two masters were actually on duty at any one time, you maybe begin to understand the difficulties they faced at times.

The whistle blowing orders, many times a day, (three times a day for meals alone) was a powerful control device, which all boys soon accepted as normal. Like training a dog, to whistle commands, we too needed and always wanted to be fed. Hunger at Ashford was an almost daily feeling and everyone suffered equally. We were constantly reminded the whole country, because of the war, were on short rations. We were also told frequently how lucky we all were, as there were millions less fortunate than ourselves. Our problem, not knowing any different to argue the toss, was we in Ashford never saw these 'unfortunates'.

The different dormitory arrangements covered a total of four floors, which were divided into three age groups. The first housed the very youngest up to eight years old, with one ward set aside for babies up to three years old. In this group, the buddy system, already mentioned, flourished. The second group, with separate dormitories, housed Intermediates from eight to twelve years old, on the third floor. The last group housed the seniors of twelve to sixteen years old. Situated on the top floor, they required little or no supervision.

Each floor also had its own night time ablutions or toilets with the most seniors having extra facilities of showers and even a bath in their upstairs bathrooms.

The daily routine at Ashford had a sameness of repetition about it, punctuated in its construction by three meals a day, morning, noon and evening. All housework and cleaning duties were carried out by the boys themselves, dorm by dorm, before breakfast.

The day started at 6.30 a.m. every morning, six days a week, where every boy charged downstairs in their pyjamas, for early morning ablutions, before making their own beds and doing housework. All before breakfast at 8.00 a.m.

During this vital routine one master toured the dorms with the other on inspection outside the ablutions downstairs. Any boy found lacking in his household chores could find himself on other duties for as long as a week, which in itself was a good incentive to make sure you did your share of the housework properly.

Our main grouse by all within Ashford, was the constant feeling of hunger, so to miss a meal was a very harsh punishment indeed. There were no fat boys at Ashford and for any boy wanting to slim, well, lets say he was a nutter.

So this was Ashford, my home for the next thirteen years, and I better learn to like it!

CHAPTER THREE
Accommodation

The main long building block comprising the whole of the boys entire accommodation with a double image in both size and layout for the girls entire accommodation, separated only by easily the single largest building known as the Grand Dining room with all its offices appendages, must have been a good mile long. Both girls and boys wings stood a good one hundred feet tall, built before 1903, during the Victorian reign. The vast playground areas in front of each wing was well laid out with only two sides of this vast area open on two sides which were fenced in by Victorian iron railings. The four upper floors were made over, exclusively, to sleeping dormitories with their night time ablutions.

On the ground floor below this night accommodation was the large dayroom with tuckshop at one end. The main shower rooms ran alongside this area of the dayroom which then led onto a quiet room or reading room and a number of games rooms where table tennis and billiards could be played.

Along one side of this quadrant of a yard was a long row of multipurpose workshops or trade departments that jutted out at right angles to the main block going all the way across one side of the playground to the outside toilets and driveway. If, when you reached the main drive, you turned right you would eventually come to the infirmary.

If on the other hand you turned left you would firstly pass the indoor heated swimming pool just before the power house. Opposite the power house on the other side of the drive were all the rear entrances to the kitchens and laundry.

Continuing along the drive you come to the girls mirror image accommodation block, with all the school or education buildings opposite. Lastly the church, which sat in a large plot on its own with the drive terminating in a wishbone shape fork, just ahead of the main gates and gate lodge house.

The drive from the main gates all the way to the infirmary is just over three miles long. From one hundred foot high gable ends were elaborate fires escapes into the playground area. The interior of most of the buildings in Ashford had typical high ceilings, corniced with Victorian mouldings and high arch topped windows. The interior décor was plain pastel shades on flat surfaced walls, usually cream, with a dark paint job below the dado rail. Except for the shower room which itself could be described as a purpose built wet room, all other floors were timber planked.

All repairs and running maintenance within the school were done in sittue by all the various trade departments. From expert tailors, cobblers, joiners, engineers, builders and decorators were just a few in-house skills. We also had our own blacksmith, farmers and gardeners as well as teachers for the school block and medical team for our own infirmary.

The power house had to have its own squad of workmen working their own complicated shift rota system. In short, Ashford was totally self sufficient, dependant on no outside help for either services or products.

Naturally as boys we were not the least bit interested in the complex organisation it took to run such an institution. We were far more engrossed in the little boys' world of our own imagination, attached to our basic instincts we needed to survive such a depressive regime.

To notice, or even understand the organisational skills employed to run such a beast was of no consequence to us. The intricate inter-relationships of individual mates, groups or even rival gangs within the school, was of far more absorbing stuff and certainly of more interest to us mere plebs.

I for one never met a single boy who was delighted to find himself at Ashford. Most of us didn't understand the reasons for being in such a dump anyway. All boys dreamed at one time or another of being whisked away by some wealthy relative turning up out of the blue. It never happened or if it did, it was such a rare occasion. The skies over Ashford turned a shocking shade of pink before a herd of vivid blue elephants in single file crossed, forming a beautiful arc in the sky before our very eyes. We learnt from bitter experience, with time, to accept our lot. Very few of us know what a real family unit meant and given time our family was Ashford. It was our home, our solar system of the universe and even the family we knew we would never have outside this realm we found ourselves a part of.

We all through a lengthy period of adjustment after the initial shock dulled our senses of finding ourselves in such a strange environment wore off. There was no alternative, and with the ravages of war raging about our heads, we became thankful even at least, for the protection, false or otherwise, that Ashford offered.

When the devil drives the wagon it gets easier to make some kind of secret pact with evil, in exchange for ones own soul!

There were many good times of course, just not enough of them! Or so it seemed in ones early years. We were all given two pence a week in old money, which we could spend in the tuck shop on comics or sweets. My purchases, when I couldn't cadge, borrow or steal were drawing materials, pencils, paper and the like to feed my craving of art.

Sundays were always the highlight of an otherwise boring week where fruit and jelly or custard was served for lunch after morning church service, which was compulsory. Other enjoyable times, enjoyed by all who participated, were the scrumping expeditions to feed our constant hunger. Especially when they were daringly achieved successfully with no one getting caught.

The knowledge of the possible consequences for being caught in the act added more spice of living dangerously, making the game even more worthwhile and exciting.

Or, when the hand of providence saw fit to give us a power failure. It may only last minutes or longer, but for that time without electricity, especially when we were taking showers, was wonderful. I remember several occasions with Hitler's double supervising our ablutions, which somehow Sims always managed to turn into a bit of a chore. After only a few minutes in complete darkness when the power did return, having failed to extract himself quickly enough during such an emergency, Sims could be found standing alone in a shower having been forcibly put there by the older boys. The culprits, needless to say, could be found as far away as possible towelling themselves down having just stepped out of the showers. Probably the same one that Sims found himself in. Standing there soaked from head to toe and fully clothed would bring joy to any small boys heart. Sims with a face like thunder, squelching away like a drowned rat, would rant away like a lunatic possessed with everybody in sight playing possum.

The fury would squelch his way out of the shower room shouting his tales of woe and once out of earshot, a crescendo of pure jollyment and laughter would break loose spontaneously as an audience laughing at a pantomime punchline.

There were many such naughty adventures at Ashford but the shower conundrum only ever happened to Mr Sims. I wonder why? These funny sorties were too infrequent but did serve to redress some of the balance of power. These sources of enjoyment, though uncommon, enriched our little lives and got better in the telling to each other.

The system of "big boys", at least until you passed your eighth birthday, was mandatory within the Ashford regime. It was this very system of nurturing that big boys, if chosen, took very seriously indeed. Not to be chosen was almost an insult, of distrust by the powers that be, on your ability to function as surrogate siblings to care for someone more junior than you and in need of help. You might even say it was a vital part of the social fabric of the Ashford ethos of caring, that without question, benefited every child passing through the Ashford experience.

The trouble with my big boy Bobby was, that when either one of us got into trouble we got punished together for committing the crime together as one.

CHAPTER FOUR
Only The Geese Were Getting Fat

We were well into the month of December, 1939 with the completion of my first full month now behind me at Ashford. You could say the honeymoon period for me was over, at least so Mr Sims informed me in no uncertain terms, having been a cats whisker away from my first thrashing. My misdemeanour was to answer Sims back by poking my tongue out at him. Bobby, my big boy, took the brunt of Sims wrath for my insubordination.

I was advised by Bobby, my mentor, to adopt a more pacifying role in my attitude towards m'lord whenever possible. "Better still" said Bobby "stay clear of Sims as it was obvious he didn't like me very much."

With the first signs of Christmas upon us, a very large and beautiful Christmas tree had been erected on the stage in the Grand Dining Hall by lunchtime. Festooned with dozens of coloured lights and decorated all over with silver and gold tinsel was a wonderful sight to behold. The excitement of the occasion was more than enough to uplift the spirits of any child.

With all the iron railings having been dismantled throughout all of the school areas, the new open look was welcomed by most. This was done purely to help the war effort as well as helping to build new war machines for the country we were told.

The teenagers of both sexes were delighted of course because it removed barriers, which previously hampered their love life. The building of air raid shelters was well underway, which for most of us seemed like a bonus as an additional asset towards a more adventurous play areas.

These were joyous times in the final week run up to Christmas Day, with everybody involved in the hand making of Christmas decorations for the dayroom areas. Carol singing practice was well underway in readiness for the religious festivity, which was taken very seriously. We all entered into the merriment of the occasion with great gusto and determination to enjoy ourselves to the full. Like everything else at Ashford, with any great event, the undertaking was masterfully accomplished.

Even the staff, including our warders, entered into this sacred event walked about with smiling faces as they carried out their daily duties. The temporary disposal of their normal stern gazes was put on hold, which for most of us was somewhat disarming. If you were brave enough and big enough you could even hold a conversation with some members of staff.

Naturally, many of us exploited this god sent opportunity to indulge in all kinds of skulduggery. We were only kids after all, so why not, it was Christmas! Most of the staff lowered their guards, so this was a better time than most to take advantage. The fruit was ripe for harvest you might say.

The final countdown toward the big day was painfully slow in coming. Each and every day of that last week towards Christmas Day went agonisingly slowly.

When one is so little the perception of time itself is simply the hands on a clock face, which to children, have no real meaning. After what seemed an eternity, the wonderful day finally dawned, but not without sleepless nights. Early Christmas morn arrived and at the bottom of our bedsteads was one of our own woollen stockings filled with all sorts of goodies. In my stocking was an orange, an apple and a banana, which I had never seen before. There was also a matchbox toy lorry, which made me yell for joy. There was also a bag of mischief sweets and some nuts completing my delight. Everybody was chatting with each other in excitement and a great deal of swapping and bargaining taking place.

Bobby sat on my bed, like my big brother, with just as much glee as the rest of us. I gave him my unwanted sweets, not being a sweetie fan, and in return he gave me his colouring in book, which he clearly felt I should have got anyway. There would be no housework for two days, Bobby told me, nor would there be any school classwork.

With the prospect of two wonderful days of holidays, times could only get better I thought.

No early morning rise at 6.30 a.m. which meant we could all slum it, at least until breakfast at eight. Even breakfast today would be different to the normal bowl of porridge. Instead, sandwiches, sponge cake and lots of lemonade would be served in the dayroom.

Happiness spread quickly like an outbreak of chicken pox and even boys you didn't particularly know or like, were only too willing to join in the banter.

This was more than just a holiday; this was a kind of freedom with total gay abandonment from routines and tedious food rations. I felt I could soar with joy and fly without fear of getting my wings clipped, at least for a couple of days. Why is it that when you are enjoying yourself so much, time itself runs away like an express train. For lunch in the Grand Hall we had three courses starting with oxtail soup then chicken, sausages, lots of roast potatoes, sprouts and all the trimmings. Home made trifle for afters with gallons of orange juice to wash it all down.

We also had crackers and paper hats to wear but most of all the freedom to talk. The endless din of merry chatter the banter of jokes and laughter was music to all our ears. No commands by whistle this meal time and if you wanted to pig out with second or even third helpings, there was ample fruit, jelly or custard for the asking.

For once our little tums could be stretched, fit to burst. There were certainly no complaints of hunger this day, only groans of joy from over indulgence.

For those that had finished stuffing their faces they could leave the Great Hall and return to the dayroom at their leisure, where party games were organised by some of the female kitchen staff.

Alas, especially small infants unable to withstand the pace, bed time called out at six. In fairness, especially those children under three, were by now desperate for their beds. Christmas Day sped by far too quickly but Boxing Day had still to arrive.

Most of us who had lost sleep on Christmas Eve were ready to collapse into a dream like coma come bedtime anyway. Boxing Day was equally as good, especially at lunchtime when the head master Mr Bailey, nicknamed Fatty Arbuckle, took centre stage to perform his annual present giving ceremony. Dressed in drag, as Santa, the head called each boy onto the stage to collect a present.

This performance took most of the afternoon, but none seemed to mind. To the majority of children this was one of those rare occasions we saw the head in a jovial mood. Many of the older lads said it was the one day of the year that Fatty Arbuckle did any work.

A little uncharitable I thought, even if it was true. He certainly filled his Santa costume with his ample rotunda bespectacled like figure, he looked quite dashing. Mr Bailey was big, and I mean big, so much so he could certainly not see below his own waist without standing in front of a full length mirror.

Sitting on big shoulders sat an egg shaped bald pate, highlighted by thick horn rimmed glasses. A ruddy complexion was always part of his make-up. It was rumoured that he was more than partial to a drink or two and we are not talking lemonade.

The less kindly souls among us just said he was an alcoholic. At first I thought this was some kind of medical affliction until Bobby put me wise.

In reality I was sure he would be far to busy administering his empire to ensure the smooth running of the school. Being an old educated scholar of all Dickens work he was often compared to Mr Beagle, one of Charles Dickens favourite characters. Mr Bailey would sometimes be seen emulating Beagle, right down to the same pompous mannerisms.

One thing couldn't be more certain, I knew of no boy at Ashford that wanted to be called before him for punishment. Fortunately for most of us mere mortals, the senior housemasters were more than willing to do the heads bidding.

We were already into the depths of the winter of 1940 with only the cold dark winter nights to look forward to, along with a new term starting at school. Meanwhile we had only the memories to cherish of Christmas past.

My fourth then fifth birthday each year on the twelfth of April disappeared over the horizon. Meanwhile my move from the infants to the Primary School signalled a new age of responsibility. My previous female teacher was replaced by male masters who were dedicated to the Victorian dogma of learning. The regime at Ashford was well geared for adaptation in both education and conformity of classwork. Now, the learning process was driven at an earnest pace with seriousness that none could fail to notice. A tougher more rigorous approach to education was followed to a well established curriculum. The Victorian moral code of conduct left us no more time to grow up once you reached the age of five years old.

Now it was made crystal clear from five upwards, was the time of responsibilities for ones own behaviour becoming paramount. Responsibility was thrust upon you, ready or not. The sands of time were already running through the hour glass and there was absolutely nothing anybody could do to stop it. However one of the perks of this move into primary classes was the Saturday morning Cinema Club.

This always took place in the Grand Hall where the screen was set up on the stage. The films, all in black and white, showed cartoons as well as cowboy flicks and after every showing the boys could be seen at play acting out their favourite cowboy heroes in the playground.

Remembering always that the Second World War raged heavily on the outside, the constant boom of distant guns and bombs hitting their intended targets in nearby London, was a strong reminder to us all of real dangers. It was sometimes difficult for us to remember that the war was not orchestrated just to give us boys an added sense of adventure. Although most of us did feel it added thrill to our lives.

With the air raid shelters long completed it was amazing how many other uses were found for these dark secret places. You could, with just a little imagination, be exploring darkest Africa, although older boys were more likely to be exploring their girlfriends' body shapes. There was the usual smut of sexual innuendos, which could be found in any boys' playground and probably in girls' playgrounds too. The teenagers and sometimes even younger lads at sometime in their sexual development, desired to put theories into sexual practice. As the song said, it started with a kiss!

Sooner rather than later, these powerful sexual urges often resulted in more stronger prowess of sexual activity. The big no no was full blown sexual intercourse and only on the rarest of occasions, was a girl caught pregnant and was promptly dispatched from Ashford.

Signs like "Keep Off The Grass" had no meaning to most of us. Unfortunately at Ashford many of the misdemeanours committed were girl related, as we shall see as I grow older. However, at the tender age of seven, my sexual interests were at this time none existent. But Bobby, my buddy, warned me these feelings would radically change in time.

For the time being I was more interested in activities like swimming, scrumping or lying in wait for an express train to flatten a penny into a two inch disc. The danger element attached to such bravado brought with it, its own kudos. The railway line was our nearest boundary with the orchard running alongside. With luck you could combine both scrumping with penny flattening at one and the same time. Naturally the railway line was out of bounds as was so many other attractive worthwhile places.

Plumbs were my favourite followed by pears; both were well scrumped in alarming quantities. Growing boys needed feeding, as hunger pangs were our constant companion. The chances of getting caught scrumping were always very high because one had to cross a driveway used exclusively by members of staff. It was always well patrolled to protect such a vital food source, which only made this escapade more dangerous and therefore more exciting.

After tea one evening we were instructed to see Mr Walton in his office, and both Bob and I felt sure that someone had seen the two of us scrumping or we had been dobbed in by someone trying to gain brownie points. We duly arrived outside Walton's office waiting for the axe to fall. Bob knocked on the office door waiting for the command of his master's voice.

"Come in" barked Walton. So, pushing Bobby ahead of me, knowing it was more his fault than mine, we entered.

"Ah you two, you're both down on my list for our swimming gala in a few months time" said Walton.

The sheer relief on both our faces was clear to see.

"I will let you know" Walton continued, "when training starts".

Walton looked at one to the other of us, then said

"Have you got something you want to tell me?"

"No sir" we said in unison

"Right" said Walton "you can both scarper and get showered".

With unusual speed we disappeared, relieved it was nothing more serious.

Naturally we were chuffed to be considered suitable for such an important event in one of Ashford's most prestigious sports. Ever since my first swimming lesson before the age of four I had taken to the water without fear. I steadily progressed into a competent swimmer thanks to Walton's expertise, which I found to be my element of joy. Swimming, like so many other activities at Ashford was mandatory. I was now in my mid primary school years and, although Bobby was no longer my big boy or carer, he had become my best friend. Our friendship continued to flourish along with our mischievous behaviour, which meant we were frequently punished as one, having committed the crime together. Trouble became increasingly unavoidable in the pursuit of fun, adventure and happiness.

CHAPTER FIVE
Leo; Gangs and Other Mischief

One beautiful sunny morning after a typical Ashford breakfast of porridge, toast and a mug of tea I was about to set off to classes for the day, when I was instructed by Mr Gibbs to accompany him to the day room office. Following him into his office I was confronted by Miss Richards, the matron, who was already seated.

Attached, hanging onto her sleeve, was a little black boy looking very frightened called Leonard Jackson, or Leo for short. This unusual scene before me struck me as odd because to my knowledge there was no other black child at Ashford. Leo was just four years old, smaller in height than most four year olds, with big expressive eyes.

Leo was plump in roundness of body than any other boy I knew with a chocolate coloured skin that was so smooth it shone like velvet. He looked like a brown rabbit caught in the sudden glare of headlights. When he smiled, he had the whitest set of nashers (teeth) I have ever seen, which spread across his plump face like the keyboard of an upright piano.

Matron, meanwhile, was singing his plight of woe but Leo never once released his grip on her arm. In spite of his deep brown eyes, you could willingly swim in, he avoided eye contact, with a kind of nervousness that gave one the feeling akin to being very shy.

Leo was in fact the first black boy ever sent to Ashford. At this point Mr Gibbs retreated tactfully with some feeble excuse of work elsewhere. The matron introduced me to Leo as his new big boy. He didn't look pleased at the prospect, clinging even tighter onto matron like a baby desperate to be breast fed.

A kind of courtship designed to break down all barriers of fear surrounding Leo's obvious body language began. This went on for almost an hour until Leo showed signs of being more at ease.

We all vacated the office to the play area of the day room. Both Leo and myself got down to some serious hands on play with a selection of toys until Leo became so engrossed, the matron was able to slip away unnoticed. We continued to play together until lunchtime when the boys returned from class before getting ready to eat. Now it was me that Leo clung to like a limpet on a sea wall. Like it or not, I had become Leo's big boy, bringing back a flood of memories of my first encounter with Bob, who had started out as my big boy and was now my best friend. With this in mind, I endeavoured to be as good to Leo as Bob had been with me.

Leo's family history read like a site of devastation with Leo at first presumed dead.

Besides clinging to me like a limpet, which in itself took getting used to, Leo was a thumb sucker, bed wetter and a cry baby to boot. It wasn't his fault of course, as he was found among a pile of house rubble because his house had scored a direct hit from one of Hitler's many bombs.

His whole family had been wiped out and Leo was found deep inside the bomb crater bawling his little head off. You could say his persistent crying saved his life because he was found, several days after the bomb struck, by a passer by. His bed wetting was a result of that evil nights work. It only took the sound of distant guns or bombardment, and even the sound of thunder, to trigger him off.

I wouldn't have minded so much, if it wasn't my bed he dived into, to release his bladder of piss. The matron assured me Leo would eventually grow out of it. Let's hope he grows up very fast then, I thought. At first, if I'm honest with myself, I was a little resentful at having to take on Leo because I felt it would cramp my style. I soon got into a routine that covered all of Leo's needs and within weeks he was eased out of his shell, turning into a loveable character with many sides to his personality.

Surprisingly, his colour never once incurred racial comments or act as bait for bullying. Leo's lively character and infectious grin, like a peeled banana, won him instant friendship. My turn in becoming any boys' protector, had been long in coming at seven years old plus.

In the late summer of 1943, it was described as an Indian summer, so persistently hot was it, that the pools down at the River Ash was over subscribed by many more boys than usual. This was the summer of much discontent with rival Ashford gangs battling it out for prime water front real estate.

There were four gangs to speak of within Ashford, the most prestigious of all were the Golden Eagles. Not only were they seen as the best, but because of their well known selection process, they were also the hardest to get into. They contacted you as a possible candidate. Don't ring us we'll ring you, if we choose to, was a slogan that rang very true. Their membership of over fifty foot soldiers, and an inner circle of another twelve elite that formed the committee. Every single member qualified, having completed a special task or quest, before acceptance.

If you were lucky enough to be called to fight the cause you were supposed to be honoured. Don't ask me what the 'cause' was, I haven't a clue, and I had my doubts they themselves might struggle in explaining the cause!!

Bobby my best friend was one of the committee members and even he couldn't explain what the cause was. Bob saw it as great fun with a great deal of kudos attached. When I was approached to join I felt it would be a good idea, on the strength that Bobby was already a member. I went along for the ride, and also the esteem, I saw that it would bestow upon me. Massaging my ego sounded good. It would all hang on my ability to complete whatever task they set before me.

The committee, via Bob, instructed me to make myself available this coming Saturday for interview. Very official, I thought! The venue, known as the inner circle, would be given at the last minute, for security reasons. (Very secret, hush hush and all that).

As Bob explained, the interview first, then the quest, then the full acceptance, were the three main steps to achieve entrance. There is also a three months probation period to serve before full membership is granted.

"It is really worth all this bother?" I asked Bob

"Yes" said Bob, "think of all the benefits and prestige that goes with the recognition of being a member of the Golden eagles" he explained. I wasn't convinced, but afraid to say so. The main rival gang to the Eagles was another gang called The Hawks, whose membership included some of the nastiest reprobates at Ashford, as well as some of its worst bullies. This in itself was a good enough reason for me to join, and the fact that Bob was a leading light in the Eagles inner sanctum.

The main arena for gang warfare was no less than the River Ash. For whoever controlled this resource were definitely king of the castle. There were also running battles with outsiders who wanted the three main swimming pools, bird's eggs and our poaching rights. The Ash was an unfenced natural school boundary between us and the outside world. In reality, the Ash was little more than a big stream, although its purity of waters, and natural rock pools, made it ideal play areas for skinny dipping.

No boy at Ashford wore or was given to wear underpants below our knee length shorts. Swimming outside the schools indoor heated swimming pool, properly attired in trunks was forbidden. This only became important if you got caught. Most of the arguments over the facilities the Ash offered were usually settled amicably, with rival gangs only too willing to give the Eagles some kind of forfeit, or perhaps an offer of work was called for.

This permitted both top gangs to enjoy themselves together, but should any rival gang member abuse this hospitality by standing on the bank openly pissing on those enjoying the water, would quickly bring reprisal. The privileges of using the Ash could be withdrawn for as long as a week, if the Eagles decided. There was always the danger that one of Sims informers could try to score favour with the said master by gyping. At the first opportunity, this gyper, in turn would receive a good hiding by an elected appropriate Eagle member. From time to time one of the other three gangs would dare to challenge the Eagles for top dog position, which resulted in bloody fights. Many a boy sported black eyes or a fat lip as proud wounds won in battle. The boys code of conduct within most gangs was always more than sufficient to accept defeat gracefully.

'A Lamb to Slaughter'

The day for my investiture had arrived.

I was summoned like a prisoner preparing to meet his maker for sentencing. A boy called Nasher, so called because of his very large teeth, was a member of the elite and was to be my escort to the venue. I never knew Nasher's name, as all of the elite twelve used nicknames to avoid the use of their real names, as a matter of national security. The nicknames chosen usually had some relevance to the individual character. Nasher himself won his spurs by taking a man size bite from an opponents bum in some previous battle.

We strolled across the playground towards the boys outside toilets where a lookout waved a signal for the all clear to cross the driveway towards the air raid shelters. The meeting was to take place in the second shelter, which had already been prepared in advance. This mid morning, on Saturday, meant that there were hoards of boys playing on nearby swings and in both playground and park where we were heading.

Another guard was on duty at the entrance to the shelter, where I was first blindfolded before taken in by my escort Nasher. Why blindfolded? Knowing the interior of these shelters were as black as a moonless night in winter, I was yet to understand. Once inside I was manhandled into the circle, a ring of lit candles, the heat I could feel on my bare legs. Being told to stand on the spot I was on, the blindfold was then removed. It was difficult to see anything beyond the ring of candles, and the committee were assembled well beyond my range of vision. Even after my eyes adjusted to candle light, I could see none, but they could see me clearly, standing alone. So this was it I thought, very dramatic!

After several minutes of utter silence I was addressed by a boy called Scar, so called because of a permanent scar that ran from his left shoulder upwards to the nape of his neck.

"So acorn" said Scar, "you want to join the Eagles, why?" he spat!

"Well" I said in my cockiest voice "I reckon you need me!"

Another boy introduced himself as Gobbie, because he had a big mouth, asked me "What makes you big enough?"

This rattled my cage somewhat and threw me off guard so in haste I suggested he meet me outside for him to find out! A boy called Jugs interjected "so you think you're a tough guy do you?" Jugs so called because he wore a pair of ears that stuck out like a pair of jug handles.

"Hold on you lot" said Ape, who had long arms like a monkey.

"You Acorn, hold your tongue" so I did, feeling a little deflated.

There was a pregnant pause with a fair bit of whispering between them.

Marbles was one of the strong arm members of the committee with a fearful reputation of being able to use his dukes (fists). He was called Marbles because he was always playing pocket billiards with his testicles, through a designer hole in his pocket lining. I was told to stay put while the twelve man committee retired to the far end of the shelter to discuss my fate.

There were some disagreement with certain members, but after a while they re-assembled to give their verdict. A vote was taken which was just favourable towards me, but the quest I was told, would be extra hard, because of my insolence. Once the quest, which was yet to be decided was reached, I would be informed in due course via Bob my mate, I was told.

Later that day Bob, who was on official business for the Eagles, came to see me. Bobby looked at me as if he was looking at a stranger. For the first time I was beginning to feel negative as Bob started by telling me things didn't look good. I failed at the first hurdle, I thought.

"Your quest" said Bob "should you chose to accept it, is to climb the big stack."

"The big stack" I said, looking at Bob as if he was short of a few sandwiches from a picnic.

"I told you it wasn't good," said Bob.

"The big stack" I repeated, looking puzzled "What the hell for?" I asked.

Bob's voice altered, returning to his former role, as my protector.

"You know Paul, you don't have to do this if you don't want to" he added.

He then went on to explain, "The task was deliberately set hard to make you chicken out," said Bob.

So I said, picking up the gauntlet" They think I'm all mouth do they?"

Bob said, "I hope you realize, I'm not allowed to help you in anyway.

"That's okay Bob" I said, "I understand."

"How soon would I be expected to do this quest?" I asked.

"Well" said Bob "quite soon, I think, although Nasher will take you to the base of the big stack on the night chosen. This task" Bob rabbited on "was picked because of your known climbing ability."

"Tell that shower of bastards I accept the challenge" I said.

I could see the uneasy distance between us didn't sit well with Bob as his eyes were always a give away, as the windows to his soul, and inner feeling were evident.

I went off on my own, leaving Bob standing there, also on his tod. Perhaps a more demanding task could have been set, but for the moment I couldn't for the life of me think of one

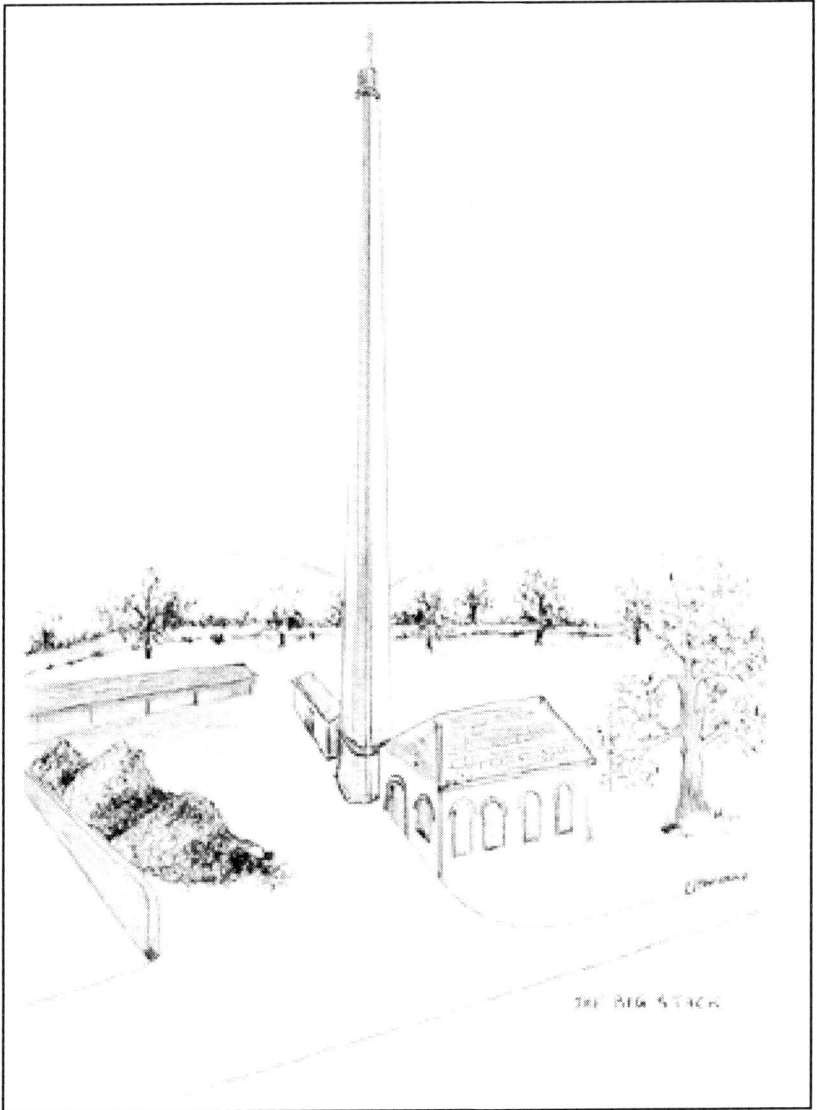

THE BIG STACK

CHAPTER SIX
The Big Stack

The big stack was in fact the tallest brick built monument in the whole of Ashford and outlying district areas. This very tall chimney also carried a lightning conductor mast, that so many of the population were reliant on, with its earthing cable buried deep into the ground, before running up its entire brick structure to the top.

The top mast rod, that glinted silver in the sunlight, was firmly bolted to the rim of the chimney at its top. The power house was a big lump of a beast, housing all the machines that was coal fed to generate electric power, the institutional community was so dependant on.

This stack was an awe inspiring cathedral like steeple, that penetrated the sky above and seemed to go on forever. This prominent landmark could easily be seen for up to twenty-five miles away in all directions. It stood well over two hundred feet tall from base to tip. The girth at the base alone some twenty foot square, set into one corner of the power house building. From this enormous base it gradually tapered to a tall candle like blunted point, with the lightning wick like rod atop.

The mountains of coal and coke to feed this beast were stacked in the open yard, like giant black sand dunes. Boys were frequently punished when caught playing on these imaginary alps, on their return from classwork, homeward bound. Playing on their private Everest left ample evidence of coal dust residue on their clothing, which was irrefutable for all to see. This un-missable imposing structure was centrally sited between the girls and boys playground areas and stood on the opposite side of the main driveway from the kitchen and laundry service entrance.

This vital asset stood at the very hub of Ashford's community. The squad of men that worked the furnaces to generate the steam engines and boilers laboured their own shift system that only they understood.

When there was a breakdown in power, which occurred quite frequently especially during the war years, all the boys were quick to take advantage and settle old scores under the cover of darkness. It was an excellent source of bedevilment, giving us all great enjoyment, for moments the power failed.

Behind the rear of the power house, and well away from the main driveway, was an area called the dovecots. The dovecots were a favourite haunt for older lads, especially those in their teens, because the seclusion was ideal for courting couples. There was a number of disused outhouses that were often pressed into service when needs must. I too, was to learn for my own benefit, much later in my school years, the advantages this place of sexual wonder offered. So, this gigantic landmark of love generated a lot more power than just electricity.

Beyond the dovecots, surrounded by lots of wild brambles, was a very large vegetable growing complex, most of which was destined to land on our dinner plates.

This was the arena, the target, the quest, where the great climb would take place.

To our knowledge this climb had never been undertaken by any boy at Ashford and no steeplejack had ascended its height since before the war.

My palms just sweated with nervous anticipation, looking up at this magnificent chimney, to its very top, that was often cloaked in smoke or cloud.

We all passed it every day on our way to class, which only enhanced what a formidable and worthwhile challenge it was.

There was a continuous iron ladder built into the brickwork that spanned its entire length to the top. This was for engineering and maintenance purposes only. Perhaps, I thought, this would help to make it a walk in the park, although I harboured my doubts.

The night for my quest finally arrived.

This said night I was rudely shaken vigorously awake by Nasher no less. At some unearthly hour, with Nashers hand firmly clamping my gob, he instructed me to put on my day clothes over the top of my pyjamas. Without delay, I got dressed, then followed Nasher across the landing to the outside fire escape. Like a pair of commandos on a secret night sortie, we quickly descended the four flights of iron stairway to the ground below. I noticed the night sky was partially lit by moonlight, with some clouds skating across the half moon from time to time.

Perfect I thought, as we skirted the far side of the playground to the driveway. After crossing the drive, we continued along the field edge, using the avenue of trees for cover. I was thinking to myself I had never been up so late, although I had no idea what time it was. Overhead, between the fluffy clouds were patches of deep dark black sky, with a hint of a twinkling star or two. The breeze was light, which I thought would keep my palms of my hands cool, as the adrenalin coursed through my body. In far less time than expected we found ourselves standing at the base of the big stack, within easy reach of the first rung of the ladder. Nasher withdrew from the body of his jacket, the all important trophy to be flown aloft.

In whispered tones, Nasher calmly handed me the flag, which was in fact a pair of pink long legged bloomers or knickers. He unfolded this triumphant garment, illustrating precisely how they were to be attached by tying knots in each leg around the lightning conductor rod.

These, I learnt later, were just one of his girlfriend conquests. I shoved them into the bodice of my brown corduroy jacket, then looked up the iron ladder for the first sixty feet or so, before disappearing out of sight into the blackness beyond. With an encouraging prod in my back from Nasher, who politely ordered me to "fucking get on with it", I stepped onto the first rung. After only five minutes or so I looked down to the ground to see that Nasher had scarpered, and now I felt really alone. Typical, I thought, as I gritted my teeth but continued upwards gaining more confidence with every rung. The first hundred feet or so went well with good cloud cover. The light wind stiffened a little as the moon found a gap between the clouds, so I paused to look about me. With the vista of buildings and rooftops below my feet, the moon reflected a sight that was beautiful as well as awe inspiring.

The thought of falling from such a height was sobering and sharpened the senses as well as focused the mind. Instinctively, I felt my hands grip the side of the ladder tighter, as a tingling sensation ran up my spine. Another bolt of adrenalin surged through my veins as I collected my thoughts commanding me to look up and continue the climb.

By now I was at least half way up the climb, when a tremble took hold of my lower legs.

Time to take a breather as I felt the wind abate and my nerve settled. I continued to climb, working my body into a steady rhythm, as I got my second wind.

Ten minutes or so later I looked up seeing the top of the chimney for the very first time!

Encouraged, I began to quicken my pace feeling more and more elated.

With less than a dozen rungs to go, I soon reached the final rung with my hands, then rested to work out in my mind the final plan of execution.

Careful now, I told myself as I reached to take hold of the mast and testing its flexibility to see if it would hold my weight. The mast felt firm and steady in my hands, as I heaved myself onto the chimney lip. Hugging the mast into my body, as if I was about to make love, I peered into the abyss of the chimney's inner core, which was very black and uninviting.

I gingerly extracted the bloomers from my windcheater and slowly tied the bottom of each leg around the mast. Tightening the knots as best I could, I slid them up the shaft, standing on tip toe, pushing them up as high as possible. Immediately the wind filled the knickers like a wind sock and the flapping sound was unnerving. I quickly lowered myself onto the top rung, and safety. I drank in the air with sheer relief, with only the reverse journey below me.

Leaving the gaping hole of that black smokeless dormant volcano, I felt a little safer.

The wind speed increased and I was certain I could feel the top of the big stack gently swaying.

I started my descent, slow at first, because I had to feel each rung of the ladder, which was now below my body, instead of above.

At around halfway down I began to feel dehydrated, as a result of burning off so much nervous energy. I continued to sweat profusely on my descent, which was taking much longer than I felt it should.

Exhaustion began to set in, as I looked down to gauge the distance still to climb down. I could now see the ground at last and thankfully I was meeting it fast.

At last I reached the ground, feeling somewhat blessed to feel terra firma below my plimsoled feet.

On reaching the ground, the urgent need to empty my bladder became a desperate task, as I fought with my extra layers of clothing to find my dick quickly, in fear of wetting myself. Having relieved myself, I looked around, saw no one and scooted back to my bed, not remembering anything about my return trip to my dorm. I fell asleep in seconds. As I dreamed away in a state of intoxication, I was awoken abruptly from what seemed a very short period of slumber by Bobby.

"Time to get up" he whispered in my ear hole.

As I begrudgingly got out of bed, we discovered I was still fully dressed including my plimsoles.

I quickly stripped to the buff, then re-dressed, as Bob said to me "You did it then?"

"Yes, I guess I did" is all I could reply.

During the housework that morning followed by breakfast, I was still having difficulty getting my head around what I had so recently undertaken a matter of hours before. I mean, did I really fasten those knickers to the top of the big stack? I kept asking myself.

The facts of my dastardly night time exploits had already filtered through to the committee of the Eagles.

At breakfast I searched anxiously amid the sea of faces to detect any sign, hint or knowing wink, that others might have knowledge of my nights work. I was pleased, but also somewhat flummoxed, that not a single boy showed the slightest knowledge of my secret climb. As we walked down the drive, with Bobby on one side and me and Leo holding hands on the other, Bob nudged me in the ribs as we came in sight of the big stack.

In unison, we both glanced upwards and a wide grin broke over Bob's face, who simply said "I knew you would do it. You had better keep mum" Bob reminded me as he left me outside his classroom.

I looked back at the big stack and could see clearly the banner flapping in a stiff breeze, although without prior knowledge you wouldn't know they were a girl's pair of knickers.

I took Leo to the infants' class, then headed for my own. As I passed along the passageway there were the usual small groups chin wagging away. I wondered if they were talking about me, as the pure wickedness of my deeds made me feel guilt ridden, swamping my body as I began to realise the possible consequences of my actions. I conspicuously walked into class, sliding into my seat with my mind clearly somewhere else.

"Ankorne" shouted Sir, which abruptly made me face reality.

"Yes Sir" I replied, looking startled

"Go and wait outside the headmaster's office" he spat out at me.

"Why Sir?" I asked questioningly.

"Because he wants to see you" came his sharp retort.

I felt sick to my stomach, and could feel my legs shaking with fear, at the same time a trickle of piss involuntary left the end of my dick. Still trying to stand on my pins, which were now wobbling like jelly, the teacher asked me if I was feeling alright.

"No Sir" I said, feeling more unwell by the second, looking for some reprieve.

"Cut along boy, smartly" he replied "and look into see the matron on your way, if you must" he added.

I left the classroom sheepishly, wondering where I could take shelter urgently. Perhaps this was as good a time as any to do a runner, I thought, as I made my way as slowly as possible to Mr Bailey's office.

"Ah, there you are Paul" said the head as he came through the open doorway of his office.

"Are you not feeling very well?" said Bailey "You look very pale." He added.

I looked up at him with my most pitiful face I could muster, appealing for sympathy.

"Wait here, I'll get the matron," said Bailey.

He returned within seconds with the matron bustling along in full flow.

"Let me look at you my darling" she cooed. "You had better come with me" she demanded as she slipped easily into her full motherly nursing mode.

My saviour, I thought, as I turned on my pathetic, sick role up to full throttle.

The rest of the morning was spent in relative comfort in matron's sick bay, licking my wounds and fearing I was not of the hook yet. Believe it or not, by lunchtime I was feeling much better but my fear was real enough.

The matron questioned me closely and concluded that the malaise was probably due to not eating my breakfast that morning. As to why Bailey summoned my presence, then was quickly called away, was just one of life's mysteries.

The matron took me through a familiar door alongside the stage to the dining room for lunch. Memories of my first day's arrival all those years ago, came flooding back.

I re-found my appetite as I got stuck into a plate of bully beef, cabbage and potatoes.

Before the usual whistle command could be given, Mr Bailey climbed onto the stage, while someone switched on the public address loudspeaker system.

A thousand faces suddenly became alert with surprise, as Bailey started to unfold a tale of great woe.

"I want to know" he started "which despicable boy or boys, are responsible for this disgusting rag at the top of the big chimney" he boomed. Bailey paused for effect or perhaps the culprit would reveal himself, he hoped.

Already his ruddy complexion turned to a strange shade of purple, as his angry body built up a fair head of steam. As his voice thundered across the great hall, the grip of my hands on the side rails of my chair grew whiter. My guilt began to wane, as I slowly began to realise Bailey at this point in time, had no knowledge as to who the little blighter responsible, was.

I did wonder, how many hours of freedom I had before my arrest.

My next four days were a worrying time, until the rag at the top of the big stack had succumbed to the elements and was no more.

Only one person knew for absolute certain who was responsible for this crime, and as a member of the inner elite, Nasher was sworn by the Eagles code.

My fear decreased, but knowing Ashford's reputation for being able to keep something as dramatic and as big as this secret for long, filled me full of doubt and foreboding. Thankfully after just a few weeks, it died a natural death. It was long overdue to put this stupid prank to bed, and I for one, was more than happy when kids in general stopped talking about the daring deed, which in any case got more and more elaborate in the telling.

I'm not sure why, but in the end I declined my membership to the Eagles, because deep down, I had a gut feeling it wasn't me. By nature, I was a bit of a loner, it was very much a part of my make-up.

Needless to say, the decision did not sit easily with the Golden Eagles, as Bob explained no one had ever refused to join this elite organisation. Indeed, it was usually the other way about. I believe Bob came in for a lot of flack and incurred great wrath, from many of its committee members as a result.

Bob too, decided he would part company from the gang also, and quite simply stated "Who needs them anyway". We were both too mature to indulge in children's games anyway, we laughed together out loud.

CHAPTER SEVEN
From Hitler With Love

The long hot summer of forty three was now over, with a very brief autumn, which turned quickly into a cold winter with biting winds accompanied by a thick carpet of snow. An ideal winter wonderland for children perhaps, but caused all sorts of difficulties for our armed services on all fronts. With the dark nights rapidly drawing in, it was almost dark by 6.00 p.m., which meant we were all confined to indoor pursuits. The war continued to rage outside, with bombing raids of Hitler's regime, steadily increasing over the London landscape. With other major cities getting their fair share as well, from the Wash and Humberside to Glasgow in the far north. Always looking for more and more targets to bomb, Germany was desperately searching for more lucrative sites to lay to waste.

Leo, my charge, was now over five years old and should be ready to fly solo, possible as early as by spring of forty six, I hope. By which time I would be eight years old, ready for my move up to the intermediate boys dorm, where I should join my best friend Bobby.

Leo, no longer sucked his thumb, nor was he considered to be a cry baby. His progress in making friends was really quite remarkable, but was still very much afraid of distant gun fire or the sounds of bombs, sent him scurrying into my bed, crawling under my bed clothes for cover.

On rare occasions he was still liable to piss my bed, without prior warning, which I never got used to. His bladder control did get better, as the matron said it would. Leo's real progress could be measured in so many other ways, and with such a disarming smile it was hard to be angry for very long, and often won some of the hardest characters over.

His cheerful disposition won him so many admirers, along with his big brown expressive eyes which if his smile failed, then the eyes were brought into play, and they were likely to succeed in shooting you down in flames.

His grin alone was like a freshly peeled banana that went from ear to ear across his chocolate cheeky face.

I once heard a member of the fairer sex with a Scottish background say "he'd get a jelly piece at any door". I thought this summed up Leo perfectly.

Have I really become that much of a sucker, I mused. It was this winter, sometime after Christmas that the air raids over the whole of the county of Middlesex, became more frequent.

Even during daylight hours, while playing outside, there was no escape as our playtime was more frequently interrupted, which just wasn't cricket.

I clearly remember on a sunny afternoon, a group of us stood watching dog fights in the sky directly above, as we gawked upwards, spell bound as our brave lads chased the hun fighters all over the place. Our group just stood there watching, long after the siren warning us to run for shelter, which was close by. Our cockiness of bravado, of the dangers being completely ignored overhead, earned us a caning for our trouble as we got caught. I myself received six of the best from Hitler's cousin, Sims, and when I complained that most of the others only received two or three strokes each, depending on how much Simms liked or disliked you, I was given extra punishment, put to work after teatime by scrubbing the red and black flagstone corridor. This led from the dayroom to the Grand Dining Room and was a quarter mile long, which took all evening until bedtime.

Bobby, my best mate, along with other friends, had warned me often that Sims was always gunning for me, which really didn't help. I must learn to keep my lip buttoned, Bob reminded me especially where Sims was concerned. This particular night I would remember well, and was to be engraved on my heart as if it happened just yesterday. By bedtime I was so dead beat, because of my extra punishment having spent hours on my knees scrubbing, I was fast asleep the moment my head hit the pillow, and long before lights out.

Sometime in the small hours of Monday morning, my blissful slumber was invaded by an ear shattering bang that also broke the big arch top window above my bed. The blue night lights at each end of the dormitory flickered for several moments, and then went out.

My bed was warm, but also very wet, as I felt Leo's body trembling in fear, with his arms tight around my chest. Amid the complete chaos of boys running amok all over the dormitory, search lights could be seen searching the night skies outside. A distinct draft could be felt as the cold winter air came pouring through the shattered windows of the dorm. The main building lights within the dormitory came on for all of twenty seconds then died.

During this brief spell of light I noticed a shard of glass, some six inches long sticking out of Leo's head, on a pillow covered in blood.

The window above my head had totally caved in from the blast, glass was strewn over the bed as well as the floor. I put my ear to Leo's chest and was convinced that he was still breathing, although by now his once trembling body was perfectly still. The night watchman came towards my bed with his torch, while kids were running up and down the dorm in panic.

"Come on Paul" he said "give Leo to me"

"No" I shouted "don't you dare touch him" I said angrily.

"Okay okay," he stuttered, "follow me as I light your path" he conceded.

I reached down to retrieve my plimsoles from below my bed, as I knew the floor would be covered in broken glass underfoot. I then got Leo carefully out of bed, cradling him in my arms, wondering why he was so quite and a still. The torch bearer headed for the nearest exit to the stone stairs, then down two flights. I carried Leo in my arms still worried about the lifelessness of his little body.

Once we arrived into the downstairs corridor we found we were invaded by our own troops, who had parachuted in and were busy searching all buildings and grounds. As I stood there wondering what next, a British soldier swept down over me, and took Leo from my arms.

"Give him to me son" he said, "this little fellow needs the hospital" he added, then passing on among the racket of kids crying and yelling their heads off, he was suddenly gone from view. I never saw Leo again.

Later that same morning after the air raid and terror of that night abated, the all clear sounded, but we were made to stay put until all the dorms were cleared of debris. We learnt much later that day a total of five doodle bugs had landed within the school. Two of which scored direct hits, with one on our building and the other on the classroom block further down the drive. There would be no housework for several days we were told, and in all probability no school work either, which pleased most of us, and secretly hoped no schoolwork for much longer. Even breakfast would be late that day, and wasn't served until well after nine.

This was our black Monday and to think only hours before, I was on my hands and knees scrubbing this very same floor that we now used as a shelter.

At our late breakfast that morning matron could be seen flitting from table to table, in full flight, dispensing her verbal medicine of comfort to all.

I tried going through the motions of eating, but not a morsel of food could I manage, as my last sight of Leo disturbed my thoughts. Not eating was normal for me at times of stress. With the matron in full flow, pausing momentarily at this table then another, like a butterfly landing for a moment or two from bush to bush, I was anxious to attract her attention to get news about Leo.

Administering her kindness like a modern day Florence Nightingale, she caught my attentive wave and came over. Smiling all the while, she assured me that Leo was doing well and would soon be back among us, she said convincingly.

"Can I visit him" I asked impatiently, as she waved herself on shouting to me in passing "very soon" she said "soon" quickly disappearing from both view and sound. I was forced to content myself with this scrap of information, at least for the time being.

It was many days before the school returned to any kind of normality.

On the morning of Thursday, just four days after the bombing raid, I was called to Mr Walton's office. As I entered, Mr Walton told me gently to sit down, which immediately put my awareness into overdrive. I distinctly knew from Walton's demeanour along with his unusually gentle manner that something serious was about to pass from his lips.

I looked at him questioningly, staring hard in search of some clue as to what he was about to say. He returned my look, and I could see his facial expression was on the verge of great sadness. Now I knew what Walton had to say was very serious indeed.

With a low solemn voice, void of all expression, that emitted more like a hum, like a car engine ticking over in neutral, I heard the words that Leonard Jackson had died.

Once the realisation had time to penetrate my brain, I looked at Walton and said, "Dead" I spluttered, "He can't be," I cried, "the matron told me he was doing just fine".

"He can't be dead," I repeated with obvious hurt and emotion in my voice. "I was supposed to be visiting this weekend, so he can't be dead" I said somewhat subdued.

"I'm afraid he passed away during the night, I'm sorry Paul" he said, "I'm so sorry," said Walton.

There was a short silence before breaking down completely, spluttering and sobbing uncontrollably.

Mr Walton, the strictest master in the whole of Ashford came from behind his desk, stood by my side with his hand upon my shoulder. This was the first time I experienced human contact from Walton. After several minutes he told me in his gentle tone of voice, to take as long as I wanted. "Just take your time Paul, stay where you are and only come out when you're ready," he said.

Walton slipped out of the office, leaving me alone with my grief and now in my own little miserable world, which felt so unimportant, I sobbed my face off.

Two rivulets of tears streamed down my cheeks, unchecked, ending in a puddle on the floor as it cascaded splashing down to join the rest of my tears. My grief was interrupted by an inaudible rap at the door, which I chose to ignore.

A second much louder knock followed, before Bobby opened the door, then with two strides was at my side with his arms about me, consoling me with words of comfort.

"Come on Paul, please stop crying," pleaded Bob "you did your best for Leo, and you can't do anymore, no one can" he added.

Bobby was always there when I needed him most, I thought.

Bobby had obviously been forewarned by Walton, who had sent him to be by my side to help. Even though he was my best friend, Bob still saw himself as my guardian angel, but most of all in all matters he was reliable and true.

After a while he took me from that dismal place, putting his arm about me and steering me towards the games room, where Bob sat by my side as we watched senior boys play snooker. On reflection, these dark days were full of troubled times, and sadness of memories and times passed. Little boys grow up fast, always moving on to pastures new, there really was no alternatives.

The war years at Ashford were treated like some big adventure until, or when, it touched you personally, then reality kicked you in the teeth.

To the press or other news media, Leo was just another casualty of Hitler's war, becoming so much fodder to be fed to the public for general distribution, such was the nature of human failures.

My own thoughts along with all my memories would remain just that. My own, at least until the day I died.

But meanwhile, this very sensitive line was not open for discussion.

Aunt Joan
Reading

Page 53

CHAPTER EIGHT
Welcome To The Outside

One was forced to grow up fast in Ashford, and by eight years old in the outside world by this age you were put to work, chimney cleaning as well as a range of tasks that would eventually with legislation be banished.

At Ashford when you passed your eighth birthday, you were treated no longer as a junior.

At eight you had reached the age of responsibility, which also acted as a watershed in so many other ways. The new school term, which started in January of forty four, was well under way with Leo still fresh in my mind. My school report for the end of forty three wasn't pleasant reading, leaving much to be desired.

My English and maths scored the lowest in class, which was pathetic, but better success at history, geography and reading. Subjects like art, music, PT and swimming scored highest, which were all above 85%. However the most alarming part of the report were the written conclusions, which were very disturbing indeed.

Remarks stating my aggressive and disruptive behaviour and which showed traits that often rang alarm bells, it went on to conclude that perhaps a more secure environment may well be considered, for a more positive interaction of a one to one might prove more beneficial.

These remarks were made by the so called school welfare officer (today's social work) who I had never met. Her gobbledegook and psychiatric clap trap certainly besmirched my otherwise unblemished character and reputation, which did not bode well for my future.

With this shocking stigma, attached to my honourable name, I felt I had been dealt a fatal stab wound and at best, had been grossly exaggerated and misunderstood. In plain English I had been labelled the worst boy in the school, which may well have given me great kudos amongst my peers, but I never the less felt this was so unjustified.

Most of her information was in fact second or even third hand gossip, which we all know to be totally unreliable. I felt hurt, cut to the quick, and perhaps too slow, in protesting my complete innocence.

Anyway, enough rambling about some silly old cow, I was once again instructed to report to Mr Bailey's office. This particularly pissed me off, as art was my most favourite subject, which was being interfered with once more. On my way to the heads office, some of my more recent misdemeanours came flooding into my head, trying to recall what new trouble I might have to deal with.

This was one man, for some unknown reason, I dreaded most. The matron accosted me, just outside the office, who for some reason or other, adjusted my attire as well as brushed my hair. This as a rule was not a good omen.

Sweeping into fatty Arbuckle's office, where sat in front of my eyes, looked like a hen party taking place. The talk inside of this holiest of all places came to a very abrupt halt, as I was ushered in.

I knew I was in trouble, this abruptness didn't bode well I thought, looking from one face to another around the room. Mr Bailey, looking very serious indeed, was sat behind his alter like desk with two strange ladies sat either side of him. Miss Richards and myself sat together in front of this trio, feeling as if some kind of Spanish inquisition was about to take place. You could have heard a pin drop, the silence was so deafening.

All the while the two strangers were studying my every expression. Perhaps they were about to make a purchase, I thought kindly, until I saw a thick file upon the desk with my name clearly written on the front cover. Surely this thick file must have something good to say about me, no one could be that bad, could they? These two strangers before me had obviously been there for some time, they would need to have been to study such a bulky dossier I thought.

This gaggle of geese in my face was very disturbing, and I felt the aura within this office was more conspiratorial, leaving me even more bewildered.

"Now Paul" said Bailey in a voice reserved exclusively for visitors and dignitaries "this lady on my left is Miss Lowman. Miss Lowman to give her, her full title, is the Chief Inspector of all L.C.C. schools".

Now I could feel trouble in my water works, as without warning, I needed a piss.

"This other nice lady on my right is a Miss Joan Leigh Clare" said Bailey as he stood up, now feeling somewhat redundant like a spare part in an all female confrontation, and left. Now it was I who felt overwhelmed with an all female audience. Miss Lowman being the senior rank took over chairing the meeting, calling proceedings to order.

I could already feel the axe about to descend on the nape of my neck, and instinctively covered my neck with my hand. I looked at the two of them, sitting just a little too comfortably, designed to catch me off guard, before they had me transported to God knows where.

I looked at the matron for help, or guidance at least, but she was not forth coming.

Miss Lowman interrupted my thoughts "Well now Paul this kind lady is Miss Leigh Clare, who has come along to adopt you."

I was looking suitably perplexed, so Miss Lowman continued.

"Miss Leigh Clare is going to be your new aunt" she said in a matter of fact voice.

"What do you say to that Paul?" Miss Lowman asked.

I looked at the two of them as if they were speaking a foreign language, paused, then blurted out "Am I leaving Ashford?"

"Nooo" purred Miss Lowman "not exactly leave Ashford as such, but your aunt will be able to take you out of school from time to time!"

At this point my new aunt took over the proceedings. Miss Joan Leigh Clare was even taller than her friend, Miss Lowman, well into her fifties with an eagle beak nose, topped with silvery curly hair. Miss

Lowman on the other hand was younger than my aunt, more business type glasses, with just a trace of a tash on her upper lip.

I fell silent, withdrawn even, wondering what on earth they were babbling on about. My new aunt sat by, showing an interest in everything that was going on about her, while Miss Richards, the matron, just sat there speechless.

Aunt Joan, as I was to call her, wore a purplish tweed suit with a pale cream blouse fastened at the neck by a single silver brooch.

"Would you like to come out to tea Paul?" my new aunt asked with a knowing smile.

"Do you mean outside of Ashford? I enquired, as if it was a trick question.

"Yes darling" she said "we can go and sit in the car while Miss Lowman goes to fetch Maisy."

Was this some kind of ploy to get me to go with them to some place worse than Ashford, I thought, but asked a question of my aunt instead.

"Who's Maisy anyway?"

"Maisy is Miss Lowman's little girl," my aunt answered innocently.

"You mean you're not taking me away for good?" I asked suddenly.

"No darling, we are all going for tea" my aunt said.

My aunt stood up, offering me her hand, which I declined, as I followed her out to a waiting black Ford car that looked just a bit familiar. Remembering all those years ago, just such a car brought me to this awful place.

My aunt climbed into the back seat, leaving the door open for me to climb in beside her. I hesitated and my aunt could see my apprehension and quietly said, "You don't have to come if you don't want to." I noticed Miss Lowman coming out with Maisy, who climbed in beside my aunt as I held the door, then climbed in beside her. Miss Lowman got in beside the driver, nodded to him and we gently glided away, picking up speed towards the gates. The lodge housekeeper saluted us as we sped through the open gates on to the main road.

This was the very first time I had ventured outside Ashford in almost five years.

Within two miles the driver pulled up outside a posh house at 31 Ford Close in the village of Ashford.

Miss Lowman let herself into the house without using a key and waved to us all to join her. I helped Maisy out of the car, as she seemed a good two years my junior. My aunt seemed suitably impressed with my gentlemanly behaviour.

The Victorian house of large proportions was tastefully decorated with a spacious front and back garden. The hall and sitting lounge were far bigger than I imagined, and was equally impressive in both décor and antique furniture. Miss Lowman waved us all in, boding us all to make ourselves comfortable as she disappeared into the back of the house, leaving my aunt to watch over us.

With my best behaviour, I was determined to grace our surroundings with as good an Impression as possible. Miss Lowman with her elder sister re-entered the room laden with two heavy looking trays. There was so much food, with all kinds of tasty delights. I wondered if anybody should remind them, that there was a war going on outside, as my eyes popped out of their sockets, with my eyes sparkling wide in awe at so much delicious food.

"Everybody for tea" cried Miss Lowman's sister, as she laid down her heavy tray onto the sofa table next to me.

"Yes please" I squealed with delight.

The tea party was a great success, acclaimed by all, as I sat back in unbelievable comfort, patting my tummy contentedly. A long loud burp involuntary expelled from my lips, which brought raptures of laughter from all, as I sheepishly murmured my apologies.

One thing was certain; I would not need to eat at Ashford tonight. Alas the four hours or so vanished quickly, but the swell in my tum remained as evidence. As the daylight rays went down beyond the horizon, we all returned to Ashford.

My aunt assured me there would be many such visits and treats in store for the future, as she kissed my cheek and waved her goodbyes. I was still rubbing my cheek where she had kissed me, which confirmed my little boy syndrome that all females were sloppy creatures. Secretly however I enjoyed all the attention, thinking that my aunt really likes me. I thought she wasn't bad either. Towards bed times that night, Bobby quizzed me extensively, wanting to know all the details.

I told him everything except about the kissing, as I didn't want him to laugh. Knowing Bobby's affairs of the heart were similar to my own where families were concerned. You must remember in these left over time from the Victorian era, it was considered to keep all children ignorant where sex and sexual matters were concerned, as a matter of duty, as well as protecting our childhood innocence, or so they thought.

In these days' only comics or other recommended reading material such as classical literature were fit for children's minds. There was of course no television, computers, CD players or anything like exploring the Internet.

There were no mobile phones, digital cameras or DVD players. Even the wireless or radio programs were closely monitored. The very idea of talking about any sexual acts, were taboo and to actually carry out masturbation was the work of the devil. So everybody in Ashford over a certain age must have worked for the devil.

The idea of full blown sexual intercourse with a girl, was talked about frequently, but never undertaken, or very rarely. Any sexual promiscuity was treated as such an abominable crime. The thought of getting caught red handed didn't bare thinking about. To be caught in illicit intercourse was a crime compared with murder.

The boys practised masturbation, or self abuse, but even this most natural of acts of growing up, was dealt with as if you were a sexual deviant of the worst kind. This was also an age of great politeness, especially towards the fairer sex. Not P.C. today.

The importance of such manners and behaviour of ones own conduct was considered an essential, nay vital part of ones deportment. My aunt, who was very much in favour of all men treating all women as ladies, placed a great deal on this genteel age. With the arrival of spring and my eighth birthday fast approaching, my aunt inherited a lovely third floor flat from her mother, at 62a Fitzgeorge Avenue in West Kensington. I was fascinated by the Victorian wrought iron gated lift, as I had never been in a real lift before.

The area was very residential, catering for the professional working people that mostly worked in the city. With good underground, as well as bus links into the city of London, West Kensington was ideally placed for commuting.

I was soon to discover that my aunt and Miss Lowman, besides being spinsters were also life long friends that even went to University together. Outside their respective jobs, they jointly ran a special clinic in Brixton for pregnant mothers. I was also to learn much later, that my aunt obtained a total of nine degrees. Her kindnesses, as well as her manipulative skills, were finely honed, as I was to learn to my bitter experience.

The Leigh Clare family were a well established aristocratic lot, with a wealth of contacts and experience to pool. The family's personal connections to Queen Victorian were well documented, although my aunt was but a very small girl before Victoria died. She was able to relate true accounts of her family's involvement with Victoria, which I found incredulous.

Meanwhile my aunt set about correcting and improving my education, which she felt was absolutely appalling. Besides showing me most of the historical sites of London, which were too numerous to learn parrot fashion, I found her knowledge of London was inexhaustible. At the end of each day in London with her as my tutor, I was only fit to drop. Her range of knowledge was so vast most of the time, I simply found it mind blowing.

She introduced me to fine arts, which we both shared a passion for, and also to reading the classics. My aunt particularly showed interest in all my artistic aspirations, with great encouragement. Every birthday or Christmas, besides my main present, she always included a classic book to read, then quizzing me about the book on my very next visit.

She was herself a very accomplished artist and some time as a special treat, she would allow me to look through some of her art portfolios. Her work was breathtakingly beautiful, especially her life drawings depicting the human body in all its guises, which is always a difficult subject to perfect. It gave me great pleasure to study and practise the techniques used.

When at Ashford, my reputation for continuously pestering our tradesmen, as well as my art teacher for materials such as paper and pencils, was notoriously well known. My unquestionable thirst to quench all my artistic aims, and to sharpen my art skills, knew no bounds.

The staff at Ashford did not understand this uncontrollable urge for all things artistic, and saw it as an illness and unnatural in one so small. Whereby my aunt never once discouraged me and was always more than wiling to help supply materials to meet my artistic cravings, much to the relief of many staff at Ashford.

PART TWO
8 TO 12 YEARS OLD

CHAPTER NINE
Sexual Awakenings

The dormitory arrangements within the hierarchy of the school were composed of three preset age groups. From zero to eight years old covered babies or infants, as well as the main juniors, which were the majority in this group. It was in this first grouping that the "big boy" or buddy system worked most efficiently.

The second age group between eight and twelve years old, where the age of responsibilities was most instant, this being the intermediate age, which I was now entering.

Lastly the seniors of between twelve and sixteen, which was supposed to be the era of preparation for experience to work, and to enable one to leave Ashford for survival in the world outside. This then, was the ethos or the purpose of the school, in theory. The practice, well, that was something else.

Bobby my best friend was already established within this realm, having moved up some eighteen months before, but it didn't stop him spending just as much time in my dorm as his own.

This move to the fourth and final deck was also shared with two dormitories of the most senior boys as well. It was always a question of the rotation of available bed spaces, in these two separate age groups.

I was instructed, that I myself would be moving into one of the two intermediate dorms, come next Monday. My only concern was, would I get moved into Bob's dorm or the other, where I knew few of these lads that occupied it. However I need not have worried as the prefect in each of these two dorms was responsible for choosing who they considered to be most compatible for their dormitory. Not only was I in Bob's dorm, but better still, I also had the very next bed space to him, which pleased me greatly.

This move within the school was seen as a natural progression which all boys made some time during their eighth year. It was also considered to be the age of sexual enlightenment, which all boys on their way to puberty, albeit at various or differing physical stages of development, was to find out for themselves this emotion called sex.

There was no sex education in school taught in these days, with all the hang ups from prudish Victorian times, it was very much a taboo subject, not even open for discussion.

This move into the big boys league was somewhat daunting, as from this point forward the gloves did come off. No more protection from the buddy system for example, nor from more beatings from masters inclined towards more harsher physical abuse, by way of punishment. What is it they say about "every action undertaken as an individual, in turn stimulates a reaction in response".

In short, under this draconian regime, a good thrashing was even more likely. (Nothing-new there then!) There were some privileges, Bob was quick to point out, the main one was were once again together, bedside to bedside. This was true of course, but it also meant that Bob was also more available to lead me further astray, although to be honest I was often more than willing to tag along. The important thing was, Bob said, this move up, this vital rung with the big boys, was another step nearer to getting away from this dump.

The sexual awareness eventually comes to every individual boy and Bob at just over ten years old was starting earlier than most. The human physiology of ones body cannot be ignored, with the dropping of the testes and the first signs of pubic hair growth, is hardly something that can be missed easily. Bob, who was well developed in every respect, had already moved into this stage. In such a regime that we all lived under, it was little wonder that boys found some way of relieving their sexual frustrations. Most boys sooner or later practiced masturbation or wanking themselves off, usually discreetly at night in bed, or locked in some toilet cubicle.

There was always the exception to the rule of course, where an individual deliberately set out to shock their peers, in some kind of display or performance. And amid four to five hundred boys, there were bound to be a few homosexuals. These were rare, but if caught in the act, so to speak, by the establishment, were dealt with most severely and usually ended in being removed from school to a more appropriate place, wherever that was!

At no time in my thirteen years at Ashford, did I ever see any sexual abuse take place between a member of staff and boys. The masters frequently inflicted none sexual abuse by way of thrashings daily, as punishment to maintain order. Some masters more than others. Little did I know at the time of my move into my new dorm, that my sexual awareness was to become such a steep learning curve, meteoric in fact.

The shock treatment I was about to experience first hand was so unbelievable as to leave me utterly gob-smacked. Having left a sedate protective dormitory environment, then to find one in this new dorm, was like being sent into bedlam. Here the older lads were boisterous, running around in varying states of undress, horse playing about with each other in a carefree fashion.

This complete change of behaviour was something Bob didn't warn me or prepare me for. At the time he wasn't aware himself. I was surprised the noise alone didn't attract the attention of duty staff. Indeed, Bob explained to me, the staff very seldom came onto the top deck, perhaps they didn't want to confront, what they must have surely known, took place.

The head poncho, or prefect in my new dorm was a lad nicknamed Chopper Madden, who was renowned throughout the school for his great sporting prowess. To look at Madden he looked more like a sixteen year old, with Adonis like physique to match.

Chopper Madden was the current school boxing champion, as well as the schools cross-country running champ. He was also a shining light in a number of field sports as well as one of the schools best swimmers. Clearly not a lad to be messed with, and it was rumoured that the most loathed master, Sims, also thought so.

According to Bob, Madden's easy passage through Ashford's school life, was more to do with his sporting abilities, than any academic capabilities. In other words Bob whispered in my ear, "Chopper is as thick as pig shit!"

Fortunately for me, my own swimming abilities and fearful reputation had preceded me, and I had Chopper, more than anyone, to thank for my move into my new bed space alongside Bob. This thought did not sit easy on my shoulders, and I wondered if I was expected to do something in return.

"You needn't worry" Bob assured me "Chopper is a very sexual animal, but homosexual he isn't".

Needless to say I felt uncomfortable knowing that Chopper was responsible for manipulating my bed space. There was nothing I could do to change matters, as I found my sex education about to go into orbit.

"What time is lights out?" I asked Bob, when a boy called Fred on the other side of my bed interjected, quite forcibly. "When Chopper says so!" Bob informed me that Fred was the school dancing champion. I looked doubtfully at Bob who was sitting on my bed, thinking perhaps that he was winding me up.

"Yeah" said Bobby "He's a bit of a Fred Astaire".

Just as Bob was telling me about Fred, the door at the far end of the dorm swung open and in tripped half a dozen lads from across the landing approaching our end of the dorm. A sudden hush descended over the dorm, and I was anticipating some kind of confrontation.

As they made their way towards us, Chopper asked in an aggressive manner.

"What the fuck do you lot want?"

The entire dorm watched with abated breath, as one of the six boys whispered in Choppers ear. Chopper grinned like a baboon about to be fed.

"Have you all got 'the money?'" demanded Chopper out loud.

The boys all about twelve to fourteen years old, opened their palms to show Chopper they all had the required fee. Meanwhile the money was handed over to one of Madden's cronies, called Jim, who was the only person allowed to stand within touching distance of Chopper.

"Just watch" said Bob, who was still sitting on my bed. So I did. It was obvious I was the only one who didn't realise what was going down.

Madden quickly despatched two individuals to keep look out at the doors either end of the dormitory. With no further ado, let alone any sign of embarrassment, Chopper took centre stage, standing on the end of his own bed. In clear view of the whole dorm and what unfolded next before our very eyes, beggars belief.

First he undid the cord to his pyjama trousers, which he quickly let drop to his feet, before stepping out of the rumpled heap upon his bed. Standing astride in an act of defiance, he started to do his strip tease, button by button, to some imaginary dance music. Having undone the final button from his pyjama jacket with even more evocative moves, he threw his jacket across the dorm in a devil don't care gesture, to his worshipping public.

Now he stood on his bed completely naked, and it was plain to see why they called him Chopper.

A great cheer went up by his appreciative audience, as if Chopper had just scored a vital last minute goal at a match. Spellbound, totally transfixed, I watched with my mouth agape, which for some reason amused Bob no end.

Chopper's body movements with snake like action, swinging his pride and joy from side to side were almost hypnotic to watch. He then placed his hands behind himself on his rump, and through the power of his mind only, slowly got a massive erection. The size of his dick was enormous, the likes of which I had never before seen in my life, so well endowed was he.

This act, was certainly not normal behaviour, or was it I wondered? The surprise and spontaneity of sheer audacity of this behaviour, in front of a captive audience no less, was clearly designed to shock.

This effect as far as I was concerned was a complete success. On the other hand, if Chopper had been made of dark chocolate, he would have willingly sucked himself clean, so much in love, of his own body was he.

I had never before seen such a big penis and he carried it with pride, like any sportsman coveting his trophy.

Still with his arms behind his back, his penis reached its maximum length and stiffness and was now in an almost upright position, pointing skyward. Then slowly, as if taking a bow, he allowed it to return to a more horizontal state. At this point, Jim was instructed to place a total of ten half pennies edge to edge along the top surface of Madden's cock.

Without touching Choppers chopper and exercising great care, Jim took several minutes to lay each coin one by one along the bridge like structure. Having placed all ten coins along the length of the shaft in a neat single file or row, Jim took a half step back from Chopper's permanent projectile as the audience held their breath. Bob leaned into my ear to tell me that Madden had to hold his erection, unaided for two minutes to qualify and keep the money.

"By the way" said Bob still whispering in my ear "Fred is busy wanking himself off behind you!"

After the statutory two minutes, Jim stepped back up and got personal with cupped hands below the tip of Chopper's cock. To complete his masterly performance with a final flourish, Chopper allowed his huge appendage to take a slow bow, and as the ten coins slid down his shaft, Jim collected all ten coins, as they cascaded off the end of Chopper's dick, into his cupped hands.

The appreciative audience broke into rapturous applause for Chopper's elegant performance. I turned to see Fred ejaculate his own white spunk into his cupped hand, smiling in thanks to Chopper's stimulating help to jack himself off.

I noticed he had caught me seeing his finale, but without any signs of embarrassment calmly wiped his hands onto his pyjamas. Fred was about the same age as Bobby, or perhaps a little older, and I wondered if all boys went through this shedding of white water, and why?

"Well" shouted Chopper, having got redressed, "that's your lot" and pointing to the six lads that paid him a grand sum of ten half pennies or five pence, "You can fuck off to your own dorm now". Within five minutes of the six lads leaving, Chopper ordered everybody to their beds and for the main dorm lights to be extinguished.

Between 9.30 and 10.00 p.m. the dorm fell silent, much later than the normal bed-time. I could hear several boys tossing themselves off as I lay still, unable to get to sleep with my brain in turmoil. What an astonishing character Chopper was, I mused, but what kind of den of iniquity had I found myself thrown into, I wondered.

The following morning I awoke still mesmerised by the previous evening's entertainment.

Bob, who was facing me from his bed, could tell my little mind was troubled, and matters didn't help when he got out of bed with his own erection.

Casually only inches away from my face, he dropped his pyjamas in front of me, hiding nothing, as he donned his day clothes. Not wanting to get out of bed in the space next to Fred, I too shared the same space as Bob, feeling awkward, and just a little embarrassed.

"Welcome into the big boys world" said Bob "but don't worry, I'll make sure no one takes advantage of you."

Later Bob explained that "Chopper was harmless enough, but what you saw last night was really quite mild for him" said Bob.

I did my allotted housework, feeling somewhat bewildered and confused to this new life experience, which seemed to be accepted as a kind of normal behaviour by all the other boys.

Chopper was busy telling everybody what housework to do, in a supervisor capacity, but I for one wasn't about to argue. Halfway through the morning's class, I was told to report to Mr Walton in the dayroom office.

I ran like hell all the way down the drive, across the yard and into the dayroom office, where Mr Walton was busy working with a mass of paperwork all over his desk.

"Ah, Ankorne," he said on seeing me, "a bit out of breath aren't you?"

"Yes sir" I said still trying to catch my air.

"Right" he said "You will be going into training for our annual swimming gala in about six weeks from now."

"Yes sir" I smiled, feeling chuffed that I had been chosen.

"Okay" said Walton "cut along to class."

Which I did.

CHAPTER TEN
Sporting Progress

Mr Walton had entered me for several categories, in the forthcoming annual swimming gala with intensive training for this event, due to start in less than two weeks in earnest. The training was to be a set three nights a week for a full month before gala day. My particular training was to cover three main areas. Springboard fancy diving, breast stroke over four lengths and underwater distance swimming, which was a new category to be introduced this season.

All sporting fixtures were taken very seriously at Ashford, and even more so during the war years.

The everyday almost continuous bombardment that reigned above our heads, often seemed surreal. My entire life at Ashford so far, had been lived in this war torn environment. Most of us took this war for granted and some of us assumed it was there to add spice and adventure to our lives. Because of the more recent bombs dropping on the very home we lived in, it served to remind us of our own mortality.

I was reminded frequently, by the death of Leo, that life on a day to day basis was for living, because none of us could be certain as to what the morrow might bring. Leonard Jackson was not the only casualty of this bloody war, nor would he be the last.

The bomb craters that appeared overnight as if by magic in some of our playing fields, were a constant reminder of Hitler's evil intent. The ever increasing air raids over the London skyline seemed to get closer to us week by week, in spite of the fact that we were a good sixteen miles away. We were also continually informed by press and radio, that Hitler had an inexhaustible supply of bombs.

The whole of the boys side of the school was divided into four main house names, after famous warships. HMS Warspite, led by Mr Walton himself and I was very much a part of, HMS Warwick, HMS

Repulse and HMS Edinburgh. These were all ships fighting the battle of the Atlantic, but all our adopted warships were sunk to the bottom of the sea in the months ahead.

This only served to highlight the sheer stupidity of war, the pure futility of it all.

With these horrific times that we were all forced to live under, it was little wonder that we in turn became aggressive, and repugnant little animals ourselves. Life was far too short for any childhood, which was stolen from us anyway, at a very early age within and by the Ashford regime.

The blame game of war was used as an excuse for brutalising little children such as ourselves, who's only crime was to lose our parents because of the very war we were fighting. The playing fields of England or more precisely Ashford, in turn became our arena, for aggressive fighting behaviour. This competitiveness, encouraged by our so called betters, was just another way we could give vent to our real feelings. All sports at Ashford, were taken extremely seriously and only winners got recognition.

I for one detested, most big team games, such as football, rugby and even cricket.

I was in my element of any sport that demonstrated the skills of one's own abilities, such as climbing, swimming, fencing or even boxing. There were areas of the schools curriculum that were compulsory, such as dancing, swimming, church and schooling of course.

One Saturday afternoon, for example, I was pressed ganged against my better judgement, I hasten to add, into making up a team shortage of numbers to play football. Worst still I was put to play in goal.

With so much inactivity of such a vital position, there was also the possibility I could die of boredom.

A much bigger player, twice my size in body, was about to take a pot shot at goal. I was just as determined he wasn't going to get past me, regardless to his size. I barred his way, gritting my teeth as he fired a real slammer of a kick, which caught me squarely in my goolies, and the sheer brute strength and velocity of the shot carried me and the ball, several feet into the air and into the back of the net. Bobby who was acting as one of the referees at the time, came running to see just how much I was faking my injury, as I dropped to the ground like a stone.

The impact of which left me gripping my privates in agony, as I was stretchered off in pain, as my testes began to swell alarmingly. After a while with my eyes watering and in unbelievable pain, Bobby came to me while I was writhing on the grass, to give me words of encouragement.

"I think I'm going to need more than a few kind words" as I pulled down my shorts to look at the damage. My balls were already several times larger than they should be, and my dick looked very angry indeed. Bob, being alarmed stopped the game and called for an ambulance. A few minutes later I passed out, and I awoke in one of our own hospital beds in the infirmary, with Bob by my side.

For some reason, he seemed more upset than I , trying to steel my thunder I thought.

"The doctor is on his way," said Bob.

By now my cock had taken on a life of its own, rebelling against such abuse no doubt, and was alarmingly big and standing bolt upright like a guardsman on parade. I refused to let any female nurse and even the matron come near me, screaming at them to go away. The only male doctor who was also the only surgeon attached to the infirmary, duly reported to examine the damage. Even he was made to draw the screens, before I allowed him to carry out a close inspection.

Once everything was in place, he started his full, and very extensive examination.

As he peeled back the bed clothes and saw this thing more than twice its size throbbing upright in obvious pain, he looked at me, then my dick, and back again at me, as I reddened in utter embarrassment.

"I'm not doing anything, honest" I said.

He pummelled my dick as if it was a lump of raw meat (which it was beginning to look like) and gently squeezed my balls, which had swollen to as big as a large hens egg. His bedside manner wasn't very sophisticated, as I felt more belittled and humiliated. The, now numb, semi conscious behaviour of my penis, now much larger than I had ever seen it before, and still getting bigger by the minute, was very alarming.

"Pull your foreskin back," instructed the doctor, but it was far too painful to do so.

"I might have to cut it off," said the doctor.

"No you won't" I insisted "you are not having my manhood" I said with venom, covering up at the same time.

The doctor smiled, explaining he was talking about circumcision, not cutting or removing my penis. Not understanding his medical jargon and thinking him more as a butcher than a doctor, the subject was no longer open for discussion. The screens were drawn and the butcher told the matron to give me very hot baths, every two hours at least until he came back to look in and see me in the morning. Here I was, thinking that cold showers were supposed to be the remedy to dissuade arousal. No female staff were allowed in the bathroom, while I was undergoing this treatment every two hours. Bob came back that same evening and the nursing staff put a lobster cage in my bed, to take the heavy weight off this very sore part of my anatomy.

Bob was obviously very worried, as to possible long term affects to my manhood.

"Can I take a peek?" he asked, as I eased back the bedclothes so as not to disturb the cage above my dick.

"Wow" said Bob, "what if it stays that big?"

"Don't be stupid Bob" I said "its bound to go down" I said unconvincingly.

"What's circumcision?" I asked Bob, questioningly.

He looked at me in disbelief, then quickly looked about him to see if it was clear, before pulling his own dick from his shorts.

"That's what your dick will look like" said Bob "after you have been circumcised, the same as mine" Bob smiled.

"Isn't it sore?" I asked.

"Now who's being daft!" replied Bob.

"Well" I said "I am quite happy with the way my dick is, and I don't want any butcher taking any skin off my cock.

Bob just laughed, before the matron threw him out.

After about six very hot baths, I began to see a difference and with some feeling coming back into my old man, I was encouraged to continue the treatment. Having my sleep disturbed to continue these very hot baths, and by the second day, things were looking up, or should I say down.

The doctor came by and after telling him to handle my genitals with a lot more care, he took heed with more gentleness, although he was not best pleased to be told his bedside manner was not up to much

He seemed happier at my reduction, but was still hinting he might have to operate, as I could still not get my foreskin to go back. I knew he was not jesting, so after he had gone, I asked the nurse to bring me some cream for lubrication, which surprisingly, she thought, it was with the doctors directions, so she did. Later when I felt brave enough and with the help of such lubricant, I managed to reverse the offending skin until it was eventually tucked safely behind the corona ridge.

I endeavoured to keep it there in spite of the soreness, as I was determined to show the doctor on his next ward rounds, circumcision was not necessary. As a surgeon, he took just a little too much delight in wielding his scalpel I thought, and was determined that come what may, I would not be leaving any part of my anatomy behind.

The very thought of him cutting into my one and only sex toy, was more than enough to make me feel sick.

The following evening, Bobby came back to visit and was told by the matron not to be noisy or tire me out. Bob wanted a blow by blow report and I proudly pulled down my bed clothes to illustrate the success of my foreskin.

"So" said Bob "you have been circumcised at last, was it done today and was it very sore?"

"Don't be such a prat" I said, as I pushed my foreskin forward to prove my point.

"Is your cock sore?" I asked Bob wondering why he asked me if mine was sore, having thought I had been done.

"No, of course not" said Bob "I was circumcised just after being born" Bob explained "because of my Jewish faith. The swelling has gone down, although it would be great if it stayed big" said Bob.

"What do I need a big cock for?" I asked Bob "I'll be more than happy when it returns to normal. I don't want to be circumcised either," I added "I'm quite happy as a Christian anyway". Bob looked a little upset.

I knew Bobby came from a Jewish background, but was very surprised to learn all Jewish boys had their foreskins removed. To what purpose was this supposed to serve, I thought. To me this seemed a very barbaric form of mutilation, to do to one of the most sensitive parts of the body. Bobby I knew was sent to England long before the outbreak of World War II, with hundreds of Jewish kids all looking for refuge. Except for a much older sister, whom Bobby never spoke of, the rest of his family including his little baby brother, were all taken by the Germans. His family just vanished, presumably taken by Hitler's Nazi party, when Germany invaded Poland.

This was all news to me, which sparked a thirst in me, to learn more. Bob was only about two at the time and his knowledge was very sketchy to say the least.

"I only remember the Germans taking away my mother who was breast feeding my baby brother at the time" said Bob very sadly, as he stared into space remembering. In truth Bob didn't even know if any of his family were still alive, or where they were taken to.

I could see this was very painful for him, as his tears started to spill down his cheeks. I hugged him as best I could, begging him not to cry.

I think Bob's own personal life experiences, is what made him a very caring person to all boys, but especially towards me, as if I was his little brother, to replace his real baby brother who he remembered so lovingly.

Feeling the atmospheres was getting just a little too morbid, I changed tack by asking him how his swimming training was going.

"Okay, I suppose," said Bob "do you think you're going to be able to resume swimming after kicking you out of here?"

"Of course" I said, " I can't wait to leave this bloody place".

"I bet you don't mind the young nurses giving you a bed bath?" said Bob, now smiling once again.

"Don't be daft" I spat out" I won't let any of them come near my cock " I retorted.

"I would," said Bob. "Give it a few years from now, then you will become just as interested in your own sex toy like the rest of us," Bob emphasised.

I was in the infirmary for another three days before the doctor was satisfied that all was back to normal. I made a mental note to stay well away from such places, and I would never play football again, either.

I was given light housework duties for a week as my early morning share, which I milked for as long as I could. Fortunately for me, my aunt made one of her flying visits, which didn't go down too well with a certain member of staff. Lucky for me, my aunt made it absolutely clear, that she had not made this arduous journey across war torn London, to be thwarted by some objectionable little man called Sims, who was very much against me in particular, getting any kind of considerations.

I naturally agreed with my aunt whole heartily. On the other hand, Sims was not accustomed to having his authority undermined, least of all by some woman. The battle-axe of the matron was called to arbitrate, but politely informed Mr Sims it was not part of his remit, to decide who should or should not be allowed to go out of school. Mr Sims looked suitably heartbroken. To be undermined by one woman was bad news, but two for him, was a Shakespearian tragedy.

As the matron pointed out to Mr Sims, it was within her realms of responsibility, which sent Mr Sims running for cover. For me this was a distinct red letter day, and one, I would remember for a long time to come, although I was more than aware that Sims would more than even the score in time. Needless to say, I had a great few hours with my aunt who fussed over me like a clucking hen, protecting her one and only chick. She showered me with a cream cake tea, knowing it to be my favourite, and on the way back into school; she gave me a bag full of mischief sweets to give to Bobby, who she knew more about, than I did myself.

I returned to swimming training with a vengeance, determined to make up for lost time. Mr Walton was impressed with my dedication, but was equally concerned that I should not over do my enthusiastic efforts.

With less than a fortnight to gala day itself, I redoubled my training efforts in getting back into peak condition. My biggest fear was letting my team and Mr Walton down, who had always encouraged my swimming. This added fear, drove me on like some demented beast. The indoor swimming pool block, was another large Victorian purpose built building, that looked more like a museum from the outside rather than a heated swimming pool.

Like most buildings at Ashford, besides being large, it was also very ornate as well as robustly constructed. By today's standards, it may seem somewhat old fashion, but for me, this was a real pool and I loved every inch.

Every thing about this place breathed an aura of excitement, from its elaborate ugly gargoyles to its ornamental murals of Roman history, and superb crisp sculptured tiling.

This wonderful place represented to me some of the most happiest times at Ashford, and I could never get enough of it. Within its portals, was a twenty-five yard heated pool, with eight swimming lanes permanently marked by deep blue tiles on a cream tiled background. At the deep water end of the heated pool, was an inviting pale green in colour and at the shallow end of just two feet six inches, were also an elaborate set of changing rooms.

These had an open run of showers, toilets, slipper baths, steam rooms and massage tables. There was no mixed bathing ever allowed, in these prudish Victorian days, so there was only one set of changing rooms built into the original designs.

The swimming baths were the exclusive domain of Mr Walton, who was solely responsible for all swimming at Ashford. Along each spacious side of the pool there were some six tiers of seating, with the highest at the back against the long side walls, graduated in levels to the front. This spectator's gallery down each long side could sit at least a thousand souls.

The pool itself was dwarfed by the vastness of this high shell of a building that was topped by a semi vaulted glass dome roof. The craftsmanship throughout was simply stunning

The joyful sounds of children's play, enjoying the pure freedom that water represents to most kids, reverberated around the pool like great music in a cathedral.

This place, this wonderful glorious sanctuary, was one of the most joyful places in the whole of Ashford. Mr Walton, who was totally in control of this facility, saw fit in his wisdom, used this venue to allow all children to behave like children, who could spread their wings and escape the rigid rules and routines of Ashford life, even if it was, only for an hour or two at a time.

With Walton in charge, no other adult or master, was ever allowed to encroach on this holiest of joyful places. The swimming gala day would soon be upon us and, to which was organised like clock work, with a rigorous timetable for every team event, carefully planned to the last detail. With most of the competing teams from each house having their fair share of swimming talent.

Mr Gibbs who led HMS Repulse had in his team some of the schools finest, and had won this event several years on the trot. Each master, leading their own team was responsible for the ultimate selection for final entry, and composed of forty per team. Mr Sims' team was full of wimps or so others seemed to think, but surprisingly, some of the very best swimmers for reasons known only to Sims himself, were not selected to swim in his team, so HMS Warwick was predicted to come last. HMS Edinburgh, Mr Hammond's team, also had a fair share of excellent swimmers and lastly my team, HMS Warspite, led by Mr Walton, also looked formidable with its share of good swimmers.

All four houses were given timetables for training during the four weeks running up to the big day. Each team also composed a spectrum of juniors, intermediates and seniors spanning all age groups. The banter between each house was boisterous and none stop. With only a few days left, the building was decked out overall, with coloured bunting and flags from all over the world, except Germany of course!

At long last the biggest day in Ashford's sporting calendar arrived, Hooray.

The organisation behind the scenes was immense, as the spectators were shown their seats by boys, who were selected as ushers for the big event.

The very small group of genuine relatives were conspicuous by their absence, which one would expect at an orphanage. The biggest and most prominent group were all the Council V.I.P.'s with the Lord Mayor of London leading his entourage of lesser dignitaries.

At the shallow end of the pool in front of the changing room area, a number of tables were set up for all the trophies. Close by the main entrance Mr Bailey, the headmaster, hovered doing his MR Beagle impression, with deep bows to the bigwigs, to whom his kowtowing actions was just a bit O.T.T. The swimmers standing behind the head, were all doing their own impressions of Bailey doing impressions. Which was very amusing to watch.

The last of the spectators were members of staff, workers and their friends. By this time, only minutes to the off, the spectators galleries were looking impressively full. The false smiles along with a great deal of small talk were soon brought to order by a long sharp blast of the whistle from Mr Walton.

Most of the audience were taken by surprise, some even falling backwards into the laps of the spectators sitting behind them. Mr Walton, having got their attention, signalled for everybody to be upstanding for the National Anthem. This was duly played, on a worn record over the public address system.

I noticed my Aunt and Miss Lowman standing solemnly to attention towards the front of the crowd. They had been shown their front row seats by no less than Fred the dancer, who looked like a fish out of water in this setting. Fred who slept in the bed one side of me, might be the school dancing champion, but a swimmer he wasn't, and he looked most uncomfortable acting as one of several ushers.

With all the pomp mustered after the playing of the anthem, the audience were not sure what was about to happen next, so remained standing. Mr Walton, now smiling, signalled for them all to sit down, as the second record of a stirring patriotic march tune blared out, as all four teams entered the arena.

Like expert gymnasts, each team marched in single file, parading in freshly laundered navy blue trunks. With a total of one hundred and sixty swimmers, across the four teams now at their designated stations, the gala got underway.

The first event covered all the sprinting races, with tremendous encouragement from a very appreciative audience. With the last of the team relay races being fought bitterly, for places in gold, silver and bronze medal positions, the springboard diving display came next.

I did my utmost to get a good score, but eventually managed a silver for my best efforts.

The competition was at its fiercest, with the whole baths filled, with prolonged periods of applause from the spectators that entered into the spirit, enjoying themselves fully. The schedule for the entire afternoon's timetable ran with such precision, no wonder Walton was looking so pleased.

The final event was introduced to the audience as a unique event, taking place for the first time in Ashford's history of all past swimming gala's.

This was the long distance underwater element, where four members from each team, would endeavour to collect up to eighteen tin plates, scattered all over the bottom of the pool.

This was the one event I had put a great deal of extra training into, and hopes of being amongst the top six. The total of eighteen enamelled tin plates were strategically placed all over the pools bottom. There was at least one placed into each corner, with sprinkling of three or four around the centre, and the rest at random anywhere else, to make it as difficult as possible to collect all eighteen.

The swim was an underwater test of endurance, holding one's breathe with a combination of speed below the surface. The real secret of longevity underwater was not to take the maximum of air into the body, which would only act as a buoyancy, causing one to struggle and force ones body up nearer to the surface, against ones need to go deeper.

By filling ones lungs with say two thirds of the air, you had room to shunt air between the gullet and the diaphragm. With less air, and therefore less buoyancy, one could move easier across the bottom, and with less resistance.

With only the top swimmers from each team left, and high scores of fifteen and sixteen plates collected already, the four competitors were each given one final chance, to better their highest individual score so far.

While I was waiting to do my last swim, my coach, Mr Walton was quietly talking encouraging words of this technique he had developed.

Now my last attempt was underway, as I swam quickly down the first long side picking up my first plates, before turning down the short shallow end. Halfway up the third leg, I cut across to the middle of the pool to gather up three more stray plates before returning to the midway point of the second long side. Having picked up all plates on the way to my third corner, I could feel my chest cavity screaming for air, so I released a little from my mouth in bubbles to the surface. I shunted the little that was left between my gullet and stomach, as the weight of the plates now began to impede my speed, of underwater movement. As I went along the fourth short, and last side of the pool, I was now reliant on my leg kicks alone, as my two hands were now fully occupied in carrying this cargo of plates.

Not seeing any further plates and with lungs fit to burst, I erupted from the deep water, shooting clear of the water surface like a human missile, with my mouth open as I broke the surface screaming for air. The piles of plates grasped to my midriff, in two leg kicks I was beside the pools kerb, and then placed my pile onto the pool side, next to the diving board.

After catching my breath in one movement, I heaved my body onto the poolside.

The deafening applause assaulted my ears as it swamped over me. Mr Walton was walking the length of the pool, peering through the water to the bottom below. He came back to my pile of plates and sung out the numbers as he counted, one by one, plates. The audience shouted the numbers out, along with Walton's count of eighteen.

Walton unexpectedly broke into such a grin, which took most of us by surprise, as it was not part of his normal character.

"Eighteen plates, maximum" declared Walton, still beaming as the audience broke into yet another encore of applause. I slipped off to the changing rooms, feeling more and more embarrassed.

The lengthy final proceeding, of prize giving followed. This ceremony took ages, but no one seemed to mind.

Mr Gibbs team house, HMS Repulse, won overall first place, with my own house coming a close second. Third place was Mr Hammond's house, HMS Edinburgh, also close, with the last place going to Mr Sims, who spent the rest of the day walking about with a face like thunder.

I received two medals, a bronze and silver, but best of all the new silver trophy cup, that would eventually have my name as the first winner of this event, inscribed upon it.

Having got changed back into normal Ashford garb, I was allowed to spend some time with my aunt, who sung my praises, embarrassing me even more.

Thankfully, life quickly returned to a normality in the knowledge I would be hopefully available for next years gala.

CHAPTER ELEVEN
Recurring Nightmare

After my euphoric triumph at the swimming gala, I walked around, still floating on cloud nine. With my head swollen from arrogant pride, it only added to my already cocky attitude that put a spring in my step. The aura like glow surrounding my celestial body emanated enough power to lighten any dark room.

I continued to accept congratulations for my swimming prowess long after, my sell by date, with a puffed out chest in sheer conceitedness', which in turn made me behave like a real plonker. Glorifying in my new found status, more akin to hero worship of myself, Bob was beginning to get really pissed off with this new unlikeable me. Bob clearly felt that my overactive inflated ego, was in urgent need of deflation back into the real world.

So with this in mind, Bob casually but firmly pointed out to me there were others in the gala that won a shed load of medals, and were far better swimmers than my good self. Deeply wounded feeling very hurt, but suitably chastised, I quickly realised, that Bob was pointing out nothing short of the truth. Having effectively made his point, he looked at me in disgust, then promptly walked away leaving me to stew in my own juices.

At bed time, still feeling aggrieved at Bob's cutting remarks, I turned over to avoid looking at him in the eye, so ashamed was I, for acting like a complete dipstick.

Now facing Fred, who was fully aware of my very close friendship with Bob, felt this was a golden opportunity to exploit this slight altercation, by sucking up and sweet talking me. Not wanting Fred's overtures, I decided to go to the loo, mainly to avoid Fred's effeminate advances, which made me feel uncomfortable in the extreme.

Returning to bed, just seconds before lights out, I felt it was better to face Bob, who I trusted implicitly, rather than face the unknown of Fred's real intentions. I stared at Bob, in hope, and who often read my mind, Bob gave me one of his winning smiles and a knowing wink, then said good night to me, before falling asleep.

I gathered from this that our friendship was now back to normal, thank God I thought, when I should really be thanking Bob, my best mate, for his timely dose of reality.

The monotonous routine of Ashford grinded painfully slow, most of the time, unless you were enjoying yourself. With all the schools annual sporting fixtures over for yet another year, it would soon be only internal recreations to look forward to, with the onset of winter threatening just around the corner.

Bob suggested that one last visit to our secret pool, situated in the far reaches of the River Ash, while the last remnants of summer still lingered in the air.

We called it ours, because boys being known for their laziness, were not prepared to walk the extra distance, knowing it to be at the furthest corner boundary of the school grounds. This pool of ours was up stream, some good distance away, from the three main pools used by most boys because of its nearness to the main buildings.

Our pool was certainly more isolated, but also sporting some good rock climbs on the crag on the opposite bank, and especially as Bob and I spent time building our own dam where the water exits, before tumbling downstream to the hoards below. These plebs were known to stand on the banks with each other trying to out perform the other, by aiming their pissing jets further than his mate onto the swimmers within the pool.

Skinny dipping was common practice, mainly because no boy was issued with underpants. To get ones shorts soaking wet was in itself a travesty, because playing in the river was forbidden, so wet shorts was a sure give away. This recreation was so wide spread that everybody, including staff, was fully aware of this past time, but were virtually powerless to stop it.

Between the boys and girls on this section of the river it was securely fenced off, with barb wire, and as it was also close to the nearest of the three pools, presented its own problems, but it was mainly there to prevent mixed bathing. Because of its close proximity to the nearest and also the smallest of these three pools it tended not to get used. This did not prevent the girls trying to get more than an eyeful, and could often be seen stalking the undergrowth. So it would appear that girls were just as much sex mad as the boys, who were often seen trying to get their own eyeful.

So it was, that we preferred the privacy of this more distant pool, away from prying eyes, especially by those girls that enjoyed banding about ones vital statistics to all and sundry. Bob and I made our way to our own place, with Bob undressing quickly on arrival.

I could tell it was much colder than normal, undressing more slowly, not even sure if I was going into swim. Bob spotted my hesitant behaviour, calling me a big girls blouse, taunting me, which he knew would have the desired effect. The cold shock of water took my breath away and sent my balls running for cover, disappearing into my body internally.

"Shit" I screamed, "it's fucking cold"

Bob laughed at me, then started his splashing game, designed to stimulate me into action, no less. I quickly submerged, grabbing him around his nether regions, which I knew to be effective to make him back off. This he did, submerging below the surface out of sight. I meanwhile was treading water waiting for his reappearance, which he did below me and behind me, then putting his palms under my buttocks, and with one almighty toss, propelled me clean out of the water.

Bob's strength was impressive, but enough was enough, as Bob decided to get out first.

He towelled himself off with speed, as my teeth began to chatter as I joined him. He remarked on my shrivelled up dick, which felt exposed in an arctic winter, so I pointed at his own cock that was also suffering, as we roared with laughter at one another. He handed me the towel, while he quickly got dressed, then helped me to do likewise.

Bob looked at his watch, which told us to scoot sharpish back to base, running all the way to warm up. As we neared school, Bob asked me if I was still having nightmares, which I had been suffering for over a four week period, but refused to talk to anyone about my troubled soul. He noticed my reluctance, and wisely backed off as we entered the dayroom. "Perhaps one day" Bob said quietly.

Mr Hammond was waiting outside the shower room and wanted to know why we were both late. Bob spun him some cock and bull tale about not hearing his whistle due to the wind. He willingly accepted our excuse, because we were both out of breath and assumed our excuse was true, as we had made the effort to get in quickly. He ordered us both into the showers, which we both enjoyed standing under a nice hot shower, to bring back warmth and life into our bodies.

After a while I soaped my entire body in suds, as is my want, when I suddenly felt a hand go up between my bum and grab hold of my balls. I quickly rinsed the soap from my eyes, turning quickly to see Fred, trying to recover his poise. He was sporting a full erection, as the curtain of red descended in front of my eyes. I struck out, swinging my right fist, catching him squarely on his jaw.

He went sprawling along the wet soapy floor on his back, travelling a good ten feet or more, holding his chin, which was already beginning to swell up.

"I was just reaching for the soap," he spluttered by way of an apology.

"Up my arse was it?" I threw back at him, and then recommended he stay put on his bum as his dick deflated like a punctured balloon. I was still livid, when Bob came over, having missed Fred's unwanted sexual advances.

"What happened" Bob asked "and why did you hit Freddy?"

A boy standing close by quickly filled Bob in fully, with a repeat of everything that had happened.

"You know" said Bob "I think Fred has always fancied you Paul, from the first" he added, but failed to finish his sentence as he saw by my expression I was none to pleased.

Fred was still sitting on the wet floor, nursing his chin as I went over to him.

"You had better more your bed space by bed time."

Bob was about the same age as Freddy, the dancing queen. I said to Bob "He may be the school dancing champion, but he's not going to dance with my tackle."

Mr Hammond entered the shower room, as I was finishing off dressing, asking Freddy what he was doing on his backside nursing his swollen jaw. Bob and I left Fred to concoct his own story of woe.

Dancing lessons, like swimming, was compulsory at Ashford and in fairness, most boys really enjoyed themselves, as they saw the dance hall as the only official opportunity to manhandle girls.

It was on the dance floor that I met my first girlfriend, Sylvia St. John, who was a dream to dance with, and quite a dish. I enjoyed the physical contact with her, although she was a good year or so older than myself. Bob said I was well and truly smitten and used to tease me endlessly. We just seemed to click together and I was told on several occasions she took a shine to me also.

With my ninth birthday coming up fast, my interest in girls took on a new dimension. Perhaps they weren't all as sloppy as I first thought.

Up until my aunt appeared on the scene some eighteen months ago, birthdays had no real meaning to me. However the impact this good woman had on my life, brought new and exciting experiences to savour.

I was quick to grasp the advantages of enrichment; my aunt gave to my life, especially outside of Ashford. In spite of my persistent naughtiness, my aunt soldiered on regardless. She accepted the challenge when she chose me, and I had no intentions of short changing her. After all, I had a reputation to maintain, which to her made the challenge even more worthwhile.

When I went up to bed that night, I was pleased as well as relieved, to see Fred had moved his bed space to the far end of the dormitory, about as far away as he could get. My recurring nightmare that I had suffered for some time returned that night, with even more menace, thanks to Fred. Before getting into bed, while in a state of undress, I remember showing Bob proudly my very first pubic hairs around my dick. Bob jokingly asked me to wait, while he found his magnifying glass.

"You wait and see" I told him "I'll soon sport a bush like yours" I warned, as I climbed into bed.

Feeling my manhood was coming along nicely, thank you, Bob casually smiled, more to himself, as he said "You're growing up fast, and the next thing to happen will be the dropping of your testicles" Bob assured me.

Later, I drifted into deep slumber, only to wake with Bob's hand over my mouth, trying to stop me screaming, as I was in the middle of my own nightmare.

Having calmed me down, Bob climbed into bed beside me, asking me to tell him my troubles. I clammed up, determined to remain silent, as Bob continued to soothe my brow, saying "Okay, but if not tonight, then maybe tomorrow?" he asked.

"Alright" said Bob, not receiving any answer from me, "Tell me when you're ready, there's no rush" added Bob reassuringly. Bob continued to hug me, talking away in comforting tones staying off the subject, he knew would upset me.

He told me to think of Sylvia, and the good times we would have together in future years. Bob stayed with me until I drifted back off to sleep, with no further interruption till morning. Next morning Bob was looking at me from his bed, with no mention of his disturbed night, on my behalf. As I got out of bed ready to set off for my morning ablutions, I felt the front of my pyjamas sticking to my privates, which still felt damp. I tested the damp patch with my fingers, before realising I had just had my first wet dream. Bob's expression never altered, but I was sure he picked up on my predicament, as I quickly donned my shorts. On my return to my bed, I noticed Bob had already folded my pyjama bottoms, and placed them below my pillow. He climbed out of his own bed sharing the same bed space, and as he dropped his pyjamas, he said "you know Paul, it's perfectly normal to have wet dreams, it's just another part of growing up, becoming a proper man, it happens to us all" Bob added as an afterthought.

I looked at him nodding my understanding, but thinking the dream I had later, about Sylvia may have triggered it off. Better that, I thought, than that bloody awful nightmare. After several more nights of this recurring nightmare, I could see Bob getting more and more impatient with me, so I decided reluctantly I must confide in Bob, as the burden of guilt I felt, was becoming unbearable to carry alone.

I just had to entrust Bob with my most horror of sexual horrors. Perhaps the ultimate realisation, that Bob was the only one I could impart this dreadful feeling of such frightening proportions, of the horror I witnessed that night, long ago.

I could no longer keep it to myself, the guilt I was feeling was so overwhelming, I had to pass it on to someone. Who better, I thought, than someone that knew me better than I knew myself. As I watched Bob with a partial erection, getting dressed, I made up my mind to tell him.

"Bob" I started, looking for some encouragement, and getting it, as Bob responded. "I want to tell you everything, but not here and not now," I spluttered.

"That's okay Paul, lets go to our secret place later, where we can be sure of not being overheard "said Bob. I nodded in full agreement.

So having arrived in our place, we quickly crossed the river at the shallows of the dam, carrying our plimsoles to keep dry. We settled our bodies, stretched out across the slabs that were already warm from the sun.

I was still fearful of saying anything, because of possible consequences or repercussions I might bring upon myself. Bob reassured me several times, that anything I said would be held by him in utmost secrecy.

He laid back on the slabs, holding my hand in support, then closing his eyes Bob said "in your own time Paul, there's no rush" he said gently.

"Okay" I started "do you remember about four weeks ago, I had the trots, with liquid sewage pouring from my rear end and like no tomorrow?" Bob nodded as I continued "Well one night I was particularly short and was forced from my bed in the early hours, desperate for the loo, and holding my arse in fear of messing myself before reaching the toilet. I dashed into the seniors toilet, which was nearest, just making the cubicle in time, as my guts emptied itself in a torrent, I had been sitting on the throne, just five minutes or so, when three senior boys came into the bathroom. There was a hole in the cubicle door, which you could see most of the bathroom layout from within, while sitting on the pan."

Bob nodded in recognition, knowing first hand the very cubicle in question.

"Well these three lads stood in front of my door, plain to see, as the biggest lad and one of the younger lads, handed over money to this other young boy, who checked the money before putting it into his pyjama jacket pocket."

"The boy who took the money" said Bob "is called Kenny, a raging homosexual, who sells his body for money, go on!"

"Anyway" I said, "they all got undressed, standing around the bathtub, absolutely bollock naked, playing with themselves. The big boy was extremely well endowed, at least as big as Chopper Madden, and was circumcised, like you Bob."

"I know him," said Bob "he's called Bishop to his mates."

"Stop interrupting Bob" I said, so Bob shut up.

"The two youngest, Kenny and the other lad about fifteen, with red hair, lifted up the duckboard from the floor, putting it across the width of the bath, like a bridge. Inside the cubicle I was sat in was quite dark, but the single light in the ceiling above the bath was fairly bright. Anyway, Kenny laid down on his back, on top of the duck board across the bath."

"The big guy, Bishop, stood at the end where Kenny's head was, playing with his monster above Kenny's face. The other guy stood between Kenny's legs and was busy tossing himself off. As he neared the apex of his excitement, he lifted Kenny's legs onto his own shoulders, lubricating Kenny's anus with the end of his erection that was already oozing some spunk. Kenny reached down with his hand, guiding this boy's cock into his arse. It slipped in easy, meeting no resistance."

"The Bishop boy, at the other end allowed Kenny to play with his big balls, the size of hens eggs, while his enormous dick danced its own tune, without any hands on, or help. Meanwhile, ginger, I'll call him, because he had reddish hair, was getting very excited building up a steady fucking rhythm, penetrating his full length up to the hilt. I mean, he was well enough endowed, but nothing compared with Bishop, whose shaft was very thick. Just before ejaculation, he withdrew completely, as Kenny reached up with his hand ready to takeover."

"The first spurt leaving the end of his cock, spat out, landing on the Bishop's face and neck. As each spurt lost power it was Kenny who received more than his fair share. Great, I thought, now maybe I could get back to my bed, but the two standing bumpots, changed over ends, like half time at a football match."

"I sat their transfixed, unable to prevent myself watching like some sordid peep-show, which it was. The thought of getting caught by these sexual predators was too horrific to contemplate. I dare not move now, I had seen too much for my own good, I thought!"

"Suddenly I was aware of Bishop's penis darkening the hole in my door and thought for one split second he was going to stuff it through the hole, which was about one and a half inches across the diameter. Or worse still, look in!"

"But no, he moved back between Kenny's legs, who was now on his knees on all fours, doggy fashion. Kenny by now had a full erection, through self arousal, and was busy taking the young lads penis into his mouth, although he had only just recently ejaculated his first load. Bishop took a big globule of thick white spunk from his own knob, into the palm of his hand, then wiped it into Kenny's entry."

"If he puts that giant weapon into Kenny, he's bound to hurt Kenny, I thought."

"Bishop squeezed his knob between his fingers to narrow the head shape, while Kenny below him, was bracing himself in readiness, to receive Bishop's weapon. Bishop paused to adjust his own stance for comfort, resting his dick pointing skyward, like a rocket ready for launch, between Kenny's buttocks."

"Feeling ready for entry, Bishop tapped Kenny on the bum, as he eased his squeezed arrow head shaped knob into Kenny's anus. I saw Kenny wince, as the full corona stuck, then with a firm push from Bishop, the knob head entered inside successfully, passed the ridge of no return."

"Kenny began to relax a little, taking the other boys length deeper and deeper down his throat. Bishop having stood for a good two minutes, now began to ease his shaft inch by inch deeper and deeper into Kenny's cavity. It seemed to be sliding easier, when Kenny instructed Bishop to go deeper and quicker. Kenny was now on a high, as he shouted faster to Bishop, then without warning, Kenny's own erection went into climax of ejaculation with complete uncontrollable spunk flying in all directions, without Kenny even touching his own dick."

"Bishop had paused meanwhile, with the length of his shaft outside, but retaining the knob only, internally. You could see Bishop's big testicle bag pumping and pulsating away, delivering his sperm to the penis head. Bishop let go of everything he had, emptying himself inside Kenny. Bishop then smoothly ran his length up to the hilt, squeezing excess spunk, by the sinking of his shaft so deep, the white liquid was forced backwards through the anus, dripping onto the floor between Bishop's spread feet. When he did withdraw completely, as his knob pulled free of the sphincter muscle, it made a sound like a cork leaving the neck of a bottle."

Bishop calmly left the other two, and went over to take a shower. Ginger, the other lad, was determined to reach a second orgasm, standing in front of Kenny, who was still kneeling. With practised ease, using his hand to jack himself off to a state of readiness, and just prior to ejaculation, Kenny began to suck deep throat again."

"With the boys body jerk movements, Kenny swallowed it all as if sucking on an ice cream cornet, on a casual afternoon out. I could not comprehend why I just sat by, spell bound watching the whole performance."

"I continued to sit for a further twenty minutes, long after the trio had left, in real fear of being discovered. The last image of Kenny climbing down and walking bow legged, as if he had just dismounted from horse back, was the last image I remember seeing, before he too calmly took a shower."

I lay there alongside Bob, who still had his eyes closed, wondering what he was going to say. After what seemed an eternity, Bob opened his eyes and looked at me with a bewildered expression on his face.

"So" said Bob picking his words carefully "was that the sum total of your nightmare?" he asked searchingly.

"Well" I replied "not quite, the worst bit of the dream is they caught me at half time through their performance, when Bishop came right up to my door!"

"Yes," said Bob "What happened next in your nightmare?"

"All three raped me, starting with the two young ones first then finishing off with Bishop, it was terrifying" I said. We were both silent, absorbing this new revelation.

"Is that why you end up screaming?" asked Bob. I nodded my reply.

"Look Paul, even if they had caught you, they would not have done anything to you. The only real homosexual of the three is Kenny and he only performs for money. Also" added Bob "I know for a fact, he's shit scared of you, and anyway" said Bob" I've seen a lot worse than that." Bob claimed casually.

"What did you do?" I asked Bob.

"The same as you, nothing and as long as none of them come near me, they can do what they like" said Bob.

"It's not my job to interfere in their morality "Bob said with feeling. "Your nightmare is mostly in your head" said Bob, "especially about the rape scene."

Trust Bob to put it into perspective, making a lot more sense than I even did. I was beginning to feel silly.

"How do you know the big lad was called Bishop?" I asked.

Bob smiled at my complete innocence, or was it ignorance, then opening the front of his shorts, extracted his own penis. "What does my cock remind you of?" asked Bob.

"What do you mean?" I asked "it's just a cock without a foreskin.!

"When we play chess, what chess piece does my cock look like?" Bob asked.

The penny finally dropped, as I realised most like the bishop on a chessboard, including the slit in the bishop's helmet or head. It now made sense, why Bob always referred to his dick as the Bishop.

Bob went on, "Kenny has always been an arsehole bandit, and is reputed to have more money than anyone else."

The fact that I willingly watched such sexual debauchery performed by this trio, made me feel ashamed and guilty, I explained to Bob.

"Believe me" said Bob, putting away his bishop, "I have seen a lot worse than what you saw that night and you only did what anybody else would have done, confronted with such a performance. You have no need to feel guilty" said Bob "I would have done the same, and probably tossed myself off into the bargain" Bob said most emphatically. If Bob was trying to ease my guilt, he was succeeding.

"Another thing to remember" said Bob "all three participated of their own volition, as well as pay money to Kenny for sex. You see" said Bob "if boys are willing to pay good money in return for sexual favours, that just makes them stupid, and is not your problem, so your best to mind your own. Nothing like this is ever done against ones will, and to be honest Paul, the few genuine queers in Ashford are shit scared of you anyway, so stop beating yourself up."

I don't know why, but this last statement made me feel a lot better, secure in the knowledge, perhaps, that Bob had experienced seeing much worse, which helped me to realise I wasn't alone in what I saw that night. We both got up together, as Bob put his arm around my shoulder, as we ambled back to school, laughing and joking with a carefree attitude, which gave me confidence and hope.

Best of all, the recurring nightmare never returned.

CHAPTER TWELVE
White, Crisp and Even

With my nightmares gone and virginity still intact I had a great deal to look forward to, and with a guilt free mind.

We reached deeply into the final fortnight of December Forty Four. The dull glow of daylight seeping through the blackout drapes covering all the windows in the dorm, was a brighter morning than normal.

The whiteness of a crisp few inches of new snow that covered the landscape overnight was responsible for this brightness. From the fourth floor fire escape door, the sky overhead was a deep azure blue in a cloudless heaven.

The three or more inches of pure white powdery snow, that cloaked every feature of the scenic landscape, was crisp with not a footstep to be seen.

The lower rooftops from our high vantage point, were like virgin slices of white bread. The network of spidery branches of nearby trees, traced their tendrils against the blue sky, were both eerie, but magical as one. The breathless air hung motionless, evoking a compelling urge to go out to explore.

Meanwhile more snow was forecast, but I prayed it would not interfere with my very first Christmas holiday, away from this place called Ashford. I was looking forward so much to spending quality time with my aunt, as my excitement reached uncontrollable proportions. The last thing I wanted was any kind of conspiracy, to prevent this long awaited event from happening. My fears were unfounded of course, as the transport links to London was free of all weather obstructions.

My aunt came down from London by train, arrived by local taxi to Ashford and duly arrived in school.

My aunt explained to me that we would have an extra passenger, as she had been asked by her brother David, to uplift a boy called Patrick Chaulkley. I thought my name was unusual, but Chaulkley, who was also a resident at Ashford.

Pat, as I called him, was the chosen one of Lydia and David Turner. The Turner's in their wisdom, had decided to take on Pat, like my aunt, had taken on me as her boy. Pat was younger than myself by a good eighteen months. He may have been my junior in years, but never the less, stood a clear inch or more taller than myself.

Pat had the most vivid blues eyes and a flaxen blonde head of hair, like ripened straw of gold.

He sat alone on the back seat of the taxi, as I climbed in besides him, wearing a sullen expression on his face. Once my aunt was in, the taxi headed off to nearby Ashford Station, with not a word spoken between us. Pat sat motionless, tight lipped, eyeing me with suspicion. A right barrel of laughs I thought, trying to remember where I had seen him last at Ashford.

On the short trip to the railway station, we sat studying each other, neither of us impressed with the other. I knew nothing about him, so I asked him how long he had been at Ashford. He looked at me as if I had just been dragged into his space by a bullmastiff. He begrudgingly answered with a snobbish air, looking along the ridge of his nose at me, "Over two years" he said.

"A right chatter box, aren't you" I said to him, and because he looked about to burst into tears, I quickly told him I was only joking. Pat's mouth turned up at the corners at a brave attempt to smile, by way of a response. Perhaps he had already been warned of my reputation as an undesirable, I mused, as we all got out of the cab.

Aunt Joan meanwhile, sensed the awkwardness between us, so addressing herself to Pat, she informed him that the Turner's would come by our flat to uplift him later that day.

The thought of having to put up with this plonker for most of the day wasn't my idea of heaven.

We crossed over the footbridge for the London bound trains platform. We took an express train non-stop to Waterloo, the centre of London's metropolis.

Once we arrived in Waterloo Station, we would spend several hours here my aunt explained, before taking the underground onto West Kensington where the flat was.

My aunt took us both to the non-stop cinema where we all watched cartoons and the latest news reels about the war. Slowly, the iceberg called Pat, began to thaw as he appeared from under his protective shell, he started to get quite chatty. My aunt was doing her utmost to bring us together, obviously wanting us to become good friends, using her manipulative skills to encourage the both of us. The wimp responded to all my aunt's overtures, sucking up by the bucket load.

I began to feel sick, but did my utmost not to reveal my true feelings. The smarmy git, launched his own brand of charm offensive with the ease of a real pro. With an urgent errand to run for Pat's uncle David, my aunt gave me implicit instructions to take care of Pat until she returned. This was a God sent opportunity for me to lose this git, I thought, but with my aunt's instructions still ringing in my lugs, I resisted the temptation. When my aunt returned, we all had a quick lunch, before taking the tube to West Kensington.

My aunt's flat at 62a Fitz George Avenue, was just around the corner from the newly built Olympia Exhibition Hall. As we entered the hall on the second floor of this superb Victorian residence, the warm lit hallway was most welcoming. My aunt paused at the first door on the right, indicating that this was to be my bedroom, with the bathroom across the hall opposite.

"I do hope you like it" my aunt said, as I peered inside the unlocked door to get a quick look, with Pat breathing down my neck.

"May we go in?" I asked politely.

"Of course you can darling" came back my aunt's reply. So both of us entered deeply into the room, looking about us with interest. It was much larger than I thought, furnished beautifully with choice pieces of attractive mahogany furniture. I looked at Pat's response which was positive, as Pat smiled broadly nodding his head like a donkey with approval

Perhaps, I misjudged Pat I thought, who obviously had good taste and who was now sticking to me like a pot of spilt glue. At the appointed time, Uncle David and Aunt Lydia breezed in reporting for duty to pick up their latest acquisition, Patrick, then departed even faster.

Lydia, my aunt explained, was desperate to break into the film world as wannabe actress, she was certainly glamorous enough, I noted. David, Pat's new uncle and my aunt's brother was already in the business as a film director with the studios of J. Arthur Rank, already living in the luvvy duvvy world of make believe.

Both the Turner's were already very much a part of the new jet set era, assuming a mantle of self importance, living in the clouds of their own making, far removed from reality. These bampots lived in a penthouse apartment (not flat) in South Kensington, the new place to be seen.

They were far more at ease, hob nobbing with the latest clutch of new celebs in London's society, than with the likes of us. Pat, I was soon to learn, was their latest status symbol to be paraded at special charity functions when it suited the Turner's.

Now I really began to feel sorry for the poor mutt. I feared the only reason for the Turner's to grace us with their patronage, was mainly due to my aunt's aristocratic genealogy. The Turner's superb penthouse suite of apartments (not flat) as Lydia was quick to correct me, was overlooked by two equally repugnant Pekinese pug dogs. These pampered pooches, were excessively over indulged, one couldn't help wonder if the Turner's were aware there was a war raging outside.

The apartment was very large and clinically white, but furnished with the very latest "nou vou" modern furniture, that was all the rage, but neither comfortable nor practical to sit on. I looked across at Pat, who was precariously perched on the edge of a modern priceless piece, looking scared and very uncomfortable. He was also sitting as far away as possible from tweedle dee and tweedle dum, who were both busy licking their disgusting sexual organs.

These two lap dogs were the most vicious pair of brutes you ever clapped eyes on. They sat there on plumped up velvet cushions on their very own love sofa, waiting impatiently for their next expensive tit bit.

The penthouse was a very desirable piece of real estate, with panoramic views over the London skyline, fully air conditioned with airflow and temperature controls fully automated. Pity I thought, otherwise these obnoxious pair of brutes might easily be despatched via an open window, making the world a better place.

Poor Pat didn't have a cat in hells chance, with these two lovable brutes to contend with.

The Turner's meanwhile droned their monotonous tones of utter drivel of film star chat, my aunt who had clearly had more than enough, stated we must be leaving.

Pat suddenly sprung into life and onto his feet, directing himself to my aunt. "May I come and sleep over with Paul please?" asked Pat.

David looked at the boss, Lydia for guidance, but Lydia quickly interjected saying to Pat "No darling, your mine and here you have your own aunt and uncle", implying that two was better than just one. I could see pat was disappointed, but for the time being he was stuck with the Turner's

On the way back to our own comfortable flat, my aunt felt a need to tell me a little more about Pat's unfortunate family background. Not, I hasten to say, because she wanted to, but because she felt my understanding of some of Pat's tragic past, would better equip my own understanding, to build an already fragile relationship with Pat.

Pat's mother had butchered his father in front of Pat, when he was less than four years old. The mother was convicted of murder, and who, in turn was hung. Thankfully, Pat remembered little of what must have been his own private nightmare. My aunt would not go into any more details and made me promise never to repeat anything I was told in absolute confidence.

The only outward physical damage were Pat's mood swings, afraid of darkness and wetting the bed in the past, but now seemed to be getting better, my aunt assured me. For some reason my aunt told me "Pat was initially very much afraid of you, perhaps because of stories he heard in Ashford. So you see Paul darling," my aunt appealed to me "we are all reliant on you, to help Patrick in every way possible."

Assuring my aunt I would do my very best to help Pat, I changed the subject, which I felt was getting a little too morbid.

"Why is David's surname Turner and not Leigh Clare?" I asked my aunt.

My aunt replied simply, "because her brother chose to take Lydia's surname, when they got married" she said, "instead of using the family name of Leigh-Clare". This only confirmed to me that Lydia was by far the dominant partner, but there was no doubt that David, was completely besotted and worshipped the very air that Lydia breathed.

I was beginning to feel a great deal of sympathy for Pat, not envying him one little bit, but was determined to see he received no more hurt, if at all possible. After all, my aunt was quick to point out, Pat was a kind of half brother with both the Leigh-Clare's and Turner's being interrelated, like it or not.

On return to the homely comfort of our own warm flat, my aunt switched on the coloured lantern lights of the small Victorian Christmas Tree that once belonged to my aunts' mother. In the year 1902 her mother was still riding a bicycle at the age of one hundred and three years old.

"Was it a Penny Farthing?" I asked my aunt. "No" she told me, "It was a velocipede, which was really quite modern at the time," explained my aunt.

Her mother died at the age of one hundred and five years old in 1904, my aunt explained.

"Very old then" I mentioned. "Are you nearly as old as that?" I asked innocently"

"No" my aunt replied, and then burst into laughter. Quickly changing the subject my aunt informed me "Pat was coming over to spend the day with us, so you had better have a bath before bedtime."

My aunt ran a hot bath for me, telling me she would look into to see me before I went off to sleep.

"Don't let the bugs bite," she said as she kissed me goodnight. After a good nights sleep, I found I had overslept, the first in a very long time, but without a care in the world, I felt safe away from the clutches of Ashford.

For breakfast I got stuck into bacon with real eggs and oodles of hot buttered toast with marmalade. I could easily get used to this life style, I thought, as my aunt spoiled me rotten!

Pat duly arrived as we set off for a fun packed day in London. He was relaxed and very happy, I thought. Firstly we all visited the Ideal Home Exhibition at Olympia, which was just around the corner from the flat, mainly because my aunt had designed her own house, still yet to be built, several years hence, and wanted to see the latest in modern gadgetry. Her grand plan, she explained, was to build a new house somewhere in Hampshire for her eventual retirement.

We then took a red double decker bus into town, where we all spent time at the Tate, which I really loved, before going onto the science museum, which Pat really enjoyed.

My aunt then treated us all to a slap up meal at Lyons corner house, before she collected theatre tickets for a pantomime we were going to see on Boxing Day, before returning home after a very full day.

It would seem that Pat and I were destined to spend a great deal of time together, as the Turner's had their own life style to consider. My aunt explained this to both of us over supper before bedtime. Why wasn't I surprised, I mused, but made no comment. I could tell Pat was pleased with this revelation, relaxed and easily accepting his lot.

I was sure we would both benefit from this arrangement, as I knew my aunt would see to that fact. We were both getting very excited this first Christmas Eve away from school, but as my aunt pointed out to both of us, we would both have to share the one double bed, for the time being at least.

Pat was obviously very pleased, but remembering Leo, I was less sure, especially if Pat should accidentally piss my bed, I thought. With this in mind, my aunt protected my mattress, just in case of such an occurrence.

My aunt ran a hot bath, which we shared because all hot water energy was used sparingly during the wartime. Pat, I found, had a thing about sleeping naked, which in itself was common practice at Ashford, but still at the tender age of seven and sharing a bed with myself who also preferred sleeping in the buff, just didn't feel right.

He also moved around a great deal while he slept and snored. When I complained about this to my aunt she roared with laughter, pointing out to me I was easily the worst snorer between the two of us.

When we woke up, Pat and I sneaked through to see if Santa had left us any presents below the tree. We were not disappointed, as we both spotted several presents with our names on them, before scooting back to bed, not knowing the drill.

When we heard my aunt coming we both pretended to be fast asleep, which didn't fool my aunt for one second. As she left, she shouted to us both that we could come through if we wished!! Pat was first out of bed, like a rocket, until I reminded him to put his pyjamas on, so I took advantage of beating him through to the sitting room. As Pat quickly joined us, my aunt said knowingly, "I thought you were both fast asleep," and we all burst into raptures of laughter.

"I think we should all have breakfast before we open our presents" my aunt said, pouring on the suspense.

"I'm not hungry," I said, just a little too quickly for my own good. We both put on our face of disappointment, which did the trick, as my aunt played our little game just as easily by telling us we could pick just one present each.

I looked at my aunt searchingly, wondering which present I should choose, with Pat looking on just as excited. My aunt told me to pick anyone with my name on it, so I chose one that was a book called Treasure Island. Not to be outdone, Pat chose a parcel of similar size, which was also a book called Kidnapped.

Both books were beautifully illustrated with full colour plates, as my aunt looked on, seeing our grins of delight at having received such wonderful gifts.

We were both thrilled because we were both ardent readers. They must have been difficult to obtain, because good reading material was hard to come by during the war years.

"I hope you both enjoy them very much and perhaps you can both get some good reading while you're here" my aunt hinted. The reflection in my aunts voice, told us both a very busy schedule was planned for the week, and we might find it a little difficult to get a lot of reading in, but try we would.

We ate a lighter breakfast of toast, with real butter and marmalade, being far too excited to eat much more.

After breakfast, Pat and I got down to some serious playing with a large box of Victorian games, belonging to my aunt since she was a child. The box contained many different games of snakes and ladders, draughts, ludo as well as tiddlywinks, which was one of Pat's favourites. We continued playing until we were forced to stop for lunch. Lunch was always eaten after midday or noon, but was really more like a dinner.

The whole time we were hard at play, Aunt Joan was busy in the kitchen preparing lots of food. The large dining room was dominated by a large oak, ornate table that was always highly polished and very much treasured as a family heirloom. The craftsmanship of this lovely table was simply breathtaking. Even before the table was extended, it could sit eight place settings comfortably.

The three extension pieces made of solid figured oak, stood upright against one wall in the dining room, and required two persons to lift and insert them into place. The winding mechanism to extend the table to any length required, was in itself of Victorian engineering, but with all three inserts in place, the table could be lengthened to a full eighteen feet long, sitting up to twenty four people.

My aunt had already set the table with a variable banquet fit for Royalty. The delectable choice of goods made our eyes pop out like gobstoppers, and our tongues hang out in disbelief. Never before had either of us seen so much food assembled, before our very eyes.

There was a large silver salver of cold meats, including chicken, turkey, olde English ham, bully beef and different kinds of sausages. There were trays of fresh cream cakes and a big bowl of mixed fresh fruit set in vivid red jelly and topped with custard. Roast potatoes, stuffing and brussel sprouts, and best of all, individual home made trifles that my aunt was legendary known for, and was always my favourite.

There were smaller bowls of mixed sweets, nuts and potato crisps, all set off with heavy ornate silver candelabra with lit candles. There was also real quality Victorian style crackers set at the head of each place setting.

Far too much food I thought, but learnt later that all the Leigh-Clare family contributed towards this feast.

Pat sat there in awe, grinning like a Cheshire cat gorging himself on bowl after bowl of fresh cream. We both shamelessly pigged out, fit for bursting point, even my aunt was surprised at the amount of food we demolished. An hour or so later, having over indulged ourselves to the full, my aunt asked us both politely (referring to the glutinous pigs before her) "Anybody for Christmas pudding with real cream and brandy butter?" We both looked at her in astonishment thinking she was joking, but quickly realised she wasn't! We both declined her kind offer, at least for the time being, as we thanked her, asking if we could be excused from the table.

Holding our tums, like newly pregnant mums, we waddled like ducks to a pair of comfortable armchairs, unable to move. When my aunt entered the living room, she once again asked would we like anything else to eat! We both groaned in total satisfaction, like a very happy pair of contented pigs, wallowing in mud heaven.

Well my aunt finally said "There's ample left if either of you feel peckish later on." Do you think she was trying to tell us something, as we both settled down to read our new books. The psychology behind giving us both good books to read was now obvious, as we both became absorbed for many hours of some serious reading in our different adventure stories.

Much, much later, we both managed a cup of tea and a cream cake or two, surprisingly, but continued to read. After several more hours reading, my aunt chased us both through to have a hot bath at bedtime. The pair of us frolicked around like a pair of water babies splashing water everywhere.

We both ran into the bedroom naked, then climbed into bed, snuggling down as my aunt came through to tuck us up for the night. Pat gave my aunt a big hug and a kiss, and thanked her for such a good day. She gave us her usual peck on the cheek, saying, "now don't let the bugs bite", leaving the door ajar so that light from the hall gave comfort, for Pat's benefit. He snuggled close into my back as we both fell over into deep slumber.

In the morning, Pat remembered to don his pyjamas before going through, where we sat in front of the gas fire, eating hot roasted crumpets for breakfast. We returned to the bedroom, racing each other, stripping to the buff, to put on our clothes ready to meet another exciting day. While we were getting dressed, we heard my aunt on the phone talking to David, her brother.

"Mary from across the hall has her own key" we heard her say as Pat looked at me wondering what was going on. My aunt put her head around the door, apologising for her sister in law, Pat's Aunt Lydia, who was running late, but later that day would leave a package for Pat, with my aunts cleaner, Mary, who lived across the hall from us.

"Mary had her own key, as she comes in twice a week to do for me," my aunt explained.

I looked at Pat, who instead of being disappointed was delighted, as it meant he could stay over another night as it would be far too late during black out time, to travel across London. With this explanation from my aunt, Pat nodded enthusiastically in full agreement.

We all set off taking a red double decker across London with great joy. We bounded up the stairwell to the top deck, leaving my aunt to climb more sedately, as we rushed to sit down up front.

We marvelled in excitement as the bus veered it's way through heavy traffic, winding it's tall sides, threading it's way between lofty buildings with a pilot's view, the double decker pausing just long enough to pick up passing trade, with passengers getting on and off.

We all alighted close to Buckingham Palace to watch the changing of the guards, this fine Boxing Day. Mother hen gathered her brood of two chicks with pride, answering all our questions, armed with historical facts. My aunt then took us to a small café she knew to feed our greedy little bellies with sausages and mash, followed by a huge sticky Chelsea bun, all washed down with ginger beer.

We all left the café in good time for a very special treat to see our very first pantomime of Peter Pan. This was the secret, to which my aunt kept well, as to which show she was taking us to. As we entered the auditorium, we both decided we needed a wee. My aunt asked if we could manage, as she pointed out the correct toilet doors to go through.

"Okay Paul" she said, "look after Pat" as we both headed off, Pat hanging onto me, as the lights dimmed to semi darkness. The loo was full of kids with the same idea, shouting like a nest of songbirds calling for more food.

The few individual urinals were occupied with a bit of a queue, so we ducked into a cubicle together to piss in tandem. Finishing first, I told Pat I would be waiting just outside the door for him. We then rejoined my aunt, to our seats, much to the great relief of my aunt.

Meanwhile the theatre filled up to bursting point, until not a single seat was left in the house. The orchestra struck up the music, introducing the start to Peter Pan.

A silent hush filled the auditorium, as we snuggled comfortably into the warmth of our curved seats. The magical story of this extravaganza, unfolded, holding us spellbound in a hypnotic trance, leaving us completely enthralled.

The two hours of this lavish production sped by as if it was just minutes, leaving us begging for more. I could not accept that the whole show was over so fast, and said so quite strongly to my aunt, expressing my feelings as if we had been short changed.

My aunt, who smiled with understanding, from someone so young, knowing, I believed with so much passion, was amused at my findings.

Not a word was uttered from either of us during the entire performance and like myself, Pat also felt it should have lasted at least twice as long, or even longer. Naturally we found it so enjoyable, we both felt it should have gone on and on.

We spilled out onto the pavement, reluctant to leave this wonderful world of fantasia, which we felt was very real indeed. A British soldier, standing at the head of a very long queue just outside the main doors, bent down to speak to me.

"Well poppet" he said, "where have you just come from looking so happy?" he asked.

"Peter Pan" I said with glee.

"Have you now" replied the soldier "I think I'll have to go and see for myself" he said.

"You can't" I replied smartly, "He's gone off to never never land and won't be coming back" I said with great feeling. "So there" I added for good measure!!

The soldier burst out laughing at my child like innocence. It wasn't until my aunt explained at length, exactly what a pantomime really was, I believed it was so true. I fell silent as the make believe bubble burst into reality, as I struggled to come to terms with the real meaning of pantomime.

"Can we go again? Can we go again?" I begged to my aunt.

"Perhaps one day" my aunt smiled her reply.

I didn't remember the return journey home, lost in a fantasy world of my own, wondering if I would ever meet Peter Pan again.

After tea my aunt switched on the radio to listen to her favourite station. After the six o'clock news, my aunt ran our bath then chasing us both through with authority, she said we could read our book in bed for a while. Without any resistance I went ahead, leaving Pat behind to open his present left by the Turner's.

I submerged deep into the bath feeling the warm water surrounding my body. A little while later, Pat came in without saying a word, climbed into the bath between my legs. We both relaxed silently, luxuriating, indulging in the cosy warm soapy water, deep with our own thoughts.

I stood up, wiping soap from my body with a flannel, before stepping into the bathroom floor mat. Pat remained silent, but studying my body with curiosity, when he suddenly spoke for the first time.

"Why has your dick got hair around the top?"

I smiled down at his upturned face of innocence from his question, but just handed him the soap without answering. He stood up to examine his own dick, as if he was seeing it for the first time.

"Don't worry Pat," I told him "you too will grow hair eventually. I added to reassure him, "I expect my own hair will get much thicker in time over the next few years." I was just about to leave when the voice of my aunt shouted through the door "Make sure you dry Pat off properly".

I could see Pat was in no hurry to leave the bath, as he played submarines with his dick floating on the water. Enough I thought, as I reached down between his legs, finding, then pulling the plug. Grudgingly, Pat stood up refusing to get out to dry himself off.

I towelled him down, which he found funny, giggling his head off. I sent him packing to the bedroom, while I cleaned up the bathroom, before joining him, reading our respective books in bed for an hour or so, before my aunt came in to bid us goodnight. We both thanked her profusely for such a fantastic day.

As my aunt departed forgetting to leave the door ajar, Pat cuddled up close, shivering and complaining about the dark. I slipped out of bed to leave the door ajar, enough to let light in, and then put my arms about Pat's body, which stopped shivering as he went off to sleep. I dreamt about Leo that night.

We both awoke more or less together, Pat asking me to put on the bedside light to see the time by the carriage clock on my side of the bed.

He was desperate for a pee, as he climbed out of bed with his dick in a semi erected state from a full bladder. I told him to put on his pyjamas, but in a hurry, he just held his pyjamas in front of him, then scooted across the landing to relieve himself.

I felt his bed space with my hand which was still warm but dry. After a long pee, he returned into the warmth of his bed, throwing his arms about me in an affectionate hug, that was so spontaneous, it took me by surprise.

"What was that for?" I asked Pat.

"Because I think you're great" he replied "and you always take care of me.

"Don't be sloppy, you're my half brother, what do you expect?" I said.

Secretly, I knew with that moment suspended in time, we, for whatever reason, had finally bonded. Just before eight, my aunt shouted to us breakfast was ready, so we jumped out of bed together to go through. Pat was still naked, so I reminded him to cover up.

Later that morning, Uncle David and Aunt Lydia, breezed in as if they were returning from the shop. They had come for their precious package, Pat, with such a false show of pretence love, I felt like being sick again.

Leaving as quickly as they arrived, the wicked witch rattled her broomstick as they flew away on the next gust of wind.

"Only two days left," my aunt gently reminded me, asking me what I would like to do today.

"I'm so glad you two are getting on so well together" my aunt said.

"Oh dear" my aunt suddenly exclaimed "Patrick has left his present, from his Aunt Lydia, behind."

The present in question, was a fancy pair of shorts, complete with attached braces, they would have looked pretty on any girl.

They were the latest fashion and very expensive my aunt said. You wouldn't catch me wearing them I replied. These shorts were a pale baby blue in colour, with very elaborate braces, and pretty Austrian alpine flowers running down the length of the braces front.

No self respecting boy, and certainly not at Ashford, would be seen dead wearing such a garment.

After spending what seemed an eternity on the phone with Lydia, my aunt asked me if I would like to go to the zoo.

"Yes please" I yelped with joy "I have never been to the zoo before."

"That's fine" my aunt said "you will be going with Pat and the Turner's, I hope you don't mind darling, but it will give me time to catch up with things here."

"No, that's okay." I replied, but wasn't so sure, but said nothing.

The Turner's duly arrived by taxi, as we all sped off to Whipsnade Zoo, I thought maybe a London red bus was not in keeping with the Turner's sophisticated image.

Pat sidled up to me on the seat and I wondered what he was thinking as he seemed unusually quiet.

Alas my first visit to the zoo was great fun, with Pat and Uncle David enjoying themselves immensely together, which rather left Lydia to make love to her fur coat. David was pleased that Pat and I had become good friends but Lydia for some reason did not approve, which pleased Pat even more. Pat obviously related to David, especially on a one to one basis, but with Lydia, seemed more distant.

However I noted, Pat was a real pro when he wanted something bad enough, with some of the best sucking up skills I have ever been privileged to witness. Always directing his desires to Lydia, the boss, Pat opened his big blue eyes and fluttered his Scandinavian fair eyebrows, and in his best purring voice, asked his Aunt Lydia if he could please have an ice cream. Aunt Lydia duly melted, to Pat's polite request sending David off to fetch.

Patrick, I learned, loved ice cream more than any other food. He licked it lovingly but slowly, determined to make it last. This, I could see, annoyed Lydia, which was not a pretty site. Indeed, Pat was still making love to his strawberry ice cream, long after the rest of us had devoured ours.

"Eat it up Patrick" snapped Lydia with a bite in her voice, which Pat ignored, giving even more exaggerated big licks, making a lot of lip smacking noises to boot.

By the time we had been at the zoo for a good three hours, Lydia decided it was time to make tracks home.

On our return journey to my aunt's flat, Lydia brutally told Pat "He would be back in Ashford tomorrow". Pat burst into tears, so I moved in close to cuddle and comfort him, as I saw David look sharply at his wife.

"Never mind" said David "it won't be long before you visit again" handing Pat a handkerchief.

We were slower on the return due the infamous London smog, which came without prior warning.

By the time we arrived at my aunt's it had turned into a real pea souper, as my aunt called it.

As we all stuck into a scrumptious tea prepared by my aunt, she suggested that perhaps it would be better if Pat stayed over to return with me to Ashford. The Turner's readily agreed, with Pat instantly shining like a new penny, beaming with joy.

That being settled, Pat himself couldn't get rid of the Turner's quick enough in case they changed their minds. Even his goodbye kiss was done with speed, as they went out the door. The transformation was like instant coffee. He became so relaxed, he was in danger of falling over.

We all sat in front of the fire, listening to a great play on the radio, which made us all laugh, as many a family up and down the country must have been doing, during these long war time evenings.

The hot bath was run, so I suggested Pat go ahead, as being taller than me, I thought I would give him time to stretch his limbs.

My aunt reminded me that if needed, a jerry was kept under my side of the bed, just in case Pat needed to 'go' during the night. "It's okay," I reminded her, "so far Pat had been sleeping well."

After a good ten minutes, my aunt chased me through to see that Pat was alright. So I climbed into the bath, asking pat to get out, as it was now my turn. I turned on the hot water to reheat the water, as Pat stood up in readiness to get out. I noticed he had been pulling back his foreskin, which was still back exposing his corona.

"Pull your foreskin forward" I told him.

"It won't go" said Pat" I've tried, honest I have" he said looking on the verge of tears.

"Come on" I said "let's have a look."

I soaped up his dick, which seemed a little larger than normal, but not as hard, as I worked his foreskin into place.

"There now, dry yourself off properly before you go through," I instructed him.

I laid back enjoying the bath all to myself until the water cooled. As I went across the hall, Pat was waiting just inside the bedroom door ready to ambush me with his pillow across my head. I pushed past him to get to my own pillow, to declare the start of World War Three.

We must have been making a racket, because my aunt suddenly appeared ordering us both into bed.

"You Pat" said my aunt "put on your pyjamas" and it was then that we both realised that he was still naked.

Pat begrudgingly put on his bottoms before climbing into bed. While my aunt tucked us up with the customary kiss, we both said in unison, "don't let the bugs bite" and then roared with laughter, which my aunt found amusing.

Once alone, Pat quickly discarded his pyjamas.

"Tell me Pat, why don't you wear pyjama trousers?" I asked him.

"They make my balls itch," said Pat.

He cuddled close, into my back, as we both drifted off to sleep.

Next morning, Pat must have woken first, as he gently shook me awake to tell me the time, Without warning, he hugged and kissed me several times over my face.

"What the hell do you think you're doing?" I asked.

"I love you" said Pat "and you've been very kind to me, I just wanted to thank you, that's all" he said.

"You don't need to kiss me," I said.

"Why not" said Pat, looking hurt, "you're supposed to be my brother, aren't you?" he asked.

"Okay okay, but don't ever do it in public, it's embarrassing" but I gave him a quick peck to show there were no hard feelings, which soon had him smiling again.

We went through for our last breakfast, as we were all aware this fantastic holiday was shortly coming to an end. My aunt reminded me there were still two presents on the tree waiting to be opened. They both looked the same, as I handed Pat his first. They were the same, a bumper colouring in book, with a great box of assorted colour pencils. Both our eyes lit up with sheer joy.

"Thank you Aunt," giving her a real smacker. Pat did likewise, as my aunt told Pat "It's Paul you should thank as it's his present to you" Pat came over to give me a big hug.

"Okay" I said, "but no kissing, okay!"

Pat stood back to look at me, as we made eye contact, we burst into laughter together.

She didn't miss a trick as we spread ourselves around the table for some serious colouring art work.

"What a fantastic holiday" we both said to my aunt, as we passed back through the gates of Ashford.

CHAPTER THIRTEEN
Unlucky Flick ~ For One

We both arrived back at Ashford, feeling very glum indeed, the anti-climax to such a wonderful holiday, away from this dump, was clearly affecting us both.

The moment we appeared together in the dayroom, Sims abruptly sent us both packing, post haste to take a shower. Pat was instructed, that the moment he had finished his shower, he was to waste no time joining the rest of his dorm, who were already upstairs.

We both entered the shower room together, to be met with kids frolicking and running about naked, having a great time, playing a game called Flick. Not a master in sight, these kids of ten to fourteen year olds were taking full advantage of the lack of supervision. This dangerous game involved flicking of the corner end of a damp towel, in a whipping motion at one another. The evidence clearly visible by way of large welts appearing on ones opponent's body, which is used as the target. This so called game had already reached a riotous pitch. The staff had frequently warned everybody about this games' dangers, because not less than six months before, one boy lost an eye as a result of being a victim of this game, known by all as Flick.

With three boys in particular attacking one boy on his own, it was only a matter of time before someone got hurt. Pat leaned into me, pointing to the boy under attack, and told me the boy was nicknamed Snake.

This kid called Snake, was already suffering red welts across his back, cowering towards his attackers who for whatever reason, had desire on inflicting some real harm. I shouted at the top of my voice for them to stop, which all, save one, did instantly.

The one nearest the boy called Snake, managed to get one last flick in, just as the boy Snake turned towards us. The crack of the wet towel in-flight caught Snake in his privates, and he hit the floor with a smack, screaming in agony. The attacking lout, having shouted 'bulls-eye' realised his victim was in serious trouble, which made him back away. No one went to the lad's assistance, as Snake was squirming and screaming upon the floor. Even from my distance, I could see blood mixing with shower water on the floor.

I grabbed hold of a lad, about fourteen, who assisted me in getting injured Snake flat on his back on one of the benches. The lad that helped me, promptly disappeared from view. I used a towel to mop up the injured area that was flowing with blood. On closer inspection, I could see that the foreskin was hanging loose from his penis. I quickly wrapped a towel around his shaft to stop the bleeding. I held his dick firmly, applying as much pressure as I dared, while Snake sobbed away in great distress.

"What's your name?" I asked the lad. "Brian" he replied, still crying. At first I thought the blood was coming from some internal injury, but after a while when the bleeding slowed, I made a much closer examination. The tear was bad news, starting from the underside of the corona where the foreskin ligament fastened to the underside, of the top most part of the shaft. To me, it looked quite swollen, but not being familiar with this boy's anatomy, I asked Brian to look at his own dick, to tell me how swollen it was.

I gingerly held it up for him to get a gander, concealing the tear to his foreskin. Brian thought it looked about normal in size, but was very red and sore to touch. I re-covered his penis, bandaging it with a fresh part of the towel. Now, I could understand why he was nicknamed Snake. I sent Pat off to fetch the master on duty. Thankfully, Mr Gibbs came back with Pat, who quickly took over from me. Brian was then taken to the infirmary.

I took my shower, then I went looking for my best mate Bob. First I delivered Pat to his dorm entrance, because he was already late, and I wanted to be sure he was okay. Pat beamed at me, with a look more akin to hero worship, giving me a big hug, before heading for his bed.

Not feeling in the best of moods, unable to shake the shower room incident from my mind, I went in search of Bob. As I walked towards the games room, Bob spotted me first, and rushed over to greet me, smiling one of his disarming grins, as he clapped me on the back robustly, before ending with a friendly bear hug.

"I heard you were back" said Bob, moving his finger along the side of his nose. "What's this shower room rescue you were involved in?" he asked.

"Shit," I swore "you can't fucking fart in this place without somebody knowing," I laughed. The twinkle in Bob's eyes, warned me that something was afoot, and naturally I was curious to know what was going down.

Sims swept into the snooker room with a face like thunder. "ANKORNE" he shouted at me "MY OFFICE NOW" he snapped. Bob put his hand across my shoulder, then said "I don't know, ten minutes back in school and already in trouble" quipped Bob, enjoying himself immensely!

We both raced at breakneck speed to the dayroom office to avoid Sims wrath, but he was already waiting outside the office door impatiently, waiting for me.

"You Alditch can buzz off, but Ankorne, inside my office now!"

As I entered, Sims made some snide remark about Bob and I being joined at the hip. Standing in front of Sims office desk, was the boy I recognised as the one who injured Snake so badly. Standing barefoot with pyjama bottoms only, he was obviously in great distress, trembling like a leaf. Having been in front of Sims many times myself, I knew exactly how he felt.

"Is this the boy (pointing to the boy shaking) that was responsible for injuring Brian Smith?" demanded Sims. I had no intentions of helping Hitler's cousin, Sims, but I went through the motions of being compliant.

I took a long hard look at the boy, who might collapse at any minute, he was so scared. I then looked at the pile of shit, across the other side of the desk, and who I loathed so vehemently.

"I don't think so Sir, but I didn't actually see who attacked Brian, as he was already on the floor, when I first saw him!"

Mr Sims was not a happy bunny, and my statement didn't help one bit, as he leaned across his desk, resting his clenched fists on the table top. He took a deep inward breath as he stared hard at the boys' face in front of him.

Sims shoved his face, within inches of this squirming wreck who looked as if he was about to shit himself. Sims fat nostrils flared open to allow the flames to shoot out, destroying this unfortunate quivering heap to a pile of ashes. I looked down at the floor space in front of this lost soul, as a puddle of urine spread slowly in front of his bare feet.

Sims, fortunately, from behind his desk was unable to see the boys' involuntary actions upon the floor.

"Well Baker" Sims barked, "you can be sure I'll find out the truth, and when I do, I'll skin you alive!" he said

"Get out of my sight Baker" Sims spat. Baker disappeared like grease lightning.

"You Ankorne," said Sims "you have become the bane of my life and even when you're not here, you give me sleepless nights.

"Yes Sir" I replied as he went on to spell it out to me what a serious matter this was.

"One thing is certain" trying to be flippant "he'll have a very sore cock," then wished I had kept my big mouth shut.

Sims looked at me in disbelief to have uttered such words, then reflected by saying "I suppose if you had not got to him so quickly, it might have been a lot worse" he said. I don't see how much worse it could have gotten, I thought to myself. I just stood there, waiting to be dismissed, as Sims appeared to be calming down a little.

"May I go now, please Sir?" I asked Sims, in my most pathetic voice. He looked at me blankly, telling me to get out. I took that as a yes, departing in haste to Bob, who was waiting for me at the bottom of the stairs.

We set off to the dormitories above. As we both undressed, talking all the while, I couldn't help noticing how Bob's dick seemed to have grown bigger with a forest of pubic hair. We climbed into bed, still chatting away non-stop, with Bob wanting to know all about my Christmas holiday.

Shortly after lights out, I could hear Bob tossing himself off, so I turned my back on him and went to sleep.

My first week back at Ashford seemed very dull, after enjoying myself so much over Christmas. Bob was bursting to tell me something special, which he had planned, assuring me it was a great idea. I was intrigued and desperate to know what scheme he was busy cooking up, and what new devious plan I was about to get myself into.

After tea that night, Bob told me to follow him to the playground toilets, so like a lamb to slaughter, I tailed him into the bogs. Once inside he pulled me into a particular cubicle, locking the door behind us.

Bob then stood on top of the loo, retrieving a black bundle of material from behind the cast iron cistern. He retuned to the floor, then sitting back down on the throne, he undone the black bundle.

Having donned his cape and face mask, he handed me the rest of the bundle for me to put on mine, likewise. I whispered in his ear "very dashing, but why are we dressed like Batman and Robin?"

He re-bundled the parcel, replacing it behind the cistern, and then unlocking the door, pushed me out telling me to wait outside. I don't think Bob was too impressed with my first reaction, judging by the way he threw me out.

Bob joined me outside, just as Sims came out of the dayroom. Bob checked his wristwatch, bang on time! We watched Sims climb onto his bike, lamp lit; he came across the yard, turning left around the corner of the toilet, where it joined the drive.

I looked at Bob still somewhat bewildered as to why we both stood there watching this habitual evenings ritual.

"So Sims is doing his evening rounds, so what?" I said.

"Exactly" said Bob, "you can set your clock by him his routine is so regular" Bob emphasised.

We crossed over to the swings and sat down, side by side. Still not sure what dastardly plot Bob was hatching, I waited for him to explain in more detail. Bob didn't disappoint me.

"How would you like to drive Hitler crazy?" Bob asked.

"Go on, tell me more" listening intensely.

"Well" Bob started, "with our disguises we both wait in ambush for Hitler (Bob's pet name for Sims) as he comes across on his bicycle tour. We wait up there" he said, pointing to the roof of the outside toilets, Bob paused, just long enough for me to grasp the nettle, as he extracted his favourite catapult and a small round pebble, from his pocket.

"Yes-Yes" I said getting into the spirit of bravado and dirty deeds.

"Watch this" said Bob, as he aimed at the lamp post on the corner of the drive and let rip. Twang was the reply as the stone found it's target.

"That" said Bob, "was Hitler falling off his bike."

I remained silent, thinking.

"What do you think?"

"I think you're completely mad" I replied, "It's very dangerous" I added.

"The roof's not that high," said Bob.

"It's not the roof you twerp, it's the firing of your sling shot at Sims" I said.

Bob looked at me as if I had just slapped his face, then jumped off his swing, and as a parting shot, said "I can always get someone else!" He then left me sitting alone. As my swing slowed down, losing momentum, a boy appeared from the shadows, coming towards me. This will be Bob, I mistakenly thought, as I said out loud "come back for another try, have you?"

It wasn't Bobby, but Snake, or rather Brian, who had obviously been discharged from the infirmary.

"What the fuck do you want?" I said, having been caught off guard. Brian rather taken aback at my aggressive response, quietly asked if it would be okay to have a word with me, as he needed someone to talk to.

"When did you get out of hospital?" I asked, not knowing what else to say.

"Yesterday" he said "but I've been looking for you to thank you for helping me that night."

There was an uncomfortable pause, so I took the gauntlet.

"Did they have to circumcise your dick?" I asked.

"Yes" he replied, another pause.

"Did the doctor do you?" I asked.

"Yes" again he replied looking rather sheepishly.

Talkative little bastard aren't you?" No reply.

"Look Brian, what is your problem?" I demanded, which sent him into a flood of tears.

I pulled him to me, putting my arm about him, feeling more guilty by the second, realising he had some kind of problem and I was being very uncharitable towards him, in a moment of weakness on my part. We both fell silent, as I gave him an understanding squeeze.

A few minutes passed, then Brian suddenly burst out with "How would you like to be deformed like me?" he demanded. "Now what are you babbling about?" I asked, wondering if his operation had gone badly wrong.

"It's not that" he said quietly" it's my dick, it's too big!"

"Let's get one thing clear in my head, your complaining about the size of your cock? I bet there are lots of boys who wish they had one like yours."

"Not like mine" he queried.

"Yes, just like yours" I said.

"No, not like mine" he said again, all the boys laugh at me and call me a freak, he said with feeling, taking out his dick from his shorts, to illustrate his point more forcibly.

"Now, you listen very carefully" I said, looking at his whoppa with awe "the other boys are rotten liars and are just jealous of you. Why else would they tease you? How old are you?" I enquired

"Eight next week" he said.

"Eight, is that all?" I replied, somewhat surprised, which didn't go unnoticed by Brian.

"See what I mean" said Brian " by the time I grow up, my dick is going to be far too big, no girls will want to know" he added as an afterthought.

"Believe me Brian" I said with real conviction," with a weapon like that, the girls will be flocking around you."

"Do you think so?" asked Brian with a hint of hope in his voice.

"Trust me, stop being so negative" I said" and the very next time someone slags you off, hold your dick proudly and wave it in their face, saying 'I bet you wish you had a smashing big cock like mine?' Say it with conviction, but most of all, say it with real pride and mean every word."

"Now stop waving it about before I get jealous, so put it away where it belongs" I told Brian.

Tucking it away with some difficulty, he broke into a real genuine smile, like sunlight bursting through a window. Having secured his snake back into its pit, he strode away with a pronounced spring in his step.

There goes one very happy bunny I thought, but pity the girls when Brian comes of age, or perhaps not. I had visions sometime in the future of Brian standing in front of a full length mirror and saying to himself 'Where shall we explore today, my beauty!'

Anyway I thought, I had better find Bob, to preen his ruffled feathers. Bob, being the past master at playing the game, would make it as difficult as possible for me to find him. His deviant mind, I told myself, would play me like an expert fly fisherman, before reeling me in.

Having made the cast, Bob was now waiting for me patiently to take the lure. Maybe I should play his kind of mind game, by deliberately not finding him, I thought.

However, as soon as he saw me, he gave me one of his winning smiles, which was his known signature, and he knew, he had landed his fish.

"Okay" I said, "we agree in principal at least, the idea of finding a way of teasing the hell out of Sims, was very appealing to me," I agreed.

Bob suggested a dummy run to iron out the practicalities for a quick escape route, might be a good idea.

"There is only one drawback" Bob was about to point out.

"Okay, what is it?" I asked, feeling I was now hooked.

"The day is already Friday, which means we have to wait more than a week before our first sortie" said Bob.

"That's fine by me" I said, "Because that gives us a whole week to explore all the rooftops to ensure a foolproof plan, I answered.

"After all" I pointed out to Bob, "we don't know Sims' climbing ability, which makes Sims and unknown quantity."

Bob laughed out loud, "Look Paul, with your known ability on those roof tops, Hitler doesn't stand a cat in hells chance, and you know it."

Why did I get the distinct impression I was being thickly buttered up, I wondered why he was massaging my ego.

The following evening, and while it was still quite early, we decided to put the first stage to the test, suitably clad in our new disguises, we both shinned up the drainpipe with ease. We then raced up the steep slope of the roof, passing the glass lights that the internal electric light clearly shone through. Quickly descending from the apex down the slope on the other side of the boys' toilets to the eaves below.

Bob, stopped just in front of nine-inch diameter pipe that straddled between the girls toilets on the far side, to the boys side where we were standing. This pipe bridge connecting both toilet roofs, spanned some twenty feet or more, suspended at least fifteen feet above more rooftops below. I had the distinct impression that Bob had been this way before. Bob hurriedly crossed this pipe to the eves of the girls toilets beyond.

When I joined him, he was already laying face down, looking through the window light into the girls toilets. I lay down beside him, waiting to see what our next move would be. It was even darker now as the toilet lights caused glare. It took several minutes for my eyes to adjust to this kind of darkness, as I asked Bob why we were waiting. He whispered in my ear for me to give him my hand, which I did. He took hold of my hand, then wrapped it around the shaft of his very hard dick.

It took me but a few seconds to realise Bob was wanking himself off, as his cock was very big and sticky. I quickly pulled my hand away in utter surprise. I fell silent as Bob turned onto his back, continuing to masturbate himself off.

I was about to leave when Bob suddenly got into a kneeling position as he reached the stage near to orgasm. With light shining up through the glass panel, showing his full erected dick as it ejaculated it's white mess, spitting its load all over the glass.

I felt conned and the whole exercise had been a sham, as it was obvious to me that Bob had been here before. I couldn't wait to get away feeling angry and getting angrier, as I quickly made my way down the drainpipe to our original start point.

I waited outside the toilets, with my disguise bundled up ready to give Bob as soon as he arrived. When Bob did arrive, he could instantly tell I was ready to blow my top, as I shoved my parcel into his mitts. He asked if I would wait on the swings, while he stowed the gear. I walked away, without answering him, as I was still afraid of what I might say.

As I waited for Bob, I began to cool off a little, when Bob did arrive he sat on the swing next to me, with not a word to say. He must have sensed my disapproval, and was unable to look me in the face.

I decided to take the bull by the horns. "What the fuck were you playing at Bob?" I demanded.

"Don't be stupid Paul" Bob countered "I was wanking myself off, what the fuck do you think I was doing" said Bob.

"So why did you make me hold your cock?" I demanded to know.

"Because" said Bob "you stupidly asked me what I was doing, and in the dark I demonstrated my answer to your stupid question" said Bob

"I didn't know you were going up there purely to jack off!" I spat at Bob.

Bob fell silent for several minutes, before answering.

"I'm sorry to piss on your parade, but" said Bob "you need to grow up Paul instead of behaving like a naïve little boy."

"So you have been up there before, tossing yourself off, haven't you?" I asked.

"Once before" said Bob "Do you never wank yourself off, or are you still just a baby?"

Now I really was angry, as I pushed him off the swing, shouting at him "Is that all you can think about - your dick?" I walked away leaving Bob on his backside, where he belonged.

What happened to the Bob I've known all my life, my Bob, I asked myself, as I walked alone, across the playground. As I stepped into the dayroom, rubbing my bum, which for some unknown reason felt sore.

I decided on an early shower and early bed, as I did not feel very sociable. Pat was sitting on the bench waiting for a shower to become vacant. I undressed and sat down beside him.

"You alright Paul?" he asked.

"I supposed so" I replied.

"That's one hell of a bruise on your bum" said Pat.

"Don't talk rubbish," I told Pat "there's nothing wrong with my arse."

Pat wisely decided not to push his luck, as he could tell something was not normal. I was really confused with Bob, but more importantly I was disappointed, and felt somehow used.

I knew Bob's casual approach to all sexual matters, and I also knew there was nothing homosexual about him. Bob was only eleven years old, and lately he seemed only to think of his dick, almost obsessively. He was already into girls, although I was nine years old, he seldom talked to me about the subject. Why am I making such a big deal over this, I thought, it's not that I haven't seen his dick in both flaccid and erected states many times before, or as Bob called it, his bishop.

I wondered what Bob was looking at through the girls' skylight. Maybe, I thought, when I reached Bob's age, I too would be interested in masturbation, which was supposed to be quite normal for all boys to do, once they became old enough.

When Bob did eventually come to bed, just prior to lights out, he looked mystified and very hurt. As he stripped off to the buff, he turned away from me, then I noticed a conker of a bruise on his bum. That must have happened when I pushed him off the swing, landing on his bum on the hard playground surface. As the lights went off, I turned away, feeling very hurt and upset, as I softly wept to myself.

Well after lights out, Bob came to my bedside, whispering to me if it would be okay for him to get in beside me, as he wanted to talk. Begrudgingly I said yes.

I could feel the warmth of his body as he turned on his side so we were facing each other. He held me close to him as he explained he did not mean to hurt me, and how deeply sorry he was for behaving so stupidly.

"Why did you make me touch your dick?" I asked Bob

"Did you think I wanted you to wank me off?" asked Bob

"Don't be stupid" I said "I know you're no homo."

"Well" said Bob "now when I think about it, it must have been a bit of a shock, I'm sorry." Said Bob.

"You know" said Bob "come to think of it, no other boy has ever been allowed to hold my bishop."

"That's okay, you've held mine often enough" I said.

"When?" asked Bob.

"I don't remember."

"When I was little and you used to wash me."

Bob laughed, "That's not fair and that doesn't count."

He reached with his hand and gently took hold of my dick. "Now" he said "we are now even. Goodnight" said Bob as he kissed my cheek and went back to his own bed.

I whispered over to him "What were you watching through the glass into the girls toilets?" I asked.

"I'll tell you in the morning" said Bob.

"No, I want to know now" I said like a tot having a tantrum.

"Very well," said Bob "but you come over here to my bed this time".

Once I settled comfortably Bob said, "You sure you want me to tell you Paul, because you're maybe not ready."

"Go on it may help me to understand why you couldn't stop tossing yourself off."

Alright," said Bob "you asked for it. I was watching these two girls, directly below me, they were already naked, working on each other" said Bob.

"They had this big long candle, like the one you see in church" Bob explained. "One of the girls was working the length of this very long candle into her friends pussy. I supposed the full length of this candle was about twelve or more inches long. Do you want me to go on?" whispered Bob in my ear.

"Yes" I said, now very intrigued.

"She was taking a good half of this candle inside her" said Bob "and it was beginning to shine with her wetness, After a little while, the girl holding the candle put her end into her own cunt. That's when I couldn't stop myself from getting rock hard" said Bob.

"Anyway" said Bob "they were both seeing who could swallow the longest between working it into themselves in tandem. At times" said Bob, "the whole of the candle disappeared in side their pussy, between them."

"The scene before my eyes was so erotic, I knew I had a stiffy as I put my hand down to feel."

"Okay that's enough, I'm already hard." I said to Bob.

Bob put his hand down to feel. "Now do you know what I mean?"

"Yes" I said, feeling embarrassed as I felt some fluid ooze from the end of my cock.

"I'm sorry," I said as I felt the end of my dick brush up against Bob, who also was hard.

"You might as well finish yourself off." said Bob, pulling back the bed clothes. I turned onto my back with no inhibitions with Bob at my side, wanking myself off to a full ejaculation, taking care to retrieve my spunk onto my belly. I laid back elated, as Bob tossed himself off for the second time, spitting his spunk high, but under control, so it also landed on his chest and stomach.

Bob handed me his pyjama jacket, as I wiped myself off and then wiped himself down, with his dick refusing to go soft. I whispered into Bob's ear "That was my first real wank." We lay there together, in peace.

I went back to bed and fell asleep instantly.

I slept soundly that night, long and deep, remembering what had happened the night before, only because I wasn't wearing my pyjama bottoms.

Why didn't I feel a sense of guilt, I asked myself?

Remembering the activities the evening before, when I pushed Bob off the swing, made me realise that this was the only time I lost my rag with Bob. It was I that walked away from Bob, because of my stupid misunderstanding on the roof, which I over reacted to. Yes, Bob had changed, he was growing up faster than me, and I have to try and understand this change taking place, in the both of our bodies.

I turned over in my bed to face him, he suddenly broke into that famous smile at me, then I understood, Bob's body may be changing, but below all that testosterone, it was still the same old Bob, I always knew.

I climbed out of bed to get dressed; Bob suddenly interrupted me as I was pulling up my shorts.

"Turn around" he said. "Wow, that's one hell of a bruise you have on your bum."

"I know" I said "you gave it to me when I pushed you off the swing onto your arse."

"What do you mean?" asked Bob.

"Turn over Bob, show me your butt. You too, have a fucking great bruise." I told Bob.

"Snap" said Bob, laughing.

CHAPTER FOURTEEN
Vengeance, At Last

Bob reminded me, we had just one week, to learn our craft across the rooftops, before we created havoc, against our friend Hitler. We would be reaping vengeance on behalf of so many boys I kept telling myself. The time available, before we tackled the real thing would best be spent effectively, and to explore every possible bolt hole, dead end and ideal escape routes.

Between us, we fully discussed the ground rules, we must put in place, for our own safety.

(1) No more than two weekday evenings a week, which we should vary from week to week, designed to confuse the enemy. Besides, said Bob, there were too many activities at the weekend, as well as the fact that we would be missed if we didn't attend.

(2) If either of us didn't feel up to 'par', then the other would not undertake to go it alone.

(3) We must also find a very secure place to hide our gear, because if this could ever be traced back to us, we really would be in very deep shit, the consequences, Bob emphasised would be very serious indeed.

All of the above essential points were agreed. We should enjoy ourselves to the hilt, said Bob because Sims has had this coming for a very long time. He said this remark, with the kind of hatred, I so dearly shared with him.

From the outset we convinced ourselves that this evil plan of ours, was primarily designed to allow more freedom for boys and girls to fraternise, without hindrance from the likes of Hitler, who's only aim in life was to prevent love from flourishing.

After all, the dangers of bottling up all this testosterone, that was obviously rampant in an all boys setting, was not only unhealthy, but also led to all kinds of sexual deviations among ourselves. With his regular weekly visits to a place known as the dove cotts, I suspected Bob's motives were designed more around his own selfish needs, than anybody else's. Not yet having obtained the same sexual appetite as Bob, my main motive was my love of climbing and the adrenaline rush it gave me, which for the time being at least, was far more important than sex.

Bob understood this, as he knew of my love of climbing, but warned me, my body was already building up a sex drive, which would soon come into its own demands, regardless to how much I tried to prevent or deny my sexual growth, Bob assured me

Somehow I just knew and understood what Bob was trying to tell me, as my knowledge of Bob, as a five year old when six years ago, he was my, then big boy, to the Bob I saw in front of me now eleven plus coming on twelve. In every respect, he was already becoming a boy, far in advance of his years and I suppose, I was doing my utmost to keep up with him.

Bob's sexuality was very well defined and although he loved me as clear as any brother ever could, it was our special friendship we both treasured, so much together. He was far happier satisfying his new sexual lust with girls, than he ever could be with a member of the same species. I knew instinctively, that no boy would ever be allowed to get close to him, with any kind of sexual intimacy, that on rare occasions we had both shared, and I felt just as strongly adverse, towards any boy touching me, even if I knew them well, let alone any stranger.

With the weeks climbing ahead, I was getting excited in a kind of way that only climbers would understand. Once we were on the steep slope of the roof of the toilets, we quickly went down the other side and crossed the suspended pipe bridge that linked the boys and girls bogs together. Bob couldn't resist looking down into the girl's loo, which thankfully was empty. There would be no distractions tonight I thought, as I ran along the ridge from the girl's loo towards the main buildings.

We came to the first side of the Grand Dining room, as Bob pointed out to me a well worm lead path that went around all four sides, like a quadrant. Bob wanted to go down these four sides, which ultimately came back to ridge further along the one we were both on. I reprimanded Bob, for wanting to waste time, and told him, I was far more interested in looking for a more direct way to get to our dormitory fire escape.

I led Bob all the way along the ridge to the main block via an angled but almost horizontal drainpipe, I traversed across to another vertical pipe I could see took us to within, a few feet of the fire escape handrail.

Bob said nervously he didn't feel good about the final move onto the handrail. I went first to prove how easy it was for Bob's sake. Piece of cake I shouted to Bob below, who was still having second thoughts. "Come on you big wimp," I shouted to Bob, who reluctantly started to climb the vertical pipe about twenty feet below me.

He came up fast enough, to within a few feet from where I was standing. "What's your problem now?" I asked him, as he was obviously trying to work out the last move.

"I'm sorry" said Bob, "I'm not happy about this move; I'll just go back down." He was shaking with fear and I had never seen Bob in such a state before.

"Okay" I said to Bob, "I'm coming back over, so give me some room." Bob eased himself down about three feet or so as I quickly reversed the move that was giving Bob so many problems. Once I got my body into what I knew was the ideal position, I instructed Bob to climb over me onto the fire escape landing.

"What if you fall?" Bob asked me.

"Listen you prat," I said to Bob, "do you think I would let you climb over my body if I couldn't take your weight?"

"I'm not so sure" said Bob.

"Get a fucking move on or I'll kick your arse to the roof below!"

Bob, without further ado, climbed over my body to the complete safety of the fire escape landing above. I quickly joined him to his relief.

"Fucking hell" said Bob, "I was shitting myself."

"I know" I said quietly, "it's easy for any one to lose his nerve."

Bob broke down in tears, "You wouldn't have really kicked me off, would you?" asked Bob sobbing.

"Come here, you dick head" as I hugged and kissed him.

"The only way you would have gone down is if I was with you. Now stop bubbling before you set me at it." I said.

We took off our gear and wrapped them into a tight bundle, before sneaking into the dorm landing toilets via the fire doors. Having repaired his face, I insisted he give me a smile, before we found a good place to stash the gear.

We headed back down the more conventional stairs to the dayroom. We slipped outside into the yard without a word, heading for the swings to have a con fab.

Once we returned to the dayroom, losing track of time, we were both chased by Mr Walton to take showers. I think it was the first time I looked at Bob, with real love. I think I would have killed myself, if anything happened to Bob.

We both undressed, sitting on the bench while we were waiting for a shower to become vacant.

There was a great deal of talk doing the rounds about something that happened over a week ago, and it was one of Sims' informers, that had reputedly dobbed this lad right in it. The boy that did all the squealing was called Banana Boy.

"Why do they call him Banana Boy?" I asked Bob.

"I'll show you once we are under the showers" said Bob, "because I think I see him taking his shower a good distance away. I think these shits need to learn a hard lesson," said Bob, as he was deep in thought. "There are at least four well known informers in our dorm" said Bob.

I could already see the wheels in motion, as Bob was yet working on some plot, just as two showers became vacant. We quickly dived in, before someone else grabbed them. Bob threw a soapy flannel at my chest, to indicate the boy who was just passing me, and it was very obvious why he was called Banana Boy, both in size, but also because it curved up and outwards.

While we were towelling ourselves down, Bob asked me if I would be interested in a midnight commando raid. Not knowing what evil plan Bob had in mind, I nodded my agreement, which he said he would explain to me, while we were playing chess.

"Let's go straight up to bed," said Bob with a knowing twinkle in his eye that spelt trouble. My fingertips tingled and I could feel the palms of my hands dampen with excitement. Once I got into bed, Bob joined me with his chessboard. Like along row of soldiers in a row, Bob said, "We take number five and number seven pawns away."

"This line of chess men" explained Bob "represents this row of beds, the target informers are number five and seven beds in this row. These two boys are your quarry on this side of the dorm and I'll take the other side." Said Bob. "All you have to do" said Bob "is collect these narks plimsoles and remember to tie them together before bringing them back here."

"And what am I supposed to do then?" I asked Bob.

"If you shut up I'll explain everything" which he did.

"But why the poor night watchman?" I asked.

"Because" said Bob "he will collect them all up, to hand over to Mr Sims who will then punish the owners of these plimsoles."

Now I understood, because our name is marked inside every boy's plimsoles. "You're really cunning Bob, in fact, quite a real bastard" I said. Bob just smiled his reply.

We had a full week of roof top climbing and thankfully, Bob had regained his confidence fully.

"So tonight's the night" said Bob, "and by tomorrow evening Sims should be spitting bullets, with a double whammy. Just then Banana

Boy entered the dorm and went to his bed a fair distance away, on the other side of the dorm.

"That shit" said Bob with extra feeling, "is one of Sims main cock suckers, a first class shit and one of the best informers in the business" said Bob.

Bob leaned forward to whisper in my ear "Remember Kenny?" Bob asked.

"Yes of course I do, I'm not likely to forget, am I!"

"Well" said Bob "Banana Boy is Kenny's number one arsehole stabber, they are what you call a real pair of homo's"

After running over the precise instructions, for the umpteenth time about tonight's ambush, he told me to go to sleep as normal as he would awaken me in good time. Bob was the only one with a wristwatch, so no argument.

I was briskly shaken awake just before two in the morning by Bob, who insisted on absolute silence.

"Don't even breath" said Bob "as he made me recite the numbered beds yet again. Okay" he said "off you go, and don't forget to tie the laces together," said Bob.

I slithered like a snake on my belly, propelling myself along the highly polished floor, which I knew so well as it was part of my morning housework every day.

Having gathered my victim's rather smelly plimsoles, I tied them together and returned the same way to my bed. A few minutes later, I could hear Bob, rather than see him, swishing along the floor on his way back to his bed. Bob's head popped up over the edge of his bed, from the floor, as a glint from the blue night light shone on his teeth.

He wriggled into bed like an eel finding its bed for the night. He gave me the thumbs up sign, which I returned as he grinned broadly showing of his nashers. We were all set, waiting and ready to go, when Bob once again warned me not to throw until he gave the signal. Less than ten minutes later we both heard the swing door at the far end of the dorm squeak on it's hinges as the night hawk entered. He walked slowly down the length of the dorm towards us and I could already feel the adrenaline rush through my body as my hands dampened with excitement.

In this emotional high state of excitement, I felt a good size trickle surge from the end of my dick, wetting the front panel of my pyjamas.

We both waited with abated breath, trying to synchronise our over excited breathing, in fear of giving ourselves away Just as the night hawk reached almost half way down the dorm, I held my breath in agonising suspense for Bob to give the signal of command.

With one yelp from Bob, we both let fly our first salvo. I could see my first shot hit him squarely on the front of the night hawks chest, with Bob's just a fraction later hitting his right shoulder. Taken aback by surprise and before he could recover from a slight stumble, "AGAIN" yelped Bob as we both let go our second shot of ammunition, with mine landing somewhere in the stomach region, which made him double up.

As the night hawk doubled over, Bob's missile landed in his face breaking his glasses, as we both heard them hit the floor with the sound of broken glass.

We both turned in unison away from the target area and proceeded to give our very best performance of being fast asleep, Bob throwing in the odd snore for good measure. We heard the nighthawk rush passed the end of our beds, in a desperate hurry to fumble with the main light switches.

I shut my eyes even tighter as I felt the last trickle of piss involuntary leave the end of my dick and wet the inside of my thigh. I could see the brightness of the dorm lights through my firmly closed eyelids, as the night hawk was demanding to know the boys responsible.

I could hear several boys murmuring sounds having been awoken by the disturbance, while Bob was now in full snoring mode, which I thought was a bit O.T.T. Not getting any takers, the night hawk collected up all the offending debris, and rushed out of the dorm in a temper, forgetting to turn out the lights, on his way.

When Bob knew it was safe, he turned in towards me, lifting up his bed covers, to reveal that he had one massive hard on. I whispered to him "How can you even think about your dick at a time like this?"

"I didn't" he replied, "it just happened" he said.

"You're a sex maniac," I said with an expression of disgust, as I turned away to illustrate to Bob that I wasn't amused. I think the lights eventually were switched off about half an hour later, as I drifted in and out of sleep restlessly.

With all that happened, it seemed a long night as Bob gently shook me awake and then to make sure I didn't nod off again, he turned down my bed covers. He noticed the large damp patch on the front of my pyjamas, saying to me "you little devil."

I was too embarrassed to explain to Bob it wasn't what he thought, as I stripped to put on my shorts.

Ignoring his remarks, I raced down stairs to my ablutions. Mr Sims was on duty, posted at the entrance of the washroom, and he didn't look a happy bunny.

After breakfast parade, Sims simply read out the four names of our victims, which seemed a bit pointless because all four boys in question, including Banana Boy were obviously all shoe less. Mr Sims' beloved pet squealers, were sent to stand outside his office, to stand barefoot.

"Tonight" said Bob, with a perverse lilt in his voice "is the night of double whammy and hopefully" Bob continued "Hitler will reap some of his own brimstone and fire."

Mr Sims was in a bit of quandary, because he knew that the real culprits for this evil nights work were not the four boys standing in front of him. There were the usual vultures hovering around the office vicinity, all hoping to be first to break the impending news with the gossip, for distribution on the grape vine.

The four boys or should I say, the selected lambs to the slaughter, were all given extra household cleaning duties for a week, to be performed after tea until bedtime. "That should keep them out of our hair" said Bob on our way to class. As I looked up at the big stack with some nostalgia in passing, I thought of all the evil things I had enacted since being at Ashford, quite a list! Quite a record.

No wonder I was such a bastard and thought of as the worst boy in the school. Bob looked into the windows of my brain, then simply said "you may be a bastard, but I for one love you" as if he had been reading my very thought. I smiled at him as I reached my class then went in to start my day.

At teatime I could really feel the butterflies assembling to invade my nervous system. My fingertips were already tingling with anticipated excitement. I always felt like this before a big event, especially when I was faced with some climbing challenge.

It made every fibre of my being come alive, putting me on a high equally on par with drugs, and probably sex, although I had no real experience with either.

After tea Bob instructed me to go direct to the outside toilets, while he retrieved the gear from upstairs. Just ahead of me, I saw Kenny along with three other lads go into the toilets, so I decided to wait outside for Bob. Bob wasn't long in joining me and as he too was about to head into the toilet, so I grabbed him by the arm.

"Believe me Bob" I said "you don't want to go in there, as Kenny and three others are in there already."

Bob looked at me hard, then asked me if I was alright.

"I'm fine" I said "let's just go straight up onto the roof and put our disguises on up there." Which we did.

Bob kept on looking at his watch, which made me even more nervous, "any second now" Bob said, just as Sims came out onto the yard with his bike. He switched on his bicycle lamp, cocked his leg then slowly peddled towards the corner of the drive where we lay in ambush, waiting. I felt the palms of my hands get very wet, as my body climbed onto cloud nine, in heaven.

Bob took careful aim with his trusted catapult, and I heard the whistling sound of the pebble, before it found its target on Sims upper leg. The impact, along with the utter shock, sent him crashing on his side with the bicycle inflicting some unknown other injury, as he cried out in pain.

Sims quickly stood up looking about him, to find the perpetrator, so Bob decided to give this gormless bumpot a clue, by giving him a wolf whistle, which I've heard him give to many girls. This quickly got the desired response as Sims leaped into action, with Sims yelling his head off at the two of us, and started up the drainpipe after us.

I promptly raced at full speed ahead, over the ridge to the pipe bridge. I crossed so fast, I swear my feet didn't touch, until I got to the other side and waited for Bob. Bob was taking his time as I suddenly felt panicky, until I heard Bob shouting at Sims.

In a fake falsetto voice Bob was taunting Sims "come on you fucking fat lazy bastard", get a move on as Bob within seconds joined me on the other side of the suspended pipe.

"Come on Bob, lets get moving" I said.

"No wait" said Bob, as we both saw Sims appear on the skyline ridge shaking his fists at us, still ranting and raving, before heading back down where once he came.

"Right" said Bob "now we can move, heading for the drainpipe exit down the side wall of the girls toilets that also led onto the main drive.

"Take your cape off first" said Bob, which I did and handed it to him. I sped down the pipe like a greasy pole waiting at the bottom for Bob, who quickly joined me. We both ran down the drive towards the corner of our own toilet, from where we had started from.

Peering round the corner to check first that all was clear, which it was, we quickly ambled over to our favourite swings, to watch the firework display.

We both sat down, barely out of breath, watching fat Sims having difficulty negotiating his body over the eaves onto the drainpipe. We looked at each other grinning like a pair of Cheshire cats, when we both realised that we were still wearing our face masks. We quickly de-masked ourselves shoving them into the pockets of our shorts.

Sims had just reached the ground and was approaching us with his bicycle lamp in his hand.

"Right you two" shining his lamp in our eyes "come with me."

He marched us over to the bottom of the drainpipe, with implicit instructions to apprehend anybody coming down from the roof.

"Yes Sir" we both said obediently, as if butter wouldn't melt. Out came Sims' whistle which he blew for an immediate roll call assembly, and we both watched a number of shady characters fall out of the toilets in various states of undress in a hurry to get to the dayroom, in time for assembly. It was like seeing a comic opera before our eyes as the last kid disappeared into the dayroom.

We looked at each other without saying a single word, pulling our dicks out together, pissing against the wall. Bob finished first, but mine seemed to go on forever, as Bob looked down wondering how much longer I was going to take, when I noticed for the first time, I had an erection, which I had been carrying for some time.

"You dirty randy bastard" said Bob, as I put my hand over to his dick and felt him.

"So have you," I said, "SNAP."

"One thing couldn't be more certain" said Bob tucking his hard bishop into his shorts, "we are both truly off the hook for this little escapade." as I too put away my dick.

While we were waiting, I wondered why we both somehow got a hard on, because with all the excitement and still feeling as high as a kite, sexual thoughts were the last thing on our minds. I asked Bob about it, but he didn't know what caused an unwanted erection either. "It just happens sometimes" Bob said "I don't know why either.

Fortunately, with our disobedient body appendages now behaving themselves, Sims called us both over to him at the dayroom door.

"Well" said Sims, still spitting bullets "have you seen anybody?" he demanded to know.

"No Sir" said Bob at his most politeness, while I was struggling to suppress an irresistible urge to snigger.

"Okay" boomed Sims, without a word of thanks "get inside".

Once inside the bright lights of the dayroom, we were quickly informed by Pat, my half brother, that the whole of boy's side, had been placed on curfew for a whole week. This meant that no one was allowed outside to play, as we were now strictly confined to barracks. This quickly took the smile off Bob's face.

Bob cursed continually for at least five minutes, as he got angrier and angrier.

"What's wrong with you" As if I didn't already know.

"I've arranged to meet up with my girl" said Bob, calming a little.

"Well, now you're getting your just rewards, so you will just have to go without" I added. Bob looked at me and he was not amused. Everybody was talking about these two desperados giving Mr Sims the run-around, as they had been fully informed at assembly. "Time to keep a low profile" said Bob, as we took a quick shower before going to bed.

Once in bed, Bob was still feeling aggrieved, as he said "That's fucked up my plans for the week"

"Don't you mean our plans?" I queried.

"No" said Bob "I've already missed one date with Margaret, now Wednesday is fucked also."

"I didn't realise you two were so serious" I said.

"We are not," said Bob, just a bit too quickly. After a few seconds reflection, Bob said "She gives the best blow job I've ever experienced" he said quietly.

I knew he was talking about sex, but wasn't sure exactly what, so I decided not to ask.

He looked at me thinking I was going to ask, when rather abruptly he told me to mind my own business. So I did. He climbed into bed, reached down to one of his plimsoles and extracted the lace, which he put carefully under his pillow. Having just been told to mind my own business, I resisted asking him about the lace. I turned over onto my side in an attempt to put it out of my mind. The trouble was, I couldn't. Mark, on this side of the bed I was now facing, nodded to me, as he stripped off to the buff, and got into bed.

So, Pat was not the only one that enjoyed sleeping commando style, I thought, taking off my bottoms and putting them under my pillow, in case I needed to go to the loo through the night, aware that Bob was watching me.

I turned over to face Mark who was already fast asleep. I wonder what Bob wants that lace for I thought, when without prompting, Bob suddenly said "Don't ask, believe me, you don't want to know!"

I've heard of ESP but this is just going too far, reading my thoughts, even if Bob is my best friend.

I quickly changed my thinking to Sylvia, my girlfriend, as the lights went off. I thought of Sylvia increasingly more these days, as I turned back over to my normal side for sleeping. Bob in the cold blue of the night light was facing me with his eyes shut, or was he just pretending, I wondered. Bob opened his eyes wide and stared at me directly in my face, breaking into one of his winning smiles. "Will you stop reading my thoughts," I said to myself.

He started to fold back his bedclothes with great care to below his waist and already I could see his nakedness all the way down to his knees. His bishop, as he always called his penis was pointing at me like a gun ready to be fired, as he lay on his side facing me. Being only about three feet from him, I whispered to him "Don't you come all over me," I warned.

"Just shut up" Bob spat at me in a loud whisper. So I did. He turned onto his back with his full erected bishop pointing skyward as he produced his lace from under his pillow. Now I shall see for myself, what he's going to do with this lace, watching every move, totally spell bound.

Slowly, with no apparent rush and with great care, Bob proceeded to wind the lace very precisely around the base of his bishop. Why would he do this? I wondered, does he want to strangle his cock for some perverse reason, I thought, as I watched him tie the two ends of lace into a very neat, but firm bow.

Looking at this penis of his trussed up with a neat bow, gave me the urge to burst out laughing, but resulted in a muffled snigger, which obviously upset Bob, who told me to shut my face in no uncertain terms.

"Sorry Bob" I said.

He then eased the coil of lace as far back into the root amongst his pubic hair, as far back and tight into his base as possible. I felt my own penis wince with shock.

Against the blue glare of the night light, it stood bolt upright alone, like a single grenadier guardsman on gate duty. Bob took off his watch, and handed it to me, with instructions to keep time. 10 p.m. Time for what I wondered, but never mind, I thought, I wouldn't miss this spectacle for the world.

He deliberately used his left hand, so as not to obstruct my view, as with just his thumb and one finger tip only, he gently stroked the underside of his circumcised corona of his bishop.

After about a full ten minutes, the first dribble of spunk from the slot in the bishops' head appeared, glistening like a silvery thread of silk. I watched in erotic fascination, as I felt my own loins stirring into a life of its own making.

The silver thread of spunk turned into a trickle and Bob quickly took his fingers away completely, while his bishop staggered in a drunken stupor, wandering from side to side in protest. Bob resisted temptation to put his fingers back.

I felt a dribble from the end of my own dick, as I put my hand down to feel the damage. It wasn't good, as I was very hard and could feel it throbbing with excitement, so I quickly stuffed my pyjamas under it, to ease the suffering.

Meanwhile Bob's own unattended bishop was still yawning in a dance like trance, but with the head smothered in spunk, which was steadily oozing through the slot.

Bob's balls were now very enlarged, no doubt filling his sac with a steady flow of sperm. Bob after all of fifteen minutes, began again to use his finger tips to caress his corona spreading his fluid to the neck area, just below the ridge of his knob.

I could see Bob's testicles which were now the size of large hen's eggs, pulsating like mad, moving around on there own, demanding more hands on action. The flow suddenly stopped as Bob released the stranglehold on the bishop by loosening the lace and moving it about an inch away from his pubic hair. He just lay back in ecstasy with his hands clasped behind his head, waiting. Waiting for what, I wondered as the balls started to pump its waste up his upright shaft. If Bob's penis was transparent you would have seen what I felt as I could feel my own sap rising, surging its way as if fighting for air, then it happened, as my eyes were transfixed to the end of Bob's penis. It gushed in a constant flow, not spitting, but just pouring until I thought it was going on forever.

Bob, still with his hands clasped behind his head, just lay back watching, as I was, in awe. I could feel my own erection weeping like mad. Bob looked at me grinning with pride and wonder. After what seemed ages. He undid the lace, which was now saturated. His pride stood erect not losing any stiffness, completely bathed in his white stuff, which looked almost luminous in the pale blue light.

Slowly he wrapped his whole left hand around the shaft, moving it up and down stroking its length lovingly, building up a slow but steady rhythm. After a good ten minutes, he built up a full head of steam, and I saw the whole of his body convulse and stiffen as the first blob of spunk left his launching pad, erupting clean into the blue light air, at least six or more feet above his bed. The first load landed on his chin and neck, which made me stifle a laugh. After another ten or so rapid shakes, he controlled the reducing spurts, which landed on his stomach.

With the very last drop expelled, he laid back to enjoy his sexual high, with the bishop slowly deflating to half size. The dragon had finally been slain. He casually dried himself with his pyjamas. He got out of bed with his bishop fully sated and ready for sleep. He took the watch from my hand which said it was now 11.30 p.m. "That's an hour and a half" I said with surprise. Bob looked at me, then without warning, he turned down my bedclothes. "I thought so," said Bob, taking hold of my cock; he gave it a gentle squeeze as spunk oozed out of the end. He put his fingers into the skin crater formed by my foreskin and another blob came oozing out.

"Yes" Bob said, "I think you're ready for your first wank. Would you like me to do it, or do you want to go solo?" Bob asked.

"No thanks" I said "I'll go solo, if you don't mind."

He leaned over and kissed my brow. "Okay" he said then goodnight.

Bob returned to his bed, climbed in and quickly went to sleep, leaving me to finish myself off.

Whoever said sex only lasted about five minutes, just didn't know what they were talking about, I thought, as I drifted off to sleep.

In the morning I awoke a little earlier than normal and as I opened my eyes I could see Bob was still fast asleep, looking so peaceful. I wondered why I had no feeling of guilt. Why for instance, was I not angry when Bob took hold of my cock? That really was my very first wank, which felt really good. Was I becoming a pervert, because I watched Bob making love to himself? Did I feel no shame? No, but why not? You could hardly call that normal sex I thought; maybe I'm becoming a sexual deviant.

I peered under my bedclothes to look at myself properly. My dick was placid about three inches or so long and my pubic hair was flourishing, bush-like. It looked so different than Bob's, whose was circumcised and ugly to look at, I thought. He can keep his bishop; I was more than happy with my own, thank you. Bob slowly opened his eyes, yawned, then when he saw me, he smiled like a rash breaking over his face. I must remember one day to ask him about this blow job, that Margaret gave him, I thought.

OUR SECRET POOL

Page 150

CHAPTER FIFTEEN
Hooray, The War Is Over

Well after the war was officially declared as over and, now well passed my tenth birthday, I was already looking forward to my eleventh. We were already into the second half of 1946, before any of us really took notice, of any real significance to outstanding changes, to our daily plight at Ashford.

The big thing to me with any real meaning, of changes of greatness, were only two that stood head and shoulders above all else.

The first was the removal of all vestiges of blackout material, from every window throughout the school!

Just to be able to wake up every morning and be greeted by daylight was a pure joy. Simple, I know, but the psychological effect on ones whole being, was almost akin to rebirth. The second, and I suppose to many, the most important, was the silence in the sky, without having to run for cover many times a day, not that we always did, mind you!

This was no longer there to interrupt our playtime sessions, which for boys, starved of real family love and home life, playtime was even more important to each and every one of us.

It allowed us to escape, if only for short periods, into our world of make believe, to offset the real misery of this dump called Ashford, which some of us were forced to call home.

The other and most important effect on my life was Bobby, who had been part of me since my life began.

To this day, sixty or more years later, my life before Ashford is a complete and utter blank. Not a shred or a single detail can I remember, before that very first day at Ashford. My life began only at Ashford, and from day one, Bobby became part of the very first day of, my life. He was more important to me than any other single person in my life, including my aunt, to whom I am extremely fond of, and always will be.

If I have one single thing to thank Ashford for, and there are many, it would have to be Bobby.

He, of course has many of his own thoughts, (or so I'm told) but to me, he will always remain my only true kin.

I love him deeper than any real brother ever could, and even perhaps more than I should, and I don't mean in any sexual way, or even in a plutonic way, either, it's far purer and much greater than either of those, could ever be.

Meanwhile, I was determined to improve my sex life, now that I've found I have one. My romance with Sylvia was beginning to disturb my loins alarmingly, as I found out when dancing close to her. She was a fantastic dancer, and being almost a year and a half older than me, was sexually more aware and probably more sexually active than me, as well as more sexually experienced. My only hope, and wish, was that when the time came, she would be especially more gentle with me.

Bob on the other hand was always quick to point out to me, that what Sylvia and I had together, was just puppy love, he would tease me endlessly. I use to tell Bob he was an oversexed randy bastard, that was a slave to his bishop. Although being of Jewish parentage why he didn't rename it Rabbi, I didn't know, nor understood. I would chastise him often, but he would just grin and reply "Yeh great en it" if ever the word reprobate fitted anybody like a glove, it was Bob. The word was made for him, but in spite of that and worst still, I loved him as my very own.

He would ignore my bait, always disarming me with one of his winning smiles, which was so frustrating at times, but I always went back for more, like a druggy needing another fix. Many staff and boys alike, thought we were twins, so attuned were we, into each other's wave lengths, it sometimes scared me. With me already past my eleventh birthday, I knew Bobby would soon be moving up to his final dorm, indeed he should have moved up a year ago, but for some reason, known only to Mr Walton the master responsible for all accommodation moves, Bob was still in my dorm, alongside me.

I was to learn much later on in life, that this master, who was reputed to be the strictest, but also the fairest of all masters, always thought of us both as blood brothers, even though according to all records we were not. He, for some unknown reason had a special spot for me. But only God knows why.

"Don't talk fucking stupid, is that why he's always tanning the arse off me" I would say to Bob.

"That's because he loves you" Bob would say, trying to wind me up, and succeeding.

The amazing phenomenon that neither of us could ever explain, was the same pain we sometimes felt between us. Like when a loose house brick came out of the wall of the main building more than fifty feet above me, while in the playground. It hit my big toe on my left foot, doing severe damage almost losing part of my foot. The toe was saved, but the nail was so badly damaged it has spent all my life producing a claw like talon, that drops off every four years or so, then re-grows into yet another claw like talon.

Almost to the minute, Bob's big left toe got so swollen and painful like my own big toe, you would think we were both suffering from gout. Neither of us could put on our left shoe for days. Bob was in a different part of the school to me at the time the brick smashed into my toe. He could not understand why his toe should show the same symptoms, the only difference was the end result, I lost my big toe nail and Bob just had an uncomfortable few days.

"It could have been a lot worse," joked Bob.

"How do you make that out?" I asked Bob.

"Well, if the brick from that height had dropped on your head instead of just your toe, we could have both died" Bob said.

The thing is, Bob said it as if he really believed it, which rather unnerved me.

He left me in deep thought, and I certainly didn't want to tempt fate.

The latest example happened just two days ago, exactly one month after my eleventh birthday.

For some unexplainable reason the pen in my right hand, fell to the floor, and within seconds my wrist started to swell up like a huge carbuncle, and became very sore to touch. The teacher insisted I had broken my wrist, but I knew I had done nothing to cause such an injury.

I was sent to the matron's office because there was no sign of the swelling going down. She too thought I had broken my wrist, but she wondered why, I had broken my wrist, and for what reason?

I started to get angry with the matron, wondering why she thought I would deliberately break my wrist on purpose.

"Well" she explained "Bob was at this very moment, down at the infirmary having his right wrist put into plaster, having broken it in a bad fall."

"Don't tell me, did this fall of Bob's happen about 2 p.m. or there about?" I asked the matron. She didn't answer.

"Well I was in class, which you can easily verify, at 2 p.m. when my wrist started to swell up and now the pain is killing me."

She phoned for an ambulance, and told me to sit and wait for her in her office. She was back within ten minutes, apologising, having checked out my story, and then came with me to the infirmary, out of guilt. The doctor after a very close examination, decided to take an x-ray just to be sure. The x-ray showed no broken bones!

"Where's Bob?" I demanded to know.

"He is already be back in class, or should be." The doctor said, looking at his watch.

"Has Bob broken his arm? I asked.

"Yes" said the doctor " as clean as a whistle."

The swelling on my wrist was beginning to go down, I thought but it was still very sore to touch.

"I think we should put a short plaster on," said the doctor, but I was able to persuade him just to put a heavy strapping on it instead.

"Okay, but you must wear your arm in a sling." The doctor said.

When I met up with Bob at tea time, he couldn't believe his eyes.

"Snap" said Bob, "When did you break yours?" he asked.

"I didn't" I said, "you did, mine isn't broken although the bloody thing is so painful it might as well be."

"Your just a fraud," said Bob "mines really is broken" he said, looking quite pleased with himself.

"I don't know why you're so pleased" I reminded Bob. "my sling will be off in a week, but you're stuck in plaster, for how long?

"About six weeks." Bob said, rather more quietly.

With great drama at tea time, the headmaster (Fatty Arbuckle) climbed upon the stage with an announcement, bigger even than the declaration to the end of the war, some eighteen months ago. The whole school would be going on an organised camping holiday to the seaside. The head paused for the desired effect, and got it. This wonderful bombshell of a surprise had the whole dining room in an uproar. The unstoppable, excited chatter was ear bashing in the extreme, as law and order broke down in what was normally a very subdued setting.

Even the persistent shrills of high-pitched whistles blown by members of staff at their various stations around the hall, was difficult to hear. It took some time to get this comic opera under control. Once this unruly mob was quelled to our master's wishes, the head proceeded with his address, but with a cautionary tale of woe, especially to all of us, who got over excited.

"The disruptive element among you, will be retained, and certainly will not be going on holiday!" Fatty exploded.

"That means you and I "Bob whispered in my lughole. "As long as we are together" said Bob in the same ear "I don't give a fuck." Just then Mr Walton stepped up from behind us, and without whispering, told us both to report to him after tea.

Now we are in deep shit. I told myself. Meanwhile, Bailey the head was still waffling on about some kind of contingency plan. This plan would affect all reprobates, who would be placed in an alternative residential place, which had already been agreed upon, to take these unfortunates for the duration of the two weeks holidays.

The very lucky majority, would be travelling down in style, to a delightful seaside resort called Walton-on-Naze, in Essex on July 1st this year of our Lord 1947.

Not a single boy or girl spoke until we returned to the day room, in fear of being added to this shortlist.

"Well" said Bob, as we made our way to Walton's office, "I wonder where, they will be sending us two reprobates?"

"I'm past caring" I said to Bob "as long as we stay together," I lied.

Bob knocked on Walton's office door and we both waited to face our fate together.

"Come in" shouted Walton.

I pushed Bob in first, as Walton looked over the two of us.

"Well Ankorne" said Walton "how's your wrist feeling?"

"It's much better, thank you sir, "I replied, wondering why the sudden interest.

"Good" he said "How do you feel about wet nursing Alditch (Bob) for the next six weeks?" he asked.

"Yes Sir, I am willing to try" I said, not fully understanding what exactly, he really meant, or to what extent.

"Well, Alditch," Walton turned to Bob "I could send you into care, as an alternative to going on this camping trip if you prefer, where someone else would look after you."

Bob milled this poser over in his mind, then asked Mr Walton "Will there be any girls there?"

"Most definitely not" snapped Walton, so Bob remained silent. When Walton looked at Bob, with a certain amount of distaste, then turned to me and said "If this," pointing at Bob "gives you any trouble whatsoever, you come direct to me, is that understood?"

"Yes sir" I replied.

"Now off with the two of you, I have far more important matters to attend to."

Once outside, I looked at Bob, and told him frankly, I wasn't looking forward to wet nursing him, and his talk about girls in Walton's office, didn't help matters one bit. Thankfully Bob remained silent, as he could tell I wasn't best pleased.

"I was only joking," said Bob.

"No you weren't, that's the real problem, your forever thinking of yourself, you selfish git."

Bob was sent for again, by Walton a few days later. "What was it this time?" I asked Bob, expecting the worst.

"Well" said Bob "there's good news and bad news" he said with a very solemn face.

"Okay, Okay," I said impatiently" what's the good news?

"The good news" he said " is, Walton has delayed my move up to the senior dorm, until after the camping holiday."

"Great" I said "And the bad news?" I asked Bob, who was still maintaining a dead pan expression.

"Well" then paused, obviously to drag out the suspense, "is", then another pause, "there's every chance you will be moving up with me to the new dormitory" said Bob.

I pushed him, with the palm of my hand, with this unexpected revelation.

"Easy" said Bob, "watch my arm" breaking into one of his smiles.

With less than a fortnight to go, I was called to Walton's office, only this time, I was expecting bad news.

"Ah, Paul" said Walton "Sit down will you". Now I was most concerned, as Walton was renown for putting you off your guard. It was one of Walton's tactics.

"Your aunt will be uplifting you on the last day of the camp, to take you on for a few weeks holiday."

"Thank you sir," but waited because I knew there was still more to come.

"She will be calling next Friday afternoon, to take you out for tea."

"Fantastic" I yelled.

"And," Walton waited for me to compose myself, which I did quickly," she has asked if Alditch (Bob) can also join your tea party, and I've said yes," Mr Walton added. I waited feeling very excited, to see if Mr Walton had any more to say.

He looked at me hard, with that serious face of his, then calmly asked me, if I knew the two louts that were causing Mr Sims, a great deal of misery. I stood there in front of him, with my mouth open, not knowing what to say.

I must have stood there for another twenty seconds, stunned.

"I didn't think so," said Walton, not receiving any reply.

"One more thing" said Walton, "a special flexible hose has been rigged at the far end of the shower room, so it's your job to see Alditch gets showered properly. If he gets that plaster wet I will hold you personally responsible. Is that clear enough for you Ankorne?"

"Yes sir."

"Right then cut along with you."

Bob was hanging about, anxiously waiting to find out why I was so long with Walton.

"Let's go over to the swings," I said to Bob, as we left the dayroom. We both wandered towards the swings, where we chased off a couple of kids, without having opened our mouths. We both sat down together, as I said to Bob, "There's good news and bad news."

"Okay" said Bob impatiently, "just spit it out and get on with it.

"The good news is, we are both going to tea with my aunt next Friday."

That's really good," said Bob "now what's the bad?" he asked.

Walton knows about our rooftop climbing exploits against Sims.

Bob looked into my face intensely, "What did Walton say exactly?"

So I explained in detail, word for word, to Bob. We both fell silent in tandem, like a pair of expectant dads. Eventually Bob said, "Well, we cant climb anyway until I get out of plaster, but we'll have to find a real safe place to stash the gear," said Bob.

"I'll give it some thought," I said to Bob, "but now I have to take you in and give you a shower."

"Who said I have to be given a shower by you? Bob looked quite indignant. I explained about the new shower and also what Walton said about holding me responsible for keeping your plaster dry. As we walked back across the yard, Bob solemnly said he was supposed to be meeting Margaret later, now even that had been knocked on the head.

We got into the shower room, and I undressed him and then myself.

"Listen" I said to Bob "if that bishop of yours misbehaves, I'll walk away and just leave you to it, on your own."

"Okay" said Bob, "but you will be careful when you wash it?" he asked. Cheeky bastard, I thought

"I mean it Bob, if you get a hard on when I'm washing you, I'll tell Walton to get someone else to wet nurse you and that's final. " I said it with real feeling. Bob just stood there looking at me in disbelief.

Both him and his bishop, behaved like gentlemen, thankfully. Once I got him into bed, he lay back on his pillow in deep thought.

"Can I ask you something personal Bob?" then stopped in mid sentence.

Bob turned on his side towards me and said, "Paul you can ask me anything you like, and I will answer you truthfully."

Okay," I started "when you're with your girlfriend, Margaret," I hesitated, but Bob finished off my question for me.

"Do I fuck her? Is what you were going to ask me" Bob said, as he saw me go red with embarrassment. "Not normally, but I've done it twice that I can remember." said Bob closing his eyes. "I much prefer a blow job" Bob added, who was clearly stimulating his bishop below the covers.

"What's a blow job?" I asked innocently.

"Well" said Bob, still playing with himself, "Margaret puts my bishop into her mouth and sucks it off very slowly until I come, it's mind blowing, absolutely fantastic." he said, "simply the best" he added with feeling. I leaned over to Bob's bed, who had a wry smile on his face with his eyes closed, and eased back his bed clothes. I saw he had one hell of a hard on, so I quickly covered him up again.

"Aren't you afraid of giving Margaret a baby?" I asked Bob, point blank.

Bob opened his eyes wide and looked at me in disbelief, then said "I don't fuck her puss, I fuck her arse, which she just loves, but I prefer a suck. Does that answer all your questions?" he asked, with a frustrated voice.

"I'm sorry for asking" I said, then shut up. A few minutes later Bob said "No Paul, it's me who should be sorry, I'm just fucking frustrated because I can't really wank myself off properly, with my left hand."

"That's okay, Bob" I said, "I understand your problem."

Then Bob opened his eyes again and looked at me directly in the eyes. "You know Paul, you could always do it for me" said Bob.

I exploded, "No fucking way am I going to wank you off, why should I even want to toss you off, when I've got one of my own to play with. That's all you ever think of, your own dick, you've got one hell of a cheek to even ask me" I said spluttering away trying to find the right words to say to him, but couldn't.

Bob suddenly stopped playing with himself, shocked at my strong outburst. "I'm sorry" he said in a very restrained voice, "you're right, I should not have asked you, and I will never ask you again" he said with feeling. "But one thing I will say on the subject, before it's closed for good, if you were in plaster and I knew or could feel you needed help, sexual or otherwise, I would not wait for you to ask, but I would feel honoured to give you what ever it took to please. If I couldn't help my very best friend in need, then I don't need a best friend." Bob said quietly.

I felt really hurt, and guilty of refusing Bob so forcibly, but I knew I couldn't help him, in this one matter.

"I'm sorry Bob, I can't help you out, I would if I could, but I just can't."

Surprisingly, Bob simply replied, "I know you can't Paul, I was stupid to think otherwise."

Well after lights out, I could hear Bob, sobbing away to himself very softly. I got into Bob's bed, hugging his body close to mine, only to discover neither of us was wearing pyjamas, but it didn't seem so important, now.

"Please stop crying, I can't bear to see you so upset, it was so brutal of me to sound off, the way I did."

We lay there together sharing each other's body heat. "I promise you Bobby, we will find a way somehow," as my hand moved down towards his bishop, which was limp. I put it into my palm, holding it with as much gentleness that I could manage. The bishop never stirred, so I moved down to his balls, squeezing them as if they were made of cotton wool. Bob reached down to my hand and just held his hand on top of mine. He whispered to me "Thank you Paul, " he said "but I really don't want you to wank me."

We stayed holding each other's dick for a good ten minutes or more, without any attempt at arousing each other.

"I'm okay now Paul" said Bob "we are both needing our sleep, and although I love you very much, I think you should go back to your own bed now." So I did, and Bob was snoring within minutes of me leaving.

On Friday morning, I reminded Bob my aunt would be taking us both to tea in a weeks time and we would all be leaving for summer camp the very next day on Saturday1st July.

"I know," said Bob, "and we still haven't found a place to stash our gear!"

"What about the hole at the top of the crag, at our secret pool?" I asked.

"It's a great place," said Bob "but it means you will have to do the climb solo."

"So what" I said "I've done that climb at least a dozen times before, and it's nowhere near as difficult as some of the others that I've done."

"Alright" said Bob "we'll go down after breakfast first thing, the sooner that gear is well hidden, the better I'll feel about it." Said Bob.

After Saturday morning breakfast, we both headed off, as I looked up at the sky I could tell we were in for a warm sunny day. When we arrived, we each took our capes, that we had wrapped around our bodies below our shorts, and our face masks from our pockets and made a tight neat bundle, secured at the end by a length of washing line.

Bob started to undo his plimsoles, suggesting we wade the dam across to the lower slabs, at the base of the crag. I stripped off quickly to the buff, as I tied the loose end of the line around my waist, at the foot of the crag above my head. I knew exactly where the hole near the top was, as I moved onto the first footholds on the rock face.

Bob watched me the whole time, heeding me to be most careful, especially as I was bullock naked. I looked up the long winding crack, that offered excellent hand jams as I started climbing, building up an easy rhythm.

The climb itself was not difficult, but doing it in reverse coming down would present its own problems, I knew from previous experience. I felt the tingle in my finger tips as I climbed up the first twenty feet with ease.

I looked down at Bob's upturned face, which looked a little troubled, like a big brother concerned over his one and only chick. The view of my undercarriage exposed, couldn't have been the best sight, I thought to myself as I continued to climb.

Within five minutes more, I started to pull up our light bundle of gear, ready to firmly push it into the hole. Having done this, with no real problems, I continued the last four feet or so to the top, then sitting with my legs dangling over the face I had just climbed, to the water below. I closed my eyes drinking in the warmth of the sun.

I knew that directly below my legs, was the deepest part of the water pool, so I shouted to Bob to step aside, and on impulse, jumped clean from my perch, pushing my body well away from the rockface with my hands. This was something else I had done before, to the water some forty feet or so below. As I was plummeting through the air towards the water, my body tilted forward and I hit the surface with one hell of a smack, then I blacked out.

I know what happened later, because Bob told me so. As I started to come too, I was face down on the slabs facing downhill, with the gentle slope of the slabs near the waters edge. I could see stars in my comatosed state, and I could feel someone kneeling astride my back.

As I came too, I could hear Bob crying loudly, saying over and over again "Please God don't let him die, please God, please God." I could feel his hot tears hitting my cool back as he sobbed and sobbed his heart away.

Suddenly I spluttered like a beached whale, as the last cup full of water left my gullet.

"Get off me," I cried, as I struggled to turn over onto my back. Bob quickly assisted me, then shouted at me for being such a fool, hugging me and kissing me all over through his, now, tears of joy.

He continued to curse me and thank God, in alternate sentences. It was at this point I realised that Bob although fully clothed, was soaking wet, looking like a drowned rat. I got up onto my feet, and helped Bob undress, then I made him lay down on the warm slab while I wrung the water from his clothes and laid them in the sun to dry. I was very concerned about his plaster.

Bob was already sunning his long lean body, face downwards with his legs apart trying to dry the inside of his thighs. I lay down alongside Bob, grateful to be alive, as I studied his every feature. Bob's head was turned to one side with eyes closed and a contented smile upon his face.

As my eyes wandered down his body, I noticed from the back al least, his body was completely devoid of all hair, except under his arms and pubic front, which was out of sight. As I lay on my back, enjoying the warmth of a wonderful day, I closed my eyes and started to doze off, thinking how lucky I was to have Bob, as such a good friend. Now I owed him my life.

Sometime later, I felt Bob's good left hand gently take a hold of my balls.

"You know Bob, I don't really want a wank." I said softly.

"That's okay" Bob said, "Because I do not want to give you a wank. Now shut your eyes and your mouth, and let me express myself in my own way, okay" said Bob, with profound feeling.

"Okay" I replied very softly, "if that's what you want to do.

Bob gently rolled my two balls between his finger tips and I did my utmost to resist myself from getting aroused, but failed completely. Oh well, I thought, as my penis leaped into life. He continued to stimulate my groin area, stroking the inside of my thighs with his finger tips that felt like velvet. I could hear Bob moving to a kneeling position between my opened legs and he lifted my buttocks on to his knees.

He leaned over me taking my now very hard penis into his mouth, and gently nibbled the top of my loose foreskin between his lips. Not being able to hold back any longer, my shaft started to throb as I felt the first ooze slip from the end of my penis. Bob using his lips only, eased back my foreskin, little by little until it rode back over the ridge of my corona, sliding back with ease. As my foreskin slid back another inch or so, I felt a small spurt leave the slot in my now uncovered knob.

Low down I could feel Bob's bishop leap forward, prodding my testicle sac, as Bob's mouth fully encapsulated my throbbing shaft of my penis.

My love juices were now flowing constantly as I felt I had gone to heaven. This is what it must feel like inside a woman's vagina, I thought, as Bob's bishop started to ooze all over my balls.

Bob read my thoughts, as to bringing me on too fast, so he slowly with drew his mouth from my tip end, and my cock began to dance a jig of its own, in protest. Bob realised the tip of his bishop was oozing his fluid all over my balls, and quickly pushed it down below my ball sack, to allow the spunk to run off between my legs.

Bob, having decided my penis was now ready for more needy attention, leaned forward to encompass my cock in his mouth again, the warmth moist of his cavity was most welcomed. He teased the glands on the underside of my knob with the tip of his tongue and at the same time, as I felt a large spurt leave the end of his own knob, run between the cheeks of my arse.

"Bob, I beg you, please don't put your cock into me." Letting go with his mouth, he promised me, he would not dare to do such a thing. I believed him. He got back to sucking slowly and longer until the whole of my full erection was as deep as it was possible to get. While he was doing deep throat, I felt the tip of his bishop stroke my anus as I felt another spurt leave the end of his bishop. The sensation was just too much, as I ejaculated spurt after spurt within Bob's mouth, as I was doing so, Bob quickly lifted his dick to above my balls unable to control his own orgasm any longer, with his bishop about to explode any second, he paused then lay down on top of me ejaculating uncontrollably all over my body. I reached down and wrapped my hand around him and very slowly squeezed him dry.

He was exhausted, as he lay down beside me, we were both so high, we were in fear of overdosing completely. We must have lay there together, for at least twenty minutes in total silence, waiting to come down from such bliss.

We both looked at each other, both still as hard as a rock, but in total peace with ourselves. Bob turned in towards me and kissed me, then asked me what I thought. That was my first ever blow job, and it left me so utterly ecstatically high, I wondered if I should ever return to earth.

Noticing my body was totally covered in Bob's spunk I decided to have a quick swim to cleanse myself.

"Why is there no spunk on you?" I asked Bob. He looked at me and smiled, saying, "Because I drank you dry."

"Oh," I said surprised, and lay back to dry off after the cool water returned my dick to normal size.

Bob's bishop was now at rest lying at one side asleep and at peace.

"What was it like giving your first blow job, and what did it taste like?" I added.

"It was better than I expected, mainly because I could feel your enjoyment through your cock, which surprisingly, helped me enjoy myself as well. Taste, was okay, if anything you tasted kind of sweet" he said.

"Why did you swallow everything?" I asked.

"That's easy; I wanted a part of you to become part of my own body," Bob said " no matter how little. I hope you don't mind?" He asked.

"No" I said, "I feel quite honoured in a way" I commented. "You know Bob," looking for the right words, "what we have just done is a mortal sin, and yet I feel no guilt, I wonder why?"

Bob reflected at length and reaching down to scratch his balls, he said "You know if you had died today Paul, I would not have been able to go on living" then he started to weep.

"Please Bob, please don't cry, not now, not having just celebrated life itself," I whispered.

Bob suddenly stopped crying, then hugged me saying "That's exactly what I was trying to put into words."

I got up and checked Bob's clothes for dryness, then lifted them all up and helped Bob get back into his dry clothes. I quickly got dressed myself and put my hand across Bob's shoulders, as we ambled side by side.

All Bob could say was "Thank you God, thank God you're alive, thank God!!"

I am not able to explain, even to myself, why either of us did what we did. I only know, what I felt at that moment, forever suspended in my memory of time itself. I know it was not sordid, nor did I feel any sense of shame or any guilt. I only know, that if any other boy even attempted to do with me, any similar sexual act, I would not have been responsible for my actions. Bob was not any other boy, and nor was he seducing me in the purely sexual sense.

Bob, I've known since year dot, was more than my brother, he was the very soul of my being. The most important part of my universe, more important than life itself. No, I'm not some rambling lover, jealous or afraid to whom he chooses to share his body with. Nor do I ever expect to preserve my own body for him, or anyone else for exclusive use, sexual or otherwise.

The bond for some mysterious reason, unknown to either of us, will only be finally broken when one or both of us cease to live, and regardless to the reason behind such loss. I have loved many a good woman in my lifetime, and even married and had four wonderful children of my own.

But, what Bob and I have between us transcends above all other levels that I have since experienced.

Bob was certainly oversexed with a very powerful sex drive. He was almost perversive about his bishop. He was also a sexual deviant with a very overactive libido, but one thing couldn't be more certain, he was not a homosexual.

CHAPTER SIXTEEN
A Camping We Shall Go

Both, Bob and myself, suddenly realised we had been pumping the church organ every Sunday morning for Mr Wingfield, the organist, for well over a year. At the same time I clearly remember Bob saying that he, should not be forced to pump the organ, in a Church of England church, because Bob himself, was from a Jewish faith. Mr Wingfield promptly shut Bob up for good, by telling Bob, that he too, Mr Wingfield, was also a Jew, and besides, as Bob and myself were in the back out of sight, neither of us would be part of the congregation. Over the period, we got to know Mr Wingfield extremely well, and both admired his talented gift, and respected him greatly, as a highly cultivated musician.

Mr Wingfield was well into his fifties, with a rapidly balding oval shaped pate, and a body of rotunda like proportions, that stood about five foot nine inches, in stature. He always had a kindly disposition, softly spoken, never raising his voice in anger.

His dexterity of all organ music was legendary, and his reputation as one of London's finest masters on this instrument meant he was often asked to play at St. Paul's Cathedral. We both became overjoyed in putting extra hours of rehearsals, just to be able to listen to the maestro, and willing slaved for Mr Wingfield, just to please him.

Mr Wingfield's Sunday routine never varied, with his mornings at Ashford and Sunday afternoons visiting his sick mother, in hospital. He grew fond of us, and we both thought he was a wonderful man, but we never were able to convince him, we weren't blood brothers.

We explained to him on more than one occasion, that we're not related to one another, but he insisted in referring to us as brothers. He went to great length, to learn everything he could about our background, and could tell us both things about ourselves, that even we didn't know about.

He spoke to us as if we were his sons, although his own two sons were both killed in the very recent war. His wife suddenly died within six months of losing both her children, utterly broken hearted. This gentleman played his feelings through his beloved organ, and it showed. She just gave up, Mr Wingfield said gently. Mr Wingfield was most concerned with Bob's broken wrist, and thought it might be better to get a temporary replacement. Bob would hear none of it, and wouldn't dream of letting anyone else take his place. This won admiration from Mr Wingfield, which had Bob, positively purring with pleasure.

As we both acted in relays pumping the organ lever, twenty minutes alternately about, I questioned Bob's motives. "This is a great skive" Bob said, "and I'm not letting some other plonker take my place, and besides, I enjoy it."

While I was doing my stint on the wooden pumping handle, Bob started to pump himself off. I could see his bishop protruding below his shorts, so I told Bob frankly, if he continued, I would walk out and leave him to pump the organ on his own, with one hand.

"You're a sex maniac" I spat at him, "and you're also in the house of God." I pointed out to him, "This is neither the place or time," I added. He sat there looking suitably shame faced, but stopped playing with himself immediately.

I was beginning to think his cock was the only thing Bob really worshipped. With less than a week to go, before the camp, Mr Wingfield reminded us it would be three weeks before he needed our services again. He handed each of us half a crown, for our pocket fund for the forthcoming camping holiday he explained.

We both jointly declined in uncanny unison, singing exact words from the same hymn sheet. This not only amazed Mr Wingfield, we amazed ourselves, as we turned to face each other laughing together. Mr Wingfield was most insistent, and made it clear, he would be very offended, if we refused. We both handed our pocket money over to Mr Walton to put in our pocket money fund.

He was as surprised as both of us, especially as we were only given twopence (in old £sd) a week pocket money by the school.

Half a crown, in the Forties was almost a king's ransom to us. By now, I had gotten Bob into a set routine, after I helped him shower by putting him straight into his pyjamas, purely to save me work. Bob objected, as he felt I was treating him like a child, but I knew he was really frustrated, finding that our roles with each other were now in complete reversal.

The demands Bob made on me, to satisfy his unquenchable sexual lust, with his exceptional high libido activities were also wearing just a bit thin. When we went up to bed that night, Bob asked me if I would be willing to collar his bishop, with a single lace from one of his plimsoles, explaining he would manage himself from that point forward.

I agreed to do so, but with some suspicion. Well after lights out, Bob whispered me over to his bedside. I neatly tied the lace as Bob prescribed in detail, around his very hard upright bishop, then got back into bed, leaving him to it. I noticed that Mark, on my other bedside, was discretely masturbating himself off, which was most unusual for him, so I quietly went off to sleep.

On Friday after lunchtime, my aunt duly arrived as promised, on one of her many flying visits. She was like a real breath of fresh air, after a week of turmoil, and sexual activities. As we travelled in her small car towards Staines, she talked at length about the holiday she had planned when she picked me up, on the last day from camp.

She had met Bob several times before, and liked and thought Bob was a suitable influence over me (if only she knew the real Bob). She was most concerned about Bobby's wrist, which the creep lapped up.

She talked away to Bob with ease and often spoke to us both as if we were brothers. Which she knew fine, we were not. We parked near the river in Staines, then sat on the grassy bank watching the 5th Staines Sea Scout Group on the river.

There were Scouts, sailing small dinghies and rowing a racing gig, with others canoeing having a fabulous time it made us both so envious. Mucking about on, or in water was definitely my element, I knew instinctively that as soon as I was old enough, I would be part of what I was watching, before my very eyes. Bob's eyes also lit up with pure envious joy.

My aunt was known to miss nothing, as she casually asked Bob how old he was. Bob replied in a put on posh accent, "almost thirteen ma'am," he gave my aunt one of his winning smiles. My aunt was impressed with Bob. The smarmy git, I thought, like all women, he's already got my aunt suckered.

We found a super teashop that my aunt knew well, where we both stuffed our faces with lovely fresh cream cakes. To be fair, Bob did exercise restraint, to win even more Brownie points with my aunt.

"Will you be picking up Patrick with me from camp?" I asked my aunt.

"I'm afraid not" she replied "the Turner's are taking Pat to Scotland with them" my aunt explained as she could read disappointment on my face, at this news.

After a few minutes "I thought you would maybe like to ask Bob instead" said my aunt smilingly.

Taken aback, I almost fell of my chair, I looked at Bob, who was sitting quietly looking equally surprised. We were both so dumfounded, we were speechless, which is very rare indeed.

"Well" my aunt interjected.

"Well what?" I asked my aunt, not sure what she meant.

"Well" said my aunt "are you going to ask Bob or not?"

"Of course I am" now looking directly at Bob, who was already nodding his agreement in a very excited way.

I looked back at my aunt and asked her "Do you think the school would allow Bob to come?"

My aunt looked at me lovingly, and then told me she had already arranged it with the schools, Mr Walton, but wanted to clear it with me first, before giving Mr Walton a final answer.

"Fantastic", we both sung out as one voice, then turned and hugged each other enthusiastically, before we both realised we were in public, then laughed out loud together.

My aunt looked at Bob, then me, "I must find out if you two are related, as I'm sure you're brothers," my aunt said in earnest. The four hours away from Ashford just sped by, as I gave my aunt a real big sloppy kiss, by way of thanks, and Bob the creep, did likewise.

I was still stunned, that Bob, had been invited along also. That night at bed time, I have never seen Bob so excited, as he continually babbled on incessantly, he was beginning to make my head spin, I was getting pissed off just listening to him. Even before lights out, he was lying beside me in bed, which in itself was not unusual. Long after the lights went out, he continued to whisper away in my lug, as high as a kite.

Suddenly, he got out of bed and kneeled down beside my bed, folded down my bed clothes and put my flaccid cock into his mouth, I froze, speechless. He just held it in his mouth. I gently pushed his head off me, kissed him, and then told Bob as best I could, I didn't feel like a blow job

He kissed my forehead, gave me one last hug, and then got into bed. I shouldn't think many boys slept that night before the big day, Saturday finally dawned.

I woke earlier that morning than normal, I was facing Bob who was still asleep. I turned over, thinking it was too early anyway, only to see Mark massaging his well endowed dick which is only the second time in months, I ever saw him. A very shy lad of very few words was totally unaware he had an audience of one.

I had no idea, how long he had been slowly masturbating himself. His ejaculation both in height and quantity was simply amazing. He took great care, in amassing it on his stomach, which seemed to go on for ages. He reached down between his legs for his crumpled up pyjamas, before taking great care in wiping himself off.

Suddenly Mark sensed I was watching, and went as red as a beetroot with embarrassment, quickly covering himself. He lay down in his bed, facing me, full of apologies, which is the very first time he actually spoke to me in months, he was normally so timid.

"I'm sorry Paul," he said " I didn't mean to offend you."

"Don't worry" I assured him" we all do it." I then turned over towards Bob who was still fast asleep.

After breakfast that Saturday morning a total of fifty-two green charabancs rolled up into the playground in an orderly convoy. The dark green cheeky old-fashioned coaches or buses were to be our mode of transport to our seaside resort. They were nothing like the luxurious streamlined coaches of today, oh no these vehicles were built like army tanks in construction with wooden slat seats as there only comfort.

These tortured contraptions of mobility were engineered by a well known almost revered company called Albion Motors, no less. The marvel of high-tec engineering, were similar to the, now infamous 'Green Goddesses', sometimes pulled out of mothballs to cover, in times of strike, by our Fire Service.

Never mind, at the time, we thought they were just wonderful and were all anxious to board them without delay, and whisk us all away, to the wonderful outside world of boyhood dreams. The London County Council (L.C.C.) in their infinite wisdom, and at no cost spared, provided us with this transport of delight. Each bus, was first loaded at its rear door, with a huge wicker basket and many boxes, containing, God knows what.

Each group of between ten and twelve boys were allotted a given numbered bus, which was carefully checked in by a member of staff, who also would be riding shotgun, with us. Surprisingly, the entire military exercise went like clockwork, being completed in under an hour.

The route plan was meticulous, and even members of the police force were alerted to expect this invasion of over a thousand excited brats on their travels.

As we rolled along the roads in convoy doing all of fifty miles per hour, (which was all these jalopies would do anyway) through some very beautiful countryside on a glorious sunny day, it was just great to be alive.

At a designated field stop, to allow us to empty our bladders, hundreds of boys could be seen with their backs to the road each one trying to outpiss each other, describing arches of rainbows, by seeing who could piss the highest.

The sight of hundreds of boys brandishing their hand held little pipes, by any passing motorist, would certainly be met with gawks of unbelief.

Naturally Bob was doing his best to out squirt everybody else. Shortly after this essential stop, we pulled off the road to fill our faces with a sandwich packed lunch, I noticed Bob, who was not feeling hungry, was also looking a bit peaky, and complaining how much his arm was hurting.

For the next few hours, I got so worried, I made the driver stop so I could get word to Walton, who came aboard. Bob was running a temperature, very pale and looked near to dead, as I openly started to sob uncontrollably. Bob was already out of the game, not aware what was happening about him. I cradled him in my arms, genuinely afraid I was going to lose him, I was totally beside myself.

His wrist was turning a funny colour as it swelled up, trapped inside his plaster. When I pointed this out to Mr Walton, he promptly cut the plaster with his penknife to release the pressure.

Bob started to rejoin the world of the living as he quietly asked us where we were.

Mr Walton was obviously concerned, as he made our driver pullover, knowing the school ambulance was at the rear of the convoy. Walton got out and flagged down our own ambulance, and Bob was put on board.

I became insistent I would not leave Bob's side, so Walton relented, allowing me to travel with Bob. I was told by boys on our bus later, they saw me kiss Walton, who was very red faced when he returned to the bus. I honestly don't remember this, as I was in such a state. I do remember the doctor cutting off the plaster completely and telling me, my brother was going to be just fine.

A hand splint was applied under a strapping, while a rather nice young nurse injected a large dose of antibiotics into Bob's bum, which brought a knowing smile to Bob's face, before he fell off to sleep. I continued to hold his hand, very worried.

As we approached the large town of Colchester, not far from our final destination, Bob started to take on colour in his face, although he was still running a high temperature. The doctor took another reading with his thermometer up Bob's anus, which the doctor said was falling and was very encouraging. As we bumped over the dirt road into the campsite, the doctor gave me instructions to put him in bed, and he would look in later to see him.

Walton was waiting for us, as Bob was stretchered off the ambulance into our tent. The eldest lad called George who knew me, or my reputation, was instructed by Walton to push two beds together and to help me get Bob into bed, so between us, we stripped Bob completely, getting him into bed. I climbed in beside him. Bob was beginning to come round, albeit for a few moments only. George knew Bob well, and could see I was very distressed.

"Your big brother will be okay, Paul, you wait and see" said George, with sympathy.

The doctor and Mr Walton came in together. The doctor gave Bob the quick once over.

"If his kid brother notices any dramatic changes, I'm to be notified immediately" said the doctor to Walton. "My guess, he'll be okay by morning, when I'll have that wrist re-x-rayed" he said. "It was spot on, with that younger brother of his alerting us," said the doc.

George, who made up his own bed, was asked to step outside with Mr Walton, for further instructions. There were another three lads, besides George who would be sharing our tent, making just six in all, with two spare beds left.

Within the hour, Bob was beginning to look more like himself and complaining he was feeling hungry. So George vanished to see what he could find. Meanwhile Walton returned with his own radio, a torch and a bottle of tablets, which Bob was to be given every four hours without fail.

"If you need anything else Paul, I'm just ten tents away on this same row, and George has been instructed as your runner."

Once Walton left, Bob turned to me and said "You know Paul, Walton has a real soft spot for you, I don't know any other boy he calls by Christian name." Bob continued, "If I didn't know better, you could be sucking him off." Bob was instantly sorry, as soon as the words spoken, tripped off his tongue.

"I don't know, he's seen my arse often enough, with all the beatings he's given me over the years." I said to Bob. I couldn't be offended by Bob's remarks, I was so pleased to see him recover somewhat to his old self.

"Did some one give me an injection in my bum? Bob asked.

"Don't you remember?" I asked him

"No, but it feels a bit sore." Bob replied.

"Believe me," I told Bob "you weren't complaining when that dolly bird of a nurse gave it to you!"

Bob smiled, having recollected a vague wisp of memory. Just then the same nurse came in, shaking a thermometer, and Bob sprung into life as his youthful spirit leapt into gear. She then handed me the thermometer, to do a reading, so I asked Bob to open his mouth, so I could put it under his tongue.

"No," said the nurse "up his rear end is the only way to be sure of an accurate reading. And you've to do that every four hours when you give him the medicine the doctor left. See you're looking much better Bobby, thanks to that kid brother of yours." The nurse said, and promptly left. The alteration in Bob's face couldn't have been more pronounced with disappointment.

"Right" I said to Bob "turn over."

"You're not shoving that up my arse" said Bob very firmly.

"George, come over and hold Bob down, while I take his temperature."

"Okay," Bob said "but just you, no one else."

I pulled down his covers with George standing by just in case I needed help.

"Bob!" I exclaimed, "How could you?" as George and I saw Bob's bishop standing clearly to attention on guard duty. George laughed out loud, as Bob rolled over onto his bishop quickly. I pried open the cheeks of Bob's arse and with one quick shove, I put the thermometer into his anus, up to the hilt.

Bob winced, more in surprise, than anything else.

"You're a dirty randy bastard," I told him, "you're supposed to be ill for fuck sake." George found this highly amusing.

"Don't you dare move" I told Bob, with no uncertainty, as I leaned across and relieved him of his wristwatch. After about ten minutes, I withdrew the thermometer and although still a little high, it was coming down, I was relieved to see.

"Okay" I said to Bob "turn over" which he did, still with a partial erection, so I whacked it with the back of my hand.

"Ouch" said Bob "that hurt!"

"It was meant to, so you had better get a firm grip of it (no pun intended)." But George was sitting on the side of his bed in stitches.

Bob went very red, having been suitably chastised, as George suddenly disappeared only to re-appear five minutes later, baring a heavy tray of food.

"Right" George said "you can go over to the mess tent Paul to feed your face, I'll take on this brother of yours for a while."

"Thank God for some space," I thought, as I went to feed myself. By the time I got back, there were screens around the bed, as I rushed in thinking the worst.

"There you are" said George, handing me a bar of soap and a flannel. "He has to have a bed bath, but Bob won't let me near him."

"Why can't the nurse give me one?" Bob asked smilingly.

"Good to see you haven't lost your sense of humour." I said.

"Okay George, thanks," I told him "but I'll give this drama queen a bed bath."

George looked at me, then said "Bob is no queen, but he doesn't realise how lucky he is, to have a brother like you."

"Why don't you tell George, I'm not your brother?" I whispered to Bob.

"I have many times" said Bob "but he won't believe me."

"I don't know if I should be proud or what, having a sex beast like you as a brother." I told Bob, who looked very wounded.

I spread out the big bath towel on top of my side of the bed and Bob quietly spread himself upon it. I dipped the flannel into the bucket of hot water, soaping it up to a good lather.

"Turn over" I instructed Bob "I'll do the backside of your body first." He hesitated, but did so. I soaped the whole of his neck, shoulders and back first, and noticed the bruise on his bum from his first injection, washing his anus area as gently as I could, before moving down to his legs. I rinsed him off, before getting him to turn front side up.

I was relieved to see he was behaving himself; I washed his whole front, leaving his bishop to himself. Once he was rinsed and dried off, he got back into bed.

"You know Paul," Bob said "you know my cock, better than I know it myself."

"I don't think anyone could know your dick better than yourself, with the amount of time you spend playing with it!" I told Bob.

He looked at me with solemn eyes but remained silent. Bob quickly fell asleep, so I left him, to jaw with George, as I sat on the bed beside him.

"You know Paul, "George said " I wish I had a brother like you."

"Why?" I asked him.

"Come on, most of Bob's mates know about your antics" George said.

"What do you mean?" I asked.

"The big stack for one" he whispered, "and the fights you have got into over the years protecting smaller, less fortunate kids. Leo Jackson for one, among many" said George.

"Who told you all this rubbish?" I asked George.

"Not Bobby, your brother, that's for sure, although he's very fond of you, your reputation within the school is well known anyway."

"Well George" I told him quite sternly "Bob is not my brother for starters, and if my reputation is well known, why doesn't everybody know that fact."

"Yeh Yeh," said George "I've heard it all before."

I stood up, and walked outside to get a breath of fresh air, before I lost my rag.

At half past nine that evening, it started to get dark, so I headed back towards my tent, just as Walton looked out of his tent.

"How's your brother?" he asked. I stopped dead in my tracks, looked at Walton, with a question on my lips.

"Why does everybody think Bob is my brother?" I asked instead.

"I can't really answer that question in truth," said Walton, ducking back into his tent. Now I really was mystified, but also very pleased. As I walked into the tent, to undress ready for bed, I was relieved to hear Bob snoring gently in deep slumber.

At ten o'clock, it seemed a pity to wake him, for his tablet and even worse still, to check his temperature.

I gently shook him awake, giving him his tablet, which he took without water at his own insistence, but when I asked him to turn over for his temperature, he wasn't as keen but did so without much fuss. I used the torch to find his anus, and very gently slipped in the thermometer, which this time did not make him flinch. I cuddled into his back, as he reached over to give my arm a squeeze, and just as quickly fell asleep again.

Ten minutes later, I extracted the thermometer, which now read normal, then turned over away from Bob, who was now snoring away, as I drifted off myself.

At almost 2 a.m. exactly, Bob shook me awake, desperate for a pee. I retrieved the bottle from under the bed, switched on the torch, while I held the bottle as Bob unceremoniously put his bishop in the bottle, peeing so much, he must have been fit to burst.

I gave him his tablet, then he turned over for his temperature to be taken without being asked.

We both settled down for the rest of what was left of the night, at least until his next tablet at six. He turned into my back, resting his strapped wrist on my hip.

I gave him his 6 a.m. tablet, then lay back awake, while Bob fell asleep again. I quietly got out of bed, to go and have a shower, taking Bob's urine bottle with me to empty and wash out.

Just after 7 a.m., I slipped back into the tent, pretending I hadn't noticed George wanking himself off and slipped back into bed. Bob honed into my body like a heat seeking missile as I drifted or rather dozed off, wondering why I was so tired.

Just before 8 a.m., the doctor popped in to tell me to have my brother ready for 9. He was followed by George with a fresh bucket of warm water for Bob's ablutions, but looking rather sheepishly, thinking perhaps I had seen him earlier. Not letting on, I thanked him for the water.

I got Bob up, washed him down and dried him off, before dressing him ready for the doctor. His behaviour was immaculate. He leaned forward, and kissed me on the forehead.

"What was that for?" I asked Bob.

"I don't really know," said Bob smiling. I just felt like it.

George came in with a huge tray of breakfast, and while he took away the bathing water, I folded the screens away. On the dot, the doc came by at nine, telling me that Bob was only going for an x-ray, and there wasn't any need for me to go.

I went for a good breakfast of sausage, eggs, tomatoes and lots of hot buttered toast, all washed down with huge mugs of hot tea. I went back to the tent, stripped off the bed to let them air off, as Walton put his head around the tent door, telling me to bring my swimming trunks and join his swimming party.

Mr Walton doesn't do request, I reminded myself, as I joined the swimming group of fifty or more.

Mr Walton, the swimming master, led off the group as we casually walked through the attractive seaside of Walton-on-Naze. As we headed down the brae, leading to the seafront, I caught my first dramatic view of the ocean, which was so stunning it took my breath away. I hardly took in the compactness of this small town, as my eyes opened wide with awe at the sea spread out before me. I had never seen the sea before, I pinched myself in disbelief. What a fantastic sight God has created. So this was what all the kids talked about with so much excitement. Wow, I yelped out loudly, forgetting that most of my group had already seen it.

Well worth every minute of waiting, I thought, as I raced down to the beach, to meet the North Sea rollers, of pure magic breaking upon the shore. I unashamedly undressed to the buff forgetting it was a public beach, not caring who saw me, in haste to get my swimming trunks on. My mates laughing with glee, sharing my uninhibited joy, as if I was a toddler again.

I ran to meet the pounding white surf as it crashed and broke upon the sandy seashore. I was soon completely at home, as I swam out into the deep, enjoying myself like never before. Two hours, like the pounding surf upon the beach, disappeared as fast as the outgoing tide.

Alas, even my favourite lunch of sausages and mash potatoes was an anti-climax after that swim.

Bob came over, sporting a new plaster, beaming from ear to ear. He explained to me, they found a secondary break and had to reset the whole wrist.

"If I get as much as a drop of water on this plaster" said Bob "it's a hanging offence" warned the doctor.

Bob must have done more damage than he realised, when he jumped into our deepest pool, to save my worthless neck, I thought, now feeling guilty over all the reprimands I gave him over the past week or more. Just when Bob, felt he had got back his freedom, Mr Walton reminded Bob, he had already been told by the doctor he was to stay in bed, at least until Tuesday morning, when the doctor would come by, and just maybe, discharge him.

So, Mr Walton asked Bob what the hell did he think he was doing sitting at the table gassing away, disobeying the doctor's orders. Bob disappeared like a scolded cat, and I went very quickly myself, before Walton had a chance to turn on me.

Bob was already undressed, ready for bed as I walked in, and George told me quickly, that he had been instructed to make up the bed before getting his own lunch by Walton.

"I'm sorry Paul," he said, as if he had just done something wrong.

"That's alright George," I said, who then departed with haste.

"He can be a real bastard" Bob said with feeling.

I assumed he was talking about Walton, as I helped him. We spent the afternoon listening to Walton's radio and playing chess, but Bob, I noticed, tired very easily, he fell asleep just before tea time. So I left him to rest, as I disappeared to grab some tea. At tea, I met George and told him Bob was asleep, and I would take him something to eat later.

"Thanks Paul," he said grateful to be relieved of this tiresome chore.

"See you later Paul," he said as he went on his way. That night, I was thankful not to administer to Bob every four hours, and my sleep was uninterrupted until early morn. Bob was snoring into my back fast asleep, when I felt a dribble between my legs, I put my hand down to feel, only to discover Bob's bishop as hard as a rock just under my balls.

"Bob" I whispered several times to no avail, so I grabbed my folded pyjamas from under my pillow just in time, as he fully ejaculated between my legs and all over my balls. I could feel his body jerk in spasms emptying himself between my inner thighs. The dirty bastard I thought, as he slept on. I waited, until I thought he had completely finished. I mopped up as best I could. Then trying to be careful, I extracted his, still very hard, bishop from between my legs. As I did so, he woke up asking me, what I thought I was doing, I took hold of his good hand and placed it on my own soft dick, then put it between my thighs and told Bob, it was him and not me that caused all the damage. He felt his own bishop that was still rock hard.

"Please Paul, I didn't know I was coming, I was dreaming of Margaret." He said. He started to sob.

"Come here you loony," I consoled him, "I know you didn't do it deliberately" I said, "So stop crying, there's no need," as I wrapped his bishop in my pyjamas.

"I'm really sorry Paul, honest I am" Bob said.

"That's okay, go back to sleep" I told him. I dozed off myself, as George woke me up with his bucket of hot water.

"Shall I put the screens up for you Paul?" he asked.

"Yes please," I replied "and thanks." There was two for a strip wash today, I thought, as I washed myself off first, before waking Bob.

After sorting him out, I made him sit on my bed, as I remade Bob's bed up as a single. Once he was settled, I remade my own bed up as a single, separating the two.

After breakfast, Mr Walton arrived with two strange lads, and showed them to the only two spare available beds. They were both sixteen years old, they told us, and with several of there mates, were from Barnardo's, in one of the small London Barnardo homes.

They introduced themselves as Bill and Benjamin or Ben for short. They were both fairly big, even for sixteen I thought. Bob told me to go for my morning swim and he would see me later around lunchtime. So I left Bob, chatting away with the Barnardo boys, but for some unknown reason I felt uncomfortable about it. Fortunately, I met George, and asked him to keep a very close eye on Bob, with these two strangers in the tent.

"No worries" said George, "I'll stay with Bob till you return" George assured me.

So I went swimming, feeling a little less concerned about Bob's care.

Cuckoos, In The Nest

It was a lovely Tuesday morning, with the sunshine bathing the whole of the campsite of row upon rows of tents, as I quickly enjoyed my morning shower, before attending to Bob's needs. As I entered the tent, there were loud snores coming from the Barnardo boys corner of the tent.

Shortly before 8 a.m. the doctor gave Bob the once over, proclaiming Bob fit enough to leave his bed. Bob was overjoyed, but the doctor gave Bob a catalogue of do's and don'ts, warning Bob of dire consequences should he ignore doctors orders. He suddenly turned on me, remembering the hassle I gave him, when he threatened to circumcise me all those years back, after my altercation with a football.

"You," he said to me "will be held personally responsible for you're brother, should anything else go wrong," he warned me.

Both Bob and I looked at the doctor promising him we would behave ourselves. See that you do, he remarked, then left. We went over to the mess tent, Bob enjoying a big cooked breakfast as I sat alongside him laughing and joking with each other. There was a gang of men, putting up outside lights all over the campsite and everybody was talking about it.

I remarked to Bob, "I hoped they were not going to be bright, as I enjoyed sleeping in comparative darkness."

"There is already a night patrol in operation" said Bob "to keep the boys away from the girls field, and two lads were caught last night after 10 p.m." Bob remarked.

"How do you know all this?" I asked Bob.

"The grapevine" Bob replied.

"You know Bob, because of boys like you and your reputations of all being sex maniacs, they need this kind of security."

"Yeh" said Bob, "great en it!!" giving me one of his winning smiles. Bob then looked at me, and said, "You know Paul, you are going to be just as bad, given time, you have already got an over-active libido." He said casually.

"And whose fault is that?" I said.

"I'm coming with your swimming group into town, this morning to see what this one horse town has to offer." Bob said smiling.

I looked at Bob, with alarm bells going off in my head and said, "Well just make sure you stay out of trouble." Bob smiled.

We met up at lunchtime, Bob grinning like a two tailed cat, trying to wag both at the same time, bursting to tell me something.

"Come on" I said to Bob "what is it?"

"Not here" said Bob "I'll tell you when we get back to the tent."

"I don't think I want to hear this!" I said

"You will," said Bob, "you will" he repeated, helping himself to another big dollop of custard, to put on his rhubarb pudding.

Once back into the tent, Bob couldn't contain himself any longer, bursting to give me, what he called his good news.

"Well" said Bob, all excited, lying prone on his bed, "I've arranged for Margaret and Sylvia, with ourselves to meet in town tomorrow at 2 p.m. And " Bob continued, "I've found the ideal place where we can all go." He said gloatingly. I looked at Bob suspiciously as his bishop was making a notable bump below his shorts, as his sexual imagination went into overdrive.

"You know Bob," I started " you have been out of your sick bed for less than six hours, and already you're behaving like a sexual predator, lusting to satisfy your selfish sex drive."

Bob just lay back, eyes closed, letting my reprimands wash over him.

"Well" I said to Bob "I've had enough, you can count me out and go on your own."

He opened his eyes wide, then stared at me in disbelief.

"You can't do that" Bob said, "I arranged all this for you, and I promised Sylvia, you would come" Bob said, no longer smiling.

"Well" I told Bob "he should learn to mind his own business, and that I was quite capable of making my own sexual encounters.

"Well" said Bob "you haven't had any sex with Sylvia so far, have you?"

"That's none of your fucking business," I snapped.

Bob got up from his bed, prodded me in the shoulder with his good hand and said "You know Paul, you're an ungrateful little bastard, I wish I hadn't bothered" he added, then stormed out of the tent, furious with me.

A few seconds later, in walked George, asking me what was wrong with Bob, who looked very upset. "Join the club," I said to George, "I've just given Bob a right bollocking, with a few home truths thrown in for good measure."

"I'm glad it was you and not me" said George "because I've seen Bob turn nasty when he's upset

"You haven't seen me, when I get upset" I said.

"No" George said, "but I know from mates of mine, I wouldn't like to upset you either," smiled George nervously.

I left the tent, and wandered about the campsite on my own. Bob and I avoided each other, until I helped Bob prepare for bedtime. Neither of us spoke to each other, until we each got into bed, then Bob leaned over and whispered to me that he was sorry, he should have asked me first, before he arranged anything with the girls.

I noticed that Bob had pushed our beds closer to each other with barely fifteen inches between them. I resisted talking to him, and quickly fell asleep. I was fast asleep, before all the older lads returned before 10 p.m. curfew. The newly erected lights were shining through the tent canvas from outside the Barnardo's corner, so I was forced to sleep facing Bob's bed.

I slept well, until Bob gently, but persistently shook me awake, and as I came into consciousness, Bob quickly covered my mouth with his good hand, to ensure I didn't speak out. Bob put his finger across his mouth, to indicate complete silence, then pointed towards the Barnardo boys corner, behind me. I turned over very slowly without making any sound whatsoever, to see for myself, what Bob was already watching.

There was more than enough light filtering through the tents canvas, to clearly see everything that was happening. The new field security light was only feet away from the tent, outside. The biggest boy, Ben, was kneeling astride his mate, Bill's chest, both on the one bed nearest to us, barely eight feet away. How could any boys, let alone total strangers, perform such acts in such an open forum, I wondered.

I glanced over my shoulder at Bob, who was just as goggle eyed as myself. Bob, pointed again, so I turned back to watch the action. Ben the taller of the two was kneeling high up on Bill's chest, with his penis just inches away from Bill's face. Within moments, Ben reached a satisfactory state, of a full erection, then eased it into Bills mouth, inch by inch at first, with Ben easing in more and more at every sucking stroke. With all of Ben's penis inside Bill's mouth, the act of deep throat took over. How Bill didn't choke, I'll never understand.

Meanwhile Bill's penis at the other end, sprung into a very full erection which in size was even more impressive of the two, and Bill was the shortest in stature of them both. Indeed Bill's penis, compared to Ben, who was well enough endowed, was frighteningly larger.

Ben continued the full length slow methodical rhythm inside Bill's mouth cavity, that was obviously well practised. Ben's body and upper torso went into spasm as he reached his full orgasm, climaxing and ejaculating everything he had, emptying himself completely inside Bill's mouth.

Once he had finished, Ben left his penis resting for several moments, before withdrawing his cock, completely from Bill. Then with casual practice of two experts, having done it many times before, Ben calmly cupped his hands below Bill's jaw, who gobbed out a handful of spunk into Ben's hands waiting to receive it. Meanwhile Bills oversized endowment, was swaying in an orgy of heightened erotic behaviour.

Ben eased down his body from Bill's chest to above Bills' swaying cock in readiness. Ben wiped his cupped hand full, around his rear entrance, and with the surplus he carefully spread it around Bill's erected shaft.

Ben arched his back and slowly, lowered his buttocks onto Bill's erected penis, without Bill's assistance. Ben eased it into his own rectum, with precision so easily, as if he had received Bill many times before, with no difficulty regardless to the girth of Bill's shaft thickness.

Ben made some minor adjustments to his own knee positions, then quickly worked into a steady rhythm as if he was bare back riding a horse, swallowing everything Bill could give him. Ben maintained this swinging motion, with Bill pushing up from below, working as a team in tandem.

With every upward stroke, Ben would expose only about six inches of Bill's shaft, and would then plunge his bum down hard onto Bill's balls, who didn't seem to mind.

Bills' body below, suddenly stiffened as he exploded inside of Ben, until he knew Bill had no more to give. Ben leaned back on his haunches, with Bill still fully inside him. Then Ben managed a second erection with Bill's help who was squeezing Ben's balls, encouraging Ben to do his utmost. Within a very short time, Ben was nearing his second climax, and with some kind of signal between them, Bill took over Ben's penis, bringing it to a second satisfactory ejaculation, with Bill directing the spitting cobra all over his own body.

Ben having done, climbed off the top of Bill, and went to bed leaving Bill to it. Bill just lay there for at least a full five minutes, admiring his prized possession, which was still on guard duty. Bill started to wipe himself down, but changed his mind, as one hand cupped around his own balls, while the other wiped up some of the surplus spunk from his body, which he smeared around his shaft that appeared to lose none of its stiffness. In less than a dozen slow strokes, he came towards his second climax. He sped up his strokes and within seconds he ejaculated with purpose in mind, watching his first erupted spurt soar over his head, as this thick globule hit the sloping roof of the tent.

He became entranced, as the rest, splattered onto his upper body. After he was sure there was no more, he proceeded to clean himself off for the second time in as many minutes. He folded back his bedclothes, and climbed in facing us.

We closed our eyes, but when I looked a little later, they were both snoring their heads off. I looked back at Bob, who signalled for me to hold the bottle, as he needed to empty his bladder. I was never so pleased to see Bob's bishop behaving itself.

As Bob climbed back into bed, I noticed the time was 2.30 a.m. George shook me awake, placing the bucket of hot water down, and erected the screens around us, ready for Bob's morning routine, which I was beginning to share as it made life easier. I gently shook Bob awake, who asked to wait a little while because he was having difficulty with his erection. I pulled the covers back to see the bishop erect, but still very dry.

"Look Bob, I haven't got time for this" I started "what's your problem?" I whispered

"I can't stop thinking of Margaret, who, I'll be doing today," said Bob.

"Okay," I said "but if it's not soft by the time I've finished my own ablutions I don't care what your bishop says, I'm doing you anyway."

When I was ready for him, he reluctantly got out of bed with his bishop refusing to obey orders, so I deliberately gave the bishop a good scrub with the soapy flannel longer than normal as I watched the bishop wince with such harsh treatment. I made Bob open his legs as I gave his testicles the same treatment, as I saw the bishop surrender back to its normal flaccid self.

As I started helping Bob get dressed, he told me I was becoming a right cruel bastard, with every day I got older.

"Well Bob," I said "it's like this, you know when Walton takes the skin off my arse, caning me, why does he do it? I asked Bob.

"Because he loves you" was Bob stocky reply.

"That's right Bob, have you received the message yet?"

He looked at me as the penny dropped, and broke into a smile.

"Now let's go to breakfast" I told Bob "I'm starving.

Once sat at the table, having cut up Bob's food for him to eat with his one good hand, I asked Bob, if what we saw last night, was real, Bob quickly replied, it was no dream, then nudged me to keep mum as George sat down beside us.

George was talking away to Bob, while I was lost in my own thoughts I started to wonder what my first sexual encounter with Sylvia might be like this afternoon. I was so lost in thought until I felt a slight ooze leave the end of my dick involuntary as Bob looked at me, as if reading my dirty thoughts.

His good hand slipped below the table and grabbed hold of my dick giving it a very hard squeeze, which made me wince, but also had the desired effect, as I quickly went back to normal. This so called E.S.P. we sometimes had between us, could be a right pain in the neck, I told myself.

I went off for my morning swim leaving Bob, talking to George. Just before lunchtime I met Bob in the tent and asked him how he knew I had an erection at breakfast time?

"I don't know exactly," said Bob "but my own bishop leaked a touch and mine was soft, so I knew it must have been you, who had a hard on, thinking about Sylvia."

"Do you always known, when I get aroused?" I asked him.

"No of course not" said Bob "don't be such a dipstick, that was the first time."

"That's alright then" I said, feeling somewhat relieved.

But it wasn't alright, as this E.S.P. thing continued to bug me for sometime, it was beginning to feel like someone was stealing my private thoughts! And my feelings

After lunchtime, we both headed into town to meet the girls. Bob suddenly looked at me and asked me if I was feeling okay.

"No, I'm feeling scared" I admitted to Bob.

"I know" said Bob, "but trust me, your going to be just fine."

Bob knew it was going to be my very first sexual encounter, and for some reason, I believed in Bob so much, I just knew it would turn out just fine. I don't know how I knew, I just did.

As we approached the meeting place, the girls were waiting as planned.

"Now" said Bob before we crossed the road to join them, "trust me Paul, their just gagging for it, so just follow my lead" said Bob.

"Okay, okay" I replied nervously.

Bob led off with Margaret, who never stopped talking to Bob, as Sylvia and I, arm in arm followed sheepishly behind. As we left the outskirts of the town, Bob swung a right along a tree-lined dirt track for about five hundred yards, until we came to a small clearing.

To one side of the track, there was a small stone building like an old barn. I had the feeling I had been here before, but I also knew for certain I hadn't, unless it was through Bobs E.S.P., I thought. We followed Bob and Margaret through one half of a pair of doors, Sylvia closing it shut behind us.

There was only one small skylight set into the roof, the rest of the building was totally void of any other windows. As my eyes adjusted to the dim light, while still holding onto Sylvia's hand, I could see many loose bales of hay. Bob, took Margaret behind a small stack, and waved us to the far corner, to find a dry area for ourselves.

Sylvia sat me down on a bale of hay, but not sure, of what the next move was going to be, I waited for Sylvia to show me the running order. Sylvia was more than a year older than me, and as it turned out, far more sexually advanced as well. She kneeled down in front of me, kissing me on the mouth.

Her tongue slipped easily into my mouth as the tip of her moist tongue tangoed with mine, I felt my balls tingling and without prior warning, my cock got rock hard, trying to escape the confines of my shorts.

She slowly unbuttoned my shirt, button by button as her tongue teased me sensually, exciting me of things still to come. By now, my penis was throbbing with anticipation, as Sylvia stood me up. I undid her blouse which she let slip to the floor, and I caught a glimpse of beautifully form firm pair of breasts, before she knelt down just inches away from my very hard penis, fighting to get out from my shorts.

My cock felt so hard it was now hurting, as she undid the waistband of my shorts. She quickly pulled my shorts over my erection to the ground as my pulsating penis sprang back up to almost vertical. Sylvia waited for my gyrating cock to slow to a stationary position, as I looked down at her face. I've never seen my penis so big or so hard, it was like an iron bar, no wonder it hurt.

I cupped my hands either side of her face and very gently entered her soft warm moist mouth, as my first spurt, shot to the back of her mouth, which surprised us both.

She withdrew my penis completely, and as a droplet dripped out of the hole in my corona, she caught it in free fall with her tongue. She took me over to some loose hay upon the floor, as I stepped out of my shorts. I lay back, thinking I had gone to heaven. Now completely naked, Sylvia joined me, kneeling over my head, as she put my penis back into her mouth. My eyes were just inches away from her love lips to her vagina. I pulled her breasts towards me as I sucked her nipple, like a baby feeding.

She grabbed hold of the first two fingers of my right hand and guided them into her pussy. It was lovely and sticky as I explored deep inside her. My own spunk was flowing freely not far from a full ejaculation, and she was drinking it faster than I could provide it. I pushed her face off my cock, as I felt she was bringing me on to fast.

Sylvia held my hand, stopping me moving my two fingers deep inside her. We both looked down at my penis standing bolt upright. Sylvia had managed to push my foreskin back as far as possible, exposing a good two inches of my penis I had never seen before, because it was normally covered by my foreskin. My penis was no longer sore, but was now throbbing in protest for the interruption.

I watched Sylvia come down with lips and slowly engulf the first three inches or so, then slowly go all the way , engulfing my entire length as I felt my knob go into her throat, with her mouth taking hold of one of my balls. Somehow she managed to get one and then both of my balls into her mouth cavity, as I felt my knob go passed her tonsils deep into her throat.

I could hold back no longer as I felt my testicles discharge their load like an elevator racing to the top floor. Oh my God, I thought, I'm going to choke her, as I looked down to see the whole of my genitalia engulfed completely inside her mouth.

"Withdraw," I shouted as I pulled the whole of my penis from her mouth.

A split second later, I exploded, erupting and ejaculating uncontrollably as a few seconds later her vagina had the whole of my hand swimming in the stuff. After the main ejaculation, she went down on me again determined to drink me dry. I could give her no more, and Sylvia knew it. She left me, exhausted lying on the floor, overdosing on my own high.

She came back and wiped me down, kissing every part of my body, getting me hard again.

"No Sylvia" I begged her, "please don't." and thankfully she didn't.

After a while I joined Sylvia to get dressed and as I peered over the small stack where I knew Bob was, I saw him fucking Margaret aggressively taking her doggy fashion. We left them to it, as Sylvia and I went outside to come up for air. My balls were still tingling with a slight ache, and I was still in awe, that Sylvia was able to get the whole lot inside of her mouth. I wished I could put it up her vagina, the way Bob was ravishing Margaret, I thought. One day soon, I hoped, I think I'm becoming addicted to sex, like a druggy.

Fucking hell, I thought, Bob warned me more than once, I remembered.

Sylvia, looked at me tenderly, "Paul my love, was that your very first time?" she asked.

I returned my look of love and thanks, and then said quietly "You know it was. You stole my virginity."

"You have a really super penis," she added.

She lovingly combed my hair, just as Bob and Margaret surfaced, to join us, both smiling with satisfaction. We all headed back to town, like four frolicking lambs in spring. After saying our goodbyes, the girls went off to hit the shops and compare notes no doubt, Bob added as an afterthought.

As we slowly ambled back to camp on a high, waiting to return to earth from the clouds above our heads, I pulled Sylvia's hanky from my pocket.

Bob chatted away as usual, lost in thought, I held my council, as we soon entered camp. Mr Walton spotted the two of us and asked us if we had a good day.

"We certainly have sir," Bob replied "in fact it's been one of the most wonderful days of our lives" said Bob, a bit O.T.T., I thought, but I wondered, what Walton would really say, if he knew that he was looking at the biggest pair of reprobates possible.

With ample time before tea, we lay on our beds with time to dream.

"You're very quite," said Bob "are you okay?"

"Yes" I said, "I'm still floating.

After a few minutes, I got up and sat on Bob's bed beside him. I looked him straight in the eyes, then I said to him "Did you enjoy your fuck?"

Bob looked genuinely puzzled, so I decided to elaborate.

"I saw you ramming your cock up Margaret" I said.

"That's right," Bob said "you saw me fucking her arse hole."

"Oh oh" I spluttered "I'm sorry, I thought you were shagging her cunt."

I felt a right plonker, going really red.

As we were sitting down at teatime, I noticed Bob was doing a lot of crotch scratching. I didn't pay much attention at first, but as Bob continued to play with himself, even in public, I lost the rag with him, telling him to leave his bishop alone, especially in public, and left Bob feeling disgusted with him.

I wandered over to the cinema tent where they were showing an old black and white Hitchcock thriller, which I watched. By 7.30 p.m., I was feeling shattered, so I headed back to the tent. I think that sex Goddess Sylvia, took a lot more out of me than I thought. As I wandered into the tent, Bob was all alone in bed, with a lot more movement going on below his bed covers than normal, even for Bob.

"You're not still playing with yourself?" I asked Bob jokingly.

As quick as a flash he replied, "No, I fucking well ain't, but the itch around my balls, is fucking driving me mad."

I put up the screens around his bed.

"Now what the fuck are you doing?" Bob demanded.

"Look Bob," I said, "I was going to take a look, but if you think I'm going to be handling your fucking cock on public display, you can just fuck yourself. I'll go and get the doctor instead and let him deal with you, because I'm right pissed off with you."

As I left heading for the door, fooling Bob into thinking I was going off to get the doctor, Bob pleaded with me not to go, as he turned on the water works. I slowly walked back towards Bob, took the flashlight from my bedside locker, pulled back Bob's bed clothes with a flourish, switched on the torch and looked.

On very close examination, I could see very tiny insects that looked like crabs. I lifted his balls up as high as I could, as several tiny mites ran for cover into his pubic hair. They were even crawling over his dick near to his hair line. Bob instinctively put his hand down to scratch as I covered him back up.

"Well?" Bob asked.

"You have crabs crawling all over your bishop" I told him. "Maybe you need a good wash, that should drown the blighters."

"No that won't do it "said Bob "I've heard of this before, this is a lot more serious than I first thought." As he burst into tears.

"I think" sobbed Bob "you can only get these through having sex. What am I going to do?" Bob pleaded.

"Maybe you should go and see the doctor" I suggested" he could maybe give you something to get rid of them."

"I can't do that," said Bob, "he'll know straight away I have been having sex with a girl. He would have to report me!" Bob added.

"Maybe I should ask George then?" I said to Bob, as I saw him enter the tent.

"No" said Bob "keep your fucking mouth shut."

I left him behind the screens and walked over to George, asking him if I could have a quick word outside. I started to openly scratch my crotch in front of him, asking him what did he know about crabs. George looked at me scratching myself, then looked at me again, breaking into a broad smile and said "You randy little bastard, Paul."

I looked suitably embarrassed, and serious.

"Well" said George "I had them myself, about a year or more ago. You know they bury themselves under the skin to lay their eggs," George continued "dirty wee biters too."

"Get on with it George, I haven't got all week." I said impatiently.

"Right" said George "first you need to shave your dick and balls, then if you go to the chemist for a pinkish liquid which you brush on with great care. That usually kills the buggers off within 48 hours, but it's best to paint your cock twice."

"If I give you the money, can you get this stuff for me?" I asked.

"Well, yes" said George "but the chemist won't be open until tomorrow."

"Thanks George, but can you keep this to yourself, my brother Bob mustn't find out. Do you understand?" I asked him.

"Yes" George replied "you can trust me, honest you can Paul" he assured me.

"Great." I said, "Can you give me a loan of your shaving gear?"

"That's alright, I'll shave you clean" George said.

"No you won't" I replied" I'll shave my own tackle, thank you.

"Okay" George said "but you better take real care, I hope you realise just how difficult shaving yourself especially is, I ended up asking for help."

"Right, if I need help I'll ask you George, but I would sooner try it on my own first, okay."

We went back into the tent and he handed me his shaving gear from his locker.

"Thanks George, I'll take great care, I promise."

George then left the tent, as he had some one to meet he explained. I explained everything to Bob in great detail.

"Do you mean," Bob asked "George thinks it's you, that's got crabs?"

"That's right," I said, scratching my balls in Bob's face.

"You're a cunning little bastard" Bob said, once again smiling.

I handed Bob the shaving gear. "There you are, you had better get on with it, while it's quiet. I don't know anything about shaving" I told Bob "if I try to do it, I'll probably cut your dick off!"

"You will have to get someone else to do it" I told him "it's too dangerous for me to attempt such a task."

Bob started crying again. I sat down beside him, cuddling him and begging him to stop crying.

"What am I going to do, if you won't help me Paul?" Bob asked

"I had no alternative, but to try. Alright" I shouted at Bob, who was beginning to try my patience to the extreme.

"Okay" I said, giving in to Bob too easily "stop your crying and I'll give it a try, but don't blame me if I cut your cock off altogether, now stand up and hold the torch."

From the water in the bucket left from the morning ablutions I lathered up George's shaving brush, and started to lather up Bob's bush.

"Hold that fucking torch still" I shouted at Bob, as I took hold of Bob's penis in my left hand pulling it towards me, then gingerly at first, and starting at his stomach, started to remove his pubic hair. Rinsing the safety razor out often. This surprisingly was easier and faster than I thought. Pulling his bishop up high I got most of the hair off with very few problems.

I put the half folded towel on the bed and instructed Bob to lay back, with his legs as high as he could manage. Once he was in the best position, I told him to hold the torch as still as possible, as I very carefully shaved off the fine hair from his balls, holding each one as gently as possible.

"There," I said "I think that's it", rinsing off the razor as I spotted a few crabs left, running towards Bob's anus.

"Hold very still," I said to Bob "this is going to hurt" and knowing Bob's only good hand was holding the torch, I quickly shoved my finger into Bob's anus.

"Ouch" said Bob "that hurt."

"I'm sorry," I said, as I pushed my finger in deeper, picking the little crabs off one by one, while they were searching for somewhere to hide.

"I won't be too long Bob, I promise." I put each crab I caught between my fingernails, into the bucket of water, until I could see no more. I slowly pulled my finger out.

"For fuck sake, why did you shove your finger up my arse?" Bob asked.

"Why do you think," I said to Bob "to stop the crabs from invading your insides. Do you want these little bastards laying their eggs inside you?"

"No" was all Bob could manage to say.

"Right" I said, " lay down, with your legs apart, till I check you over."

I took the torch from Bob, and gave his genitalia the once over.

"There's just the one bit I missed" as I told Bob to pull his bishop up towards his belly button. With the last of the soap from the brush I slapped it on the underside of his shaft about an inch or so from his scrotum. I took hold of the razor, which by now was getting quite blunt, because with the very first stroke with the razor it nicked a cut about half an inch long across the underside of his shaft. The blood started to flow freely.

"Shit" I said to Bob "I've cut you."

Bob never made one complaint. I put a corner of the towel over it, but it just kept bleeding. Still, Bob never uttered a word. I knew the healing and congealing quality of spittle, so with no more ado, I put my mouth over the wound applying pressure directly with my tongue.

I held my mouth and tongue sideways onto this lower part of the shaft for a good few moments, until finally the bleeding stopped. We both waited for a few minutes to make sure it wasn't going to start again.

"Okay, Bob" get back into bed, and please, don't scratch that area, otherwise you could start the bleeding off again."

Bob got back into bed, speechless, but watched every move I made as I cleared and tidied away.

"I'll get that solution onto the vital area tomorrow, once I get it from the chemist" I told Bob, as I went to clean up George's shaving gear. Once I had safely put George's gear away in his locker, I got undressed and crawled into bed, bushed.

Just after 8.30 p.m., George put his head around the screens, putting a jar discreetly on top of my locker. We looked over to see Bob was asleep, and I whispered to George "I'll see you later". I slipped on my pyjama bottoms and nipped out the other side of the screens to have a quick word with George.

"I thought you couldn't get hold of this stuff until morning?" I asked George.

"That's a freebee," said George "from an admirer."

I looked at George. "Don't ask, Paul, you don't want to know, believe me." Said George, then walked out of the tent.

I went behind the screens again and Bob opened his eyes, now that he knew, he needed to pretend to be asleep, no longer.

"Come on" I said to Bob as I shook the bottle before opening it. The brush was attached to the inside of the lid. Bob stood there with his legs wide apart, as I liberally painted him all over with a nice baby pink colour.

"Turn round and bend over" I instructed Bob, and he did as he was bid.

"There now, stand there for a moment to allow it to dry properly."

Bob looked down at himself. "I must be the only boy in the school with no pubic hair and a baby pink dick," he said.

After ten minutes, I surrounded Bob's bishop with the palm of my hand, and after giving it a squeeze, I opened up my palm to make sure it was baby pink free.

You'll do," I said to Bob "now get into bed, and for fuck sake, don't play with yourself!"

I put the screen away, fell into bed, then also fell asleep just as quick, what one does for one's friends, is simply too amazing to put into words, I dreamt.

Next morning, I was awoken by George who by now, was just as much a slave to the morning routine for Bob's sake as I had become. I gave him the thumbs up sign, which he returned with a smile. That was one of the best night's uninterrupted nights sleep in a long time, and I felt freshly recovered.

When I washed Bob down that morning, avoiding his infected areas, I was pleased to hear that he was now itch free. He stood there totally submissively, behaving himself in such a way, like an entirely new Bob.

Once he was full dressed, he leaned forward and cupped my face in his hands and very gently kissed me on my forehead.

"What was that for?" I asked Bob, who had a tear in his eye.

"I don't know really "said Bob, very softly, "I just felt like it."

That morning after breakfast was the only day over the whole two week period, I didn't go for my usual morning swim, which I loved doing so much. Instead, Bob and I took a long cliff top walk via Frinton, all the way to Clacton-on-Sea.

Bob hardly spoke a word all day, as we went on the sands at Clacton, eating fish and chips for our lunch. Bob gazed out to sea, lost in thought with me along side him, and although none of us spoke a word, we felt a serene kind of contentment, between us.

We got back in plenty time before tea, having had a wonderful day. 48 hours after his first paint job, I applied a second and final coat with a very thorough clean off a few days later. Except for his baldness, he was now back to normal.

I saw Sylvia several times again throughout that wonderful time, enjoying myself to excess.

Bob refused to see Margaret, ever again, and for that matter any other girl, at least for the duration of that holiday. For the time being, he was going celibate, or so Bob told me, but I knew this couldn't last forever, it was only a question of time. I knew his experience of infestation had a profound effect on Bob, which made him feel contaminated and dirty. He loathed even talking about it, so we didn't.

We both headed for our last breakfast at camp, knowing my aunt would soon be arriving to take us both away for a further two weeks holiday, which Bob was now getting very excited about, almost returning to his once former self.

As we went back to our tent for the last time, we caught a glimpse of the two Barnardo boys getting into a van like mini-bus that already had about eight others aboard. I gave George a big hug a paper poke containing sweets, simply known as mischiefs.

We said our goodbyes to the rest of the motley crew and left. We saw my aunt talking to Mr Walton, who looked very pleased with himself.

"They are talking about us," said Bob.

We stowed our gear into the boot of the car. My aunt asked Bob if he would like to sit up front with her, as he was the eldest of us both. Very politely he asked my aunt, if she wouldn't mind if he sat in the back of the car with me.

"Of course not darling" she told Bob "you will be good company for Paul."

We bumped our way down the dirt road out of camp, leaving a thin dust cloud in our wake.

PART THREE

CHAPTER SEVENTEEN
Aunt Joan

My aunt's little car sped in an easterly direction from Colchester heading for the New Forest. My aunt had just purchased a two acre plot of ground, that adjoined her brother, Harry's, land, who was a retired civil servant, having spent most of his working life in the Foreign Office, abroad. Bob, sat very smugly on the back seat, holding my hand, and I noticed my aunt smile to herself in the rear view mirror.

Harry, her brother, was very fond of my aunt, and she of him, had spent many years converting lovely old stables into a superb home. It was my aunt's intentions to design and build her own house in readiness for her own retirement a few years down the line.

Bob squeezed my hand affectionately, with a glow of peace with himself, upon his contended face, not even aware of his actions, as he sat comfortably on the back seat with his own thoughts.

"We will be staying with Harry for a few days, "explained my aunt. "I'm afraid you two will have to share," said my aunt "but at least you will have your own bathroom."

Nothing new there, I thought. Next to Bob, my aunt had the most influence in my life, and I loved her dearly, especially taking on such a challenge, head on. I was nothing but trouble to her, and I sometimes wondered why she kept on coming back for more. But I loved her just the same.

"You will love the New Forest," my aunt sung, "as it is rather beautiful." She added, "and I'm sure you will both find things to do." she chanted.

We stopped in the village of Burley, just five miles from Ringwood, as my aunt had been instructed to pick up a large box of groceries awaiting her, for her brother. She took great delight embarrassing me in front of all her friends, as she introduced me as 'her boy.'

HINNEY COTTAGE

We drove up the gravel driveway into Harry's spread, and I could see Bob was impressed, as his eyes stood out like gob stoppers. The olde world charm of the place, felt very comfortable with heavy oak beams, and a fantastic ingle nook brick built fireplace, central of a very large sitting room, beautifully appointed. His dog, Bruno, lumbered off the sumptuous leather settee, making straight for Bob, Bruno who floored him, before licking Bob's face clean. Harry was obviously stunned, because he had never seen his dog Bruno, behave like this before. Bob won an instant friend with Harry, who was known not to like any children.

Harry himself was very tall, well over six feet, and wore a permanent hound dog expression on his face. Clearly one of the old school, Etonian, in fact, with very Victorian attitudes.

I sensed from previous visits, he didn't like me, but because he admired his sister, my aunt, very much, I was tolerated. There was no doubt, Harry took an instant shine to Bob, though. Bruno was a very obedient animal and always slept at the foot of his master's bed. Just how Harry liked his children, I thought!

After tea, Bob and I took Bruno for a good walk through the village, and Bob was so good with Bruno, he didn't even require a lead. We got back in time for a bit of supper, before my aunt said goodnight to us both as we sunk into a lovely hot bubble bath.

I got out first, leaving Bob to lay back in luxury, as I put a small hand towel over his plastered arm, which was hanging over the edge of the bath to keep it dry.

"Give us a shout, when you're ready" I told Bob, as I went through to the huge double bed to turn down the bedclothes. This was real luxury with the big bathroom en-suite, I told myself, and this was only the guest room. I went back into the bathroom to look into the bathroom cabinet and found some talcum powder, which I used on my body, much to Bob's disgust, as he thought only sissy's used such things. Feeling a little peeved, I told Bob it was time to get out, which he was none to keen about, so I reached down between his ankles and pulled the plug.

As the bath water emptied, it became obvious why. Bob assured me he had not been playing with himself and it was because he had abstained for at least ten day, that he no longer had control over this very sudden arousal.

"Okay" I said as I started to towel him down, then noticed Bob had a bit of a rash around his whole genitalia.

"I think it must be an allergy from that crab lotion," said Bob.

"Either that or this bubble bath" I said, giving myself a quick inspection, but finding I was okay.

I went back to the cabinet and read the instructions on the baby oil, which was ideal for nappy rash, to be well massaged into the skin, in a circular motion.

"I think this might do the trick," I said to Bob, who was standing with a very hard erection.

"Take this bottle and a clean bath towel, while I clean out the bath," I told Bob.

He was already lying upon the towel with his legs wide apart, with an erection that wouldn't go away, he assured me.

"Okay" I warned him "but no funny stuff, or you'll end up doing yourself, bad arm or not."

"I'll do my best," said Bob "honest I will."

I kneeled between his legs, not missing any part of his genitalia, but his bishop, refused point blank to lose any stiffness.

"Okay, now turn over" I instructed Bob, then having finished, I pulled the covers up, leaving the towel in place to protect the bed linen. I climbed into bed, leaving the bedside light on for a while, as we chatted together. Bob was fair taken with Bruno the dog, and he thought Harry was okay as well.

After half an hour, I switched off the light and turned over onto my side ready for sleep. Bob curled into my back resting his plaster on my hip, as was his want. I could feel Bob's bishop in the small of my back, still hard.

"Has it not gone down yet Bob?" I asked.

"No it just won't" Bob replied "but I am trying, honest I am." He said in earnest.

"Okay I understand" I told him "but it's uncomfortable, poking me in the back."

Bob moved away, and I could tell he was upset. After about five minutes of silence I said "alright Bob, you can rest it between the inside of my thighs, but if it goes anywhere near my arse, you're dead."

Bob turned back in towards me, gently pushing his bishop tight between my thighs, as I felt his shaft of iron, brush the underside of my testicles. He snuggled up close and remained as hard as an iron bar, but did not move his body an inch.

We slept locked together, and sometime through the night the bishop went to sleep as well.

I awoke first, slipped into my pyjamas and went through to the kitchen, where my aunt was very busy preparing two trays.

"Good morning Paul, darling, that's your tray ready" she said. "Saves me a journey, I'll take this one through to Harry, breakfast at 8 a.m." said my aunt, then disappeared.

I looked at Bob's watch, still on my wrist, just before 7 a.m. I took the tray through to the bedroom, as Bob was climbing into bed, having just been to the bathroom. We drank our hot mugs of tea with biscuits, with Bob talking away excitedly. I slipped out of bed to put the tray out of reach, then climbed back in, lying flat on my back staring at the ceiling thinking of Sylvia, as I could feel my groins below my pyjamas, misbehaving.

I don't know how Bob knew, he just did, as he found the opening in my pyjamas, enclosing his hand around my erection. I moved nearer to check him out but Bob was totally flaccid.

"Who's a naughty boy then?" said Bob laughing, as we both removed our hands quickly from each other.

"You know Bob" I said "one way or another, these past six weeks, I've handled your bishop ten time more than I've handled my own. By the way, how's the rash?"

He pushed down the covers for me to inspect.

"It's almost gone" I remarked to Bob.

"Good" he said, "one more massage tonight should do the trick" Bob said, with an evil glint in his eye.

"I don't think that will be necessary" I said, which wiped the smirk off his face. "We'll see," I added.

We went through to a hearty cooked breakfast of ham and eggs, lots of buttered toast and marmalade. Harry was being pleasant for once, asking Bob if he slept well, and Bob was quick to reply, by complimenting Harry for having such a super comfortable bed.

Harry remarked how well behaved Bob was, to his sister, my aunt. Bob, lapping up all the praise being poured over him, as I thought, if only they both knew the randy little bastard, as well as I did.

My aunt suggested, we go into Christchurch for the day after breakfast. Bob asked Harry if he could take Bruno with us also, which scored even more brownie points - the creep!

Christchurch then, was a super place as we watched all the different water sports galore. Bruno was the best behaved of us all, as the dog wondered why we both got so excited, with all the people playing on the water, having such a good time.

MY aunt suggested to us both, that we might like to join the 5th Staines Sea Scouts, once we got back to Ashford, as she had already spoken to Gina, the Scoutmaster in charge, on our behalf. Both Bob and myself, were over the moon with such delightful prospects, while Bruno looked on, none plussed, thinking to himself, where did these two plonkers come from. We both showed our appreciation to her, showering her with kisses, as she got redder by the minute, with such a show of affection, behaving like a pair of infants.

She quickly suggested a boat trip that was about to leave, more to cover her complete embarrassment, as we all climbed aboard with Bob carrying Bruno in his one good arm.

The coastal views were fantastic, as the pleasure boat cut its furrow through the sea swell.

An hour later, my aunt was the first off, feeling a bit queasy, while the rest of us were just fine, including Bruno the dog. I think this was the deciding factor that made my aunt realise that we were both suitable candidates for the seas scouts.

We filled our faces with ice cream, after a late lunch, with Bruno being spoilt rotten, by Bob with tasty morsels.

We returned to Harry's house, leaving both my aunt and Bruno behind, as Bob and I strolled into the village, to mooch about. Bob, without warning honed into a pair of very attractive dolly birds, and his patter flowed freely, like golden syrup, as I stood by like a spare part. The Bob I knew and loved became the comeback kid, but then I knew it was just a question of time, I told myself.

His chat up lines, to me didn't wash one iota, but there was no denying the girls just loved him, and the real niggle was, I was the attractive one, or so I thought.

We eventually went back home, with a pronounced spring in Bob's step, getting back in time for what my aunt called tupper, tea and supper combined. My aunt retired early that night, telling us we were all heading for London tomorrow.

We too, felt we had a wonderful day, but a long one at that, as we said our goodnights, Bob kissing Bruno, before our usual bath and into bed.

Bob, when I went through to the bedroom, was already spread eagled upon the towel ready for his massage, the cheeky scamp, as I went back for the baby oil. He was still behaving himself as I climbed between his legs, but I thought I would tease him a little, as I sensually rubbed oil into his balls. Almost immediately they started to get very large filling up.

"Hey Paul, go easy will you" said Bob.

I moved up to his bishop and with the oily palm of my hand, I rolled his bishop across his belly as if I was rolling out a sausage roll of pastry. He looked at me with suspicion, but continued to exercise remarkable control. I decided to tease Bob to the limit, with evil intent.

I then poured oil onto both palms of my hands rubbing it into his thighs with slow sensual silky strokes, bingo, the bishop stirred, enlarging all the time, just short of a full blown erection. With the surplus oil, I wiped it into the join between his balls, turning my hand onto its edge, as I passed over his rectum, Bob's bishop jumped for joy into a massive hard on.

"That's enough," said Bob "I don't want you to go on." He shouted at me!!

So I stopped. "I'm sorry Bob, for teasing you." as I climbed into bed beside him, I could see he was angry.

He didn't say a word in reply, curled into my back and put his good hand between my legs squeezing my balls gently as if they were made of cotton wool. I got very hard, and Bob knew it. He retrieved his hand, turned over and went to sleep, having made his point, before I too, eventually fell over and slept soundly.

I learned a valuable lesson that night, and that was Bob's way of telling me that, you don't mess with another person's sexual emotions, unless both are wiling participants.

After a good breakfast, my aunt took us all to see the building of her new house, as we crossed a small wooden footbridge across a monsoon draining ditch, that separated Harry's land from hers. I was very surprised to see the shell up, with a weather tight roof on and with my aunt, already up the ladder ready to inspect the workmanship. The foreman, stood by, looking rather nervous, as I heard some of the squad pass some remarks, about my aunt being too much of a perfectionist.

I think they were pleased to see the back of us, as my aunts reputation for keeping them on their toes was obvious to see. Some final orders were given to both the foreman and Harry, before we set off to London. We had stripped the bed, putting the sheets and pillow slip into the laundry basket, which pleased Harry, and then we were off to Aunt Joan's flat in London.

Bob moved up close to me, on the back seat of the car, as we travelled up to London and whispered in my ear, "you know I love you very much, don't you?"

"Yes" I said, "I know.

"You have always been there for me." Bob said, "Especially when I've needed you most."

I looked at Bob, long and hard, wondering why he was being so very serious, all of a sudden.

"Where else would I be?" I asked him.

"After all you have been at my side all my life" I told Bob.

After a little while, bob said "You know Paul, I had a disturbing dream last night."

Funny" I said to Bob "so did I!" "Was it about a small sailing dinghy?" I asked Bob.

"Why, yes" said Bob "but how do you know that?" he asked.

"If you shut up, I'll tell you" I said to Bob.

"My dream anyway, was about the two of us sailing this small dinghy on a river."

"Yes" Bob nodding like mad "we were both learning to sail, and I was taking over the helm from you.

I looked at Bob, who was still nodding, so I continued, "When one of us fell overboard." I stopped talking, and looked at Bob, and Bob took over the rest of the dream.

"It was me that fell in" said Bob, "and after just a few boat lengths, you spun the boat around, re-filled the sails, and headed the boat right at me."

And together we both said in unison, word for word. "I somehow stopped the boat dead, spilling all the wind from the sails, and with one heave, dragged you into the boat, like a drowned rat!" We both said with mouths agape.

"What else would you expect me to do?" I asked Bob, who was now very tearful. I noticed my aunt staring at the two of us, having stopped the car. She turned around asking Bob if he was alright. Bob quickly wiped away a tear about to fall and saying to my aunt, "I must have caught something in my eye." My aunt slipped into nursing mode, asking Bob if she should take a closer look.

"No. It's okay, thank you," said Bob. "I think I managed to get it out."

"If your sure darling" she said, looking at me, wondering what was really going on.

"It won't be long before we get to the flat darling" she said, and drove on.

Bob didn't know this part of London, never having been to our flat before, but was very impressed with the lovely old Victorian block, as we unloaded the car. We took the lift up to our floor, to save all the carrying of our gear. My aunt opened the door and switched on the hall light as Bob took our gear straight into my bedroom, then quickly ran into the bathroom opposite, desperate for a pee.

My aunt stood in the hall, surprised that Bob, seemed to know his way about, as my aunt went into the sitting room. Bob joined us smiling away, to both of us, "lovely flat you have Miss Leigh-Clare," he said.

"You haven't been here before, have you Bob?"

"No ma'am" said Bob, politely.

My aunt looked surprised, but I just shrugged my shoulders, because I didn't understand how Bob knew his way around the flat either.

Having stopped earlier for a leisurely lunch, en-route, my aunt asked us what we would like for supper. We both said together, sausages please, and then roared with laughter together. My aunt was most amused, then disappeared into the kitchen to prepare supper.

The smell of bangers under the grill, fairly whet our appetites, and in no time, she called us through to eat. The table was all set as we sat down to eat, when my aunt asked, and even before she uttered the words, both Bob's hand and mine reached for the mustard pot together. Long before the word mustard left her lips, we both handed her the pot. Now, she really did look perplexed.

Bob, having wolfed down one of my aunt's home made trifles, asked to be excused from the table, and went back into the sitting room. Meanwhile I helped my aunt clear away, and wash up.

My aunt asked me searching questions about Bob, but I knew she already knew about Bob's antecedent history.

"Well," I said, I've know Bob all my life, since my very first day at Ashford, and we've been lifelong friends ever since. Like you and Miss Lowman" I added.

"You're very loyal to Bob" my aunt said "do you think Bob would be just as loyal in a time of crisis?" she asked.

I looked at my aunt very strangely, then replied to her "Shouldn't you be asking Bobby this question?" then clammed up, feeling my aunt's intrusion.

My aunt could see I was upset, as she put her hand on my shoulder, saying, "I'm sorry Paul darling, I have no right to ask you such a question."

"Can I go now?" I asked my aunt, bluntly.

"Yes darling, and thank you for helping me with the dishes."

Bob and I played cards and listened to my aunt's radio, until she called us through to a hot bath, she had already run. As we both headed for our bath, my aunt reminded me to keep Bob's plaster away from the water.

Bob was already in the bath, before I even undressed, and as I was about to get in, Bob opened his legs wide, so I sat down between them. We chatted away about the scouts and how much great fun we could have, if we ever were allowed to join.

I could feel Bob's bishop rise against my back, and I instinctively put my hand around to check.

"I'm really sorry," said Bob "it must be the hot water."

I stood up to soap myself down, and as I put the flannel down on the side of the bath, Bob picked it up, soaping me between my legs. Fortunately, I had my back to him, so he couldn't see my rapid erection take shape. I sat down still with my back to him, but with his good hand, he felt me.

"I thought so," said Bob, taking his hand away quickly.

"Maybe I should give you a massage later" Bob said.

Not knowing what to say I remained silent. I got out of the bath and towelled myself down, and as I towelled Bob off, his erection refused to surrender. His pubic hair was just starting to come through, and his rash had gone completely. He went on into the bedroom, to leave me to clean up.

I climbed into bed beside him, then switched off the light and lay on my back looking into the blackness. Bob folded back the bedclothes, then laying the side of his head on my stomach, I lay completely still, wondering what he was up to.

I could feel his warm breath just inches away from my pubic hair. My flaccid penis began to stir as I felt my balls begin to tingle. Bob just lay there without a word.

I felt my penis spring up and over, as Bob caught it between his lips, without moving, I felt it swelling up inside Bob's mouth, as he stayed completely motionless. I quickly pulled Bob's mouth away from my cock, as I felt it starting to throb.

"No Bob" I said "please don't make me cum."

"Okay" said Bob "fair enough".

He pulled up the bedclothes as I turned onto my side to face him.

As we drifted peacefully off to sleep, I began to dream of my last time with Sylvia. Much later I drifted back into consciousness, I felt another dribble leave the end of my penis. I put down my hand to investigate. Fucking hell, these wet dreams are becoming too frequent, I thought.

Bob was lying on his back fast asleep, snoring softly. I put my hand down for a good feel, and only felt a little spunk, where has it all gone, I wondered. I put my hand across to Bob gingerly. Shit, I had covered Bob's genitalia, with all my spunk.

I quickly got out of bed putting on the sidelight at the same time. I peeled back the covers then noticed Bob had the good sense to lay the bath towel across the bed. So I folded my half over him, then put back the bedclothes, before scooting across the hall to the bathroom, where I cleaned myself off. I could hear my aunt in the kitchen moving about. I grabbed a damp flannel and a small hand towel, and scooted back to bed.

Bob was still snoring his head off, fast asleep. My aunt knocked at the door, "Come in" I shouted, and she put the tray across my lap, reminding me, we all had to be ready for 8 o'clock, as it was one of her days at the clinic. It was not yet seven, so we had plenty of time, she told me, noticing Bob was still asleep, so she left.

After the door closed, I hurriedly shook Bob awake, and as he sat up, I handed him a freshly made mug of tea.

"This is a great bed," said Bob.

I looked at him, and asked Bob if he was in a good mood. He gave me one of his winning smiles.

"I feel great." He said.

"I've got some bad news, I'm afraid to tell you," taking his mug of tea from his hand. That soon wiped the smile off his face, I noticed.

"I had a wet dream last night, and I've come all over you, by accident!" I hastened to say.

Bob looked at me, pulling a straight face, now I'm for it, I thought.

"Well," Bob started "perhaps you should have let me do you after all," was Bob's only reply.

Stunned, I opened my mouth to say something, but nothing came out. Bob smiled, then I knew everything was okay by him.

"Why?" I asked Bob!

"Well, if it was anybody else, I would have killed them by now, but it wasn't anyone else, it was you, and anyway it's no big deal." Bob said, "Now hand me back my tea."

"I was just going to clean you off." Holding up the flannel to show Bob.

"Drink your tea," said Bob "that cleaning job, will keep.

Now that' what I call understanding, as I drunk my tea, I thought.

"You know last night," said Bob "when you thought I was going to suck you off?" I looked at Bob and said quietly "Yes"

"Well, I was going to" Bob said.

"But why would you want to?" I asked him.

"I don't really know, I suppose I just want part of you inside me." Bob said.

"Honestly Bob, there's no need. I love you anyway, you don't need to, really, you don't!"

A long silence followed.

"But I feel the need" said Bob.

I took his empty mug from him, folded back the covers and washed and dried all my sticky evidence away. We both got out of bed, washed and dressed then went through to breakfast. With my aunt bustling her two grown chicks before her, we took the tube to Brixton, just a few hundred yards from the clinic.

We all tripped through the door, before 9.00 a.m. and Miss Lowman was there to greet us. She engaged Bob in conversation, asking Bob about his broken wrist, which she clearly knew about before hand.

Miss Lowman, and my aunt, then chatted away to each other like a pair of magpies. I admired Bob's way with anything in a skirt. I suddenly wondered, why he didn't get on with his older sister, who he once referred to as a slut.

With his good hand, he handed out bottles of freshly made orange juice, to all the pregnant mums, as they came into the clinic. He was very good with them, talking easily to them, not having any problem, charming each and every one of them. They were mostly coloured, but that made no difference to Bob, who was in his element at the coal face, so to speak (no pun intended) charming all the women, like a young gigolo.

I caught my aunt and Miss Lowman, talking in confidence, rather secretly, and I just knew they were talking about Bob, and probably about me, as well. The clinic was a very busy place with lots of babies feeding from their mothers' breasts. There was also a constant stream of naked babies being weighed, which was one of my jobs to record.

The two partners, Miss Lowman and my aunt, were in and out all the time, personally greeting and attending to all the clients, which they knew all by name. We were so busy, we ate our sandwich lunch on the hoof.

By the time 4.30 p.m. came, the clinic emptied, and we were pleased to join all the ladies for a much needed hot cup of tea. The staff were a friendly bunch, all getting on well as an harmonious team. Miss Lowman, put a single florin in front of Bob and myself. We both automatically pushed the coins back across the table to Miss Lowman, together, then said in unison, no thank you, we worked because we wanted to, and not for payment. We had said it together, word for word as if in one voice. We looked at each other bursting into laughter together.

All six women around the table stopped talking looking very surprised, as I noticed my aunt nudge Miss Lowman, knowingly. The lady nearest me, asked how old was my elder brother Bob. I left the table quickly, feeling very embarrassed, and waited outside the front door, to catch some fresh air.

On our way home, my aunt treated us to fish and chips at a small café just outside West Kensington Station.

Only after an hour or so inside the flat and a refreshing cup of tea, my aunt thought Bob was looking tired, so she ran a bath. As we both climbed into the bath together, we luxuriated, enjoying the heat and bubbles, with me lying cosily between Bob's legs.

We both dozed, enjoying the soak, until the water began to cool.

"Come on you two," my aunt shouted through the door "you must both be looking like a pair of well cooked prunes by now."

"Okay" I shouted, as I got out first with Bob following behind me. We dried each other off, then Bob scooted across the hall naked, into the bedroom. I rinsed the bath out, tidying up, then joined Bob.

"Goodnight you two scallywags" my aunt said.

"Goodnight" we both shouted back.

I turned over onto my side and switched out the bedside light, expecting Bob to snuggle up, but he didn't. I was thinking about our day at the clinic, when Bob pulled me onto my back. I lay perfectly still, as Bob folded back the covers and rested his head on my stomach.

"Really Bob," I said, "You don't need to."

"Shut up" Bob said gently, "shut up" he repeated. So I did.

Again, I could feel Bob's warm breath disturbing my pubic hair. Never mind England I thought, lay back and think of Sylvia instead. Bob could not only read my mind at times, I sometimes thought, he was able to pick up nervous signals through my body as well.

He waited patiently, until he knew exactly when the right moment arrived. Without touching any part of my body, he had a long time to wait. No matter, my fertile imagination of Sylvia going down on me, finally triggered an unstoppable erection, with my testicles pulsating furiously.

He caught the tip of my loose foreskin between his lips, which he then started to very slowly nibble sensually, which soon had my juices flowing. He did this for at least ten minutes in no apparent hurry to move on. Then gently using his lips only, he began to push back my foreskin bit by bit, until he knew instinctively, when it was time to move on.

With one sudden movement, still using his lips, he pushed it back all the way, enclosing my shaft for the first, two or three inches into his very warm mouth.

Bob got into a comfortable kneeling position, with one of his knees between my loins. I reached up and took hold of his testicles in the cup of my left hand. Bob ignored my move, as I gently squeezed the two together, which were like ripe tomatoes.

Without warning in one swift movement, I felt the first inch of my iron penis slide down into the back of his throat. Bob just held it stationary, as his tongue worked on the underside of my balls. I could feel my balls swelling alarmingly, as they released its white liquid cargo, travelling at a constant flow, but not spurting in full ejaculation, Bob drunk as much as I could offer. He very slowly eased it from his deep throat and I felt my spongy knob clash with his tonsils, in passing. Keeping his lips firmly clamped to my shaft, he withdrew slowly, then finally, he released me.

I lay back enjoying the high, as I put my hand on his stomach, then Bob quietly said, that his own erection was my fault, because I played with his balls. We both fell silent, each with his own thoughts, for at least fifteen or more minutes.

I don't know why I did what I did next, I just did it without thinking, and with no feeling of guilt, either.

I reached over and enclosed my hand around Bob's very hard shaft, not moving my hand at all. I just held it for about five minutes. I got up into a kneeling position, pulling Bob's buttocks up onto my knees. With both hands, I gently started to massage his balls that quickly got much larger. I tested the tip of Bob's bishop, which suddenly made it jump for joy, lengthening by at least another half inch, ignoring my own hard penis, which was still dribbling. I felt the tip of my own penis brush against Bob's anus; it sent Bob wild, as the back of his legs clamped up tight behind the small of my back. He was far too big to take into my mouth, which I knew would make me gag, anyway.

His bishop was far thicker, than I realised, so even attempting to suck him off, was a none starter.

I enclosed my hand around the shaft as he began to ooze freely. I gathered up his spunk to spread along his length. Bob reached down and took hold of my own hard penis, stroking his anus with the now very wet tip of my penis.

His bishop jumped with erotic delight, then without warning, Bob with the help from the back of his legs and the guidance of his good hand, forced me into him. My penis slipped through the sphincter muscle and passed the point of no return.

"Don't take it out "Bob said several times, frantically.

So with regret I did as he wished. I lay back into Bob's cradled legs, and I felt my penis go in even deeper. This must be like entering a virgin, as I could feel Bob's anus pulsate, around the higher part of my shaft. I started to wank Bob slowly with my enclosed hand sliding, like velvet up and down his shaft length.

"Go deeper" Bob begged, so with considerable pressure, I worked my full length penis, deep inside him. Bob started to make noises of pleasure, asking me to go a little faster.

"If I do that, I'm in danger of cumming inside of you," I told Bob in a voice that indicated disapproval.

Bob and I ejaculated together, as I held his bishop flat against his stomach wall, to minimise the ejaculated damage.

"Don't take it out, until I'm ready" said Bob, demandingly.

He leaned over and switched on the side light to survey the mess. Fortunately almost all of it was collected on his chest with one very large milky puddle.

I could feel my own penis beginning to deflate inside him, and so could Bob.

"Okay" said Bob "withdraw real slow" and as I started to do so, his own bishop jumped and his last spurt oozed onto his belly. I slowly completed my withdrawal, but the sphincter muscle, which had contracted, did not want to release my corona without a struggle. Bob, took hold of my penis in a firm grip, and with just one tug, released me. Using one end of the towel, I dried Bob off.

Just as I was about to turn off the light, Bob suddenly jumped up wrapping the towel around him and scooted out of the room. I pulled the covers up, shocked, but not feeling any real guilt, at first about what I had just done. Bob was gone a while, but I then heard the loo flush, as he raced back into the room, and climbed into bed.

I turned out the light, and Bob quickly cuddled up to me, asking me for my forgiveness. We lay there for sometime, each trying to work out why? I said nothing, because I simply had no words to say.

After what seemed an eternity, Bob asked me what I was thinking, but I just couldn't find the right words to say, and somehow felt ashamed.

"Please say something," Bob started to sob, which became unbearable, and made me feel even more ashamed.

With Bob still sobbing persistently, I just had to put my arms around him, if only to comfort him, but I too started to weep to myself silently, because I just didn't know what I could say, that would help, either of us.

After a while, Bob, who was still cradled in my arms, eventually ran out of tears.

"It just happened, Paul" Bob said after a long silence, "I didn't mean it to happen, please believe me, please Paul, forgive me, please say you forgive me;" begged Bob.

"There's nothing to forgive you for," I told Bob "it was just as much my fault, anyway." I added.

"No" said Bob "it was me that put you in, please say you can forgive me Paul?

"Okay" I said, "I forgive you, but it must never ever happen again, okay!"

"Okay" said Bob, "I promise".

And it never did.

With two days a week spent helping my aunt at the clinic, each of the two weeks holidays was very packed, and as usual, when you're having a great time, it has a way of disappearing so quickly.

I remember lazy afternoons rowing on the Serpentine, and visits to the zoo, the pictures and so many different visits to the many landmarks, all over London.

I remember spending hours in the art galleries, and going to west End theatres. So many memories Bob and I would share forever.

Our last day of the hol's finally dawned and for some unknown reason my aunt was determined to make an early start. She wants rid of us, I thought rather uncharitably. My aunt drove us direct to Staines, where she had pre-arranged a visit, with Gina the head poncho, of the 5th Staines Sea Scouts.

As we parked the car, that Saturday morning and started down the tow path from the bridge, I could feel that tingling sensation, I often got before starting a climb. We both knew exactly, where we were, the question we were both asking ourselves was, why?

My aunt was determined to keep us both in suspense as long as possible.

"I've arranged a meeting with Gina the Scoutmaster" she started.

"Yes" we cried out together, she smiled at us both before continuing, (God I wish she would get on with it) the suspense was unbearable, as I felt a very small trickle leave the end of my dick, which I quickly pinched. My aunt stopped talking, and looked down at what I was doing to myself, then casually asked, if I needed to go to the bathroom.

"No" I said to my aunt, "please go on."

"Well" said my aunt, "there may be a few vacancies, and Gina thought this might be a good day for him to take a look at you both." Only a woman could draw out the agony so long, I thought.

Halfway down the tow path, Gina stepped ashore from his boat, to meet my aunt, and his two prospective candidates. He was instantly impressed with Bob, but felt I was still a little small. Gina asked me to wait a few minutes, while he had a word with Bob.

After a few minutes, Gina bounced over to me with Bob at his side.

"Well" said Gina, to me "it seems you either come as a package or not at all, according to Bob here." Then Gina stuck out his hand which I took, "Welcome to the 5thStaines Sea Scouts" said Gina.

My aunt wrote out a cheque, giving it to Gina, to pay for our new uniforms. We were both handed a handbook of scouting life, with all the rules, especially written for tender foots, which apparently we were. We studied it on our way back to school.

My aunt explained to us, this operation for us to join the scouts had already been cleared with the school, and that nice gentleman Mr Walton, was very enthusiastic over the whole business, my aunt told us both.

By now we were both as high as a kite, at this fantastic change of events.

We arrived back at school, walking tall with our heads in the clouds. We said our joyful goodbyes, with Bob giving my aunt a big hug and a kiss, thanking her profusely, (the little creep,) but then I did likewise. And both waved my aunt off, as she crossed the yard and swung onto the main drive.

CHAPTER EIGHTEEN
Innovation v Starvation

Mr Walton was waiting for us, as he watched us wave goodbye to my aunt, who slowly drove off into the night. We were both taken into his office, the moment we stepped into the dayroom, informing us both he had several things to discuss.

"Firstly," said Walton "how did you both get on with Miss Leigh-Clare?" he asked us both, but was looking at Bob when he asked the question.

"Just super" said Bob, joyfully "Paul's aunt is a smashing lady!"

Having got all the pleasantries out the way, he felt it was time to move on.

"Now, Alditch," addressing Bob " come September, you along with several other boys will be going up by train daily to London." Bob looked pleasantly surprised.

"Your new term starts this September at Battersea Technical College, in just a months time. This is a new innovation and is already being called 'The Ashford Experiment'. You Alditch," Walton continued "have won the opportunity, because of your high marks in your last exam results. The second Ashford experiment concerns you both. The Sea Scouts, which I fully endorse, but this is the very first time that either of these experiments are being tried out, and I'm relying on you both not to let me down."

"Yes Sir" we both sung together.

"One more thing Paul," Walton turned to face me "I've decided to move you up to the most senior boys' dormitory tonight, along with Alditch here. I also have your pocket money account, which has been with me since you left camp, so if either of you need cash for equipment for your scouting activities, come and see me."

"Yes sir" we said.

"One more thing" Walton said "you Paul, will have to continue to wet nurse Alditch, for at least another fortnight or so, until his plaster is removed."

"Yes sir" I said to Walton.

"Any problems, come and see me, now cut along both of you" said Walton, "and make sure you keep out of trouble Alditch."

Once outside, I turned to Bob, saying "Walton went on a bit, but I got the feeling he knows you're the one that leads me into trouble." I said to Bob, sarcastically.

"You're right" Bob said, "Walton thinks the sun shines out your arse." We both roared with laughter.

"Well" said Bob, "we better go and sort out our new beds."

When I went up to my old dorm to empty my locker, I was surprised to see pat, my half brother, had already moved into my bed space. Pat was over the moon, and he introduced me to his best mate Brian, who was sleeping in Bob's old bed, alongside Pat.

I left them chatting away to each other as I took my gear, heading for my new dorm, where I would now stay for the duration at Ashford. Compared with the intermediate dorm, I had now left behind me, this was very much the 'grown ups' dorm, and a lot more sedate, to boot.

I was now in the big boys league of twelve to sixteen years olds, who had left their childhood years, firmly behind them.

At under twelve I was of course the youngest, but my evil bad tempered reputation, was well established, even among the most senior boys. Lots of kudos I thought, great. Within two weeks, my transition was complete, and I already felt settled. Bob was at long last, relieved of his cursed plaster, and now that it was off, he was itching to get to our most favourite spot in Ashford.

After swimming for a while, I repeated the climb to retrieve our gear without mishap, as Bob and myself hoped we would soon be using it to taunt Sims, again.

While we were sunning ourselves after our swim, Bob explained at length the new educational experiment, he was delighted to become a part of. He was genuinely looking forward to travelling up and down to London every day. Five days a week, on a season ticket, paid for by the school. Bob also thought that by extending his education to sixteen, instead of leaving school at the normal fourteen years of age, his prospects would be vastly improved in the job market. Coming up for fourteen, Bob, like most boys of his age, didn't have a clue what he would eventually do, once he left Ashford.

"You must be happy to have been chosen, in the elite for this new Ashford experiment," I said to Bob. Bob chewed the fat for a while, just scratching his balls before answering.

"I think," Bob said "it only proves, that we are not as thick as the rest of the do do's!"

I searched Bob's face intensely, for any sign that he might be masking his real feelings on the matter. Bob stood up, took a quick leak, then got dressed, before heading back to base. I was relieved, I was no longer needed to dress or wet nurse him.

On the way back into school, Bob asked me if my aunt liked the picture I gave her, for her birthday.

"She seemed to" I replied. But I said to Bob "You know what women are like, they make such a fuss about everything."

Bob nodded his head in agreement, as we got back in good time for tea.

During and after tea, that night everybody was complaining about the smaller than usual quantities of food. It was not the first time we all felt we were being short changed. None of us could understand why there was such a shortage of food, especially as the war had been over for a good two years.

By bed time, most boys were belly aching about the lack of food in their bellies. We all started to look down at the orchard, four floors below us, and all that ripe fruit, for the picking. A late night scrumping raid may be the answer Bob had suggested. We discussed all our options open to us. Going down the fire escape, with them being on the opposite of the building to the orchard, was quickly ruled out.

There was a drainpipe outside my window that would do the trick, leading us to within yards of the orchard, I mentioned to any one prepared to listen. To satisfy our dorms hunger alone, would take at least a party of three or even four, to carry enough fruit, someone pointed out.

"Well" said Bob "if we knot the leg ends of a pair of pyjama trousers together, like this," Bob illustrated "you could then put all the food inside the waist, using the draw cord like the top of a bag. And with the legs knotted at the ankle ends, you can then hook it over your head for carrying purposes, leaving both hands free."

Bob demonstrated how very effective this method was.

"Shall we have a go as a duo?" Bob said to me.

"No." I quickly replied, "Your weakened wrist would come under far too much strain" I pointed out to him, "and I don't want to wet nurse you all over again, for the sake of a scrumping raid." I told Bob quite firmly.

"Anyway a solo climber would be much faster and safer, as long as he doesn't try to carry too heavy a load" I said.

"Are there any volunteers" Bob asked "with the climbing abilities to attempt this scrumping raid?" No takers, but everyone looked at me.

"So," said Bob "it looks like you will be on your own, I hope you realise what you will be undertaking Paul, it's a long climb."

"It's not the climb that worries me" I told Bob "I just hope I can manage to scrump enough, to satisfy you greedy bastards."

With almost all of the boys complaining of hunger, and with so many stomachs' rumbling noisily, being heard by so many boys, I saw this more as a mission of mercy. Bob told the tallest boy called Albert, to give me his pyjama trousers because he had the longest legs, and his trousers would hold the most booty. Albert obliged there and then by dropping his pyjamas to the floor, then handed them to Bob, who tied both leg ends together very tightly.

"Okay Paul, it's down to you, but please be very careful" Bob said. "I'll be waiting right here at the window to help you up with your load. And for fucks sake, whatever happens don't try to carry too much of a load."

I put the knotted pyjama bottoms over my head then eased myself out on to the window ledge, under the full gaze of all the boys in the dorm, I reached out to the drainpipe and started my descent. I looked down from four floors to the blackness below, and I could see the feint silver of dim moonlight on the ribbon of driveway below me. It had been a fine day, but there was a good few clouds scudding about in the night sky overhead.

Going down was a doddle, and I made quick progress as I could feel, rather than see, Bob leaning out of the window watching my progress, rather like a worried parent waiting anxiously for his beloved child to return.

Once I reached the ground, I quickly looked about me, and I could feel the rush of adrenalin charge around my body, which made me feel good. I complimented myself thus far, but I was fully aware the return climb would be more difficult. I quickly crossed the narrow drive, which I knew was only used by staff, and with so much fruit ripening towards the end of a good summer, the staff were especially on their guard, for the likes of me.

Memories of the big stack, came flooding back, and having climbed that, at just seven and a half, by comparison, this little escapade will be a walk in the park I reassured myself. Anyway, I told myself, my reputation for never having refused a challenge was at stake here. I could feel Bob's eyes burning into me, even though I knew he couldn't see me. With my bag at the ready I selected very large apples about the size of large grapefruits, unaware I was in the cooking apple section of the orchard. My ignorance of the different varieties of fruit was never more apparent. After about nine of these whoppers, the bag already seemed heavy enough. I tightened the draw cord securely, turned the heavy bag upside down, hooking the tied legs around my neck.

The weight, I could feel on the back of my neck, and with my hands free, was just bearable. Shall I take a few out I thought to make the climb easier. No, fuck it, I thought, lets go for broke, as I started back towards the driveway.

The moon, for the moment was covered by cloud, as I checked the driveway in both directions for any staff prowlers. With fleet of foot, in spite of my illicit cargo, I re-crossed the driveway, but had difficulty in finding my drainpipe, plus I was desperate for a jimmy riddle, so I had a piss there and then, before searching for my drainpipe.

After a few moments, thankfully I did find the correct drainpipe, so I adjusted my load around my neck, before putting my hands around the pipe firmly in readiness to move my feet upwards. I looked upwards, and although I could only see the first floor window, beyond was just pure darkness.

I braced myself, gritting my teeth and made my first few steps upwards, when suddenly all hell broke loose, as I felt a dog take a bite into my rear end. I must have been at least four feet clear off the ground at this point, when I came crashing back down to earth. There was Fatty Arbuckle the head, with torch in hand shining on me while his pet Jack Russell dog, Toby, was determined to debag me of my pyjama bottoms. In spite of repeated commands to let go, this dog would not let go of me, and succeeded in taking my trousers from me, leaving me embarrassingly naked, from the waist down.

Fatty grabbed me by the scruff of the neck or rather the knotted pyjama bag, and pulled me to my feet nearly choking me into the bargain. Unceremoniously he marched me all the way back, about a mile away, to his office, with my dangly bits now feeling very exposed to the dog and darkness of the night, but with the head keeping a very firm grip of me.

He took me into his office, and locked the door behind us. Under the bright office lights, which made my eyes squint, I covered my genitals, with my hands cupped in front of me, feeling very vulnerable standing in front of the heads, alter like desk.

My load was still around my neck, Bailey the headmaster adjusted the reading light so it now shone directly at me.

He stood behind his desk looking at me through his bottle glasses, and sweating profusely. He reached under the desk to retrieve his favourite cane, which he started to flex in a menacing manner.

"Take off those disgusting pyjamas from around your neck" he ordered.

Using both hands I lifted my booty from over my head and placed them on his desk before him, then quickly covered myself up again, with my hands. He thrashed the desk in front of him with his cane, which made me jump, and his beloved pet dog Toby run for cover to his basket, but still holding onto what was left of my pyjama bottoms.

"Put your hands down by your sides" screamed Bailey, working himself into a rage.

Reluctantly, I removed my cupped hands away from the front of my penis, and again he readjusted his desk lamp, which I was conscious was now shining onto my privates, as he ogled openly at my genitalia, as his glasses steamed up.

After cleaning his glasses he whacked the table top again, only harder, as I felt a dribble of urine leave the end of my cock and run down the front of my leg. His tongue licked away a sliver of spit from the corner of his mouth. For several moments he openly studied my penis, now fully exposed to his view. I felt dirty, as he gazed at my dick, feeling he was about to sexually abuse me, and a shiver ran down my spine.

He undid the bundle of loot upon his table, then placing one by one, each apple in a neat row, slowly along my edge of his desk, his eyes as he leaned forward, across his desk never leaving my privates, made me squirm with repulsion, and fear.

Bailey stood up to his full height, and it was now clear to see the signs of his own erection below his trouser front. Using the tip of his cane, he lifted the now empty pyjama bottoms on his table, and with one quick flick, sent them soaring over my head, landing on the floor, between me and the door.

"Pick them up and put them on," Demanded the head.

I quickly turned around, bending over to pick up the bundled heap off the floor, knowing Bailey's eyes were now looking at my arse. As I turned back round to face him, now holding the trousers in front of me, I noticed the bump in Bailey's trousers had grown much bigger. I struggled to untie the knot that secured the leg ends. After many minutes, I eventually managed to undo the knot, I then quickly put them on in haste, falling over in the process. The legs of Albert's pyjama bottoms were a good six inches too long for me. So having secured the draw cord about my waist, I rolled up each leg, so they were well clear of my plimsoled feet.

Bailey picked up the phone on his desk and after a few moments he spoke to the night watchman, instructing him to come to the office and wait outside.

"How old are you?" barked Bailey at me.

"Almost twelve sir" I replied, shivering.

"Oh" said Bailey in surprise "I thought you were older" he remarked. "Much older in fact" he added.

He looked at me with disgust, as if I was something the dog had brought in! (Which in a sense, the dog Toby had). I could tell he was working himself up into a state, ready for some physical action. Bailey started to flex his whipping cane, swiping the air, as Toby the dog yelped away in his basket, and who obviously knew, what was coming next, as Bailey flexed his muscles, ready to flag the skin from my backside.

I don't know why, but I didn't feel afraid of what I knew, was to come next. I was far more disturbed and upset, when moments earlier, when Bailey was lusting and leering at my privates.

"Right," said Bailey, joining me on my side of his desk, "drop your trousers and lean over my desk, I'm now going to give you something to remember me by" he said (he had already done that).

He was now standing between my bare bum and the office door, as he prodded me between my buttocks with the tip of his cane.

"I'm going to give you six of the best, just now, but your real punishment will start tomorrow," he said and I could feel the tip of his cane move between the cheeks of my arse towards my anus which made me clench my buttocks together very hard, in fear of penetration.

"Open your legs wider," screamed the headmaster "and relax your buttocks, or it will hurt even more" said Bailey.

How the fucking hell would he know, I thought to myself. I opened my legs as commanded, but couldn't unclench my cheeks. Thankfully at last, this probing tip of his cane left my most intimate part of my anatomy as I felt, then heard the flexible rod, whistle through the air. I flinched as I felt the edge of his cane bite into my bum.

Bailey obviously thought he was losing his touch, by not getting the expected response from his first stroke. I could hear Bailey re-adjust his stance in readiness for a more vigorous performance. Clenching both my buttocks and teeth, I waited.

I waited and waited. Bailey was obviously enjoying himself, and who was I, to disappoint him, pouring on the suspense. The next three or was it four strokes, from his cane were fast and furious, as I felt each, cut into my bare flesh.

Bailey paused for effect, or was it to gather more strength I wondered, when off guard, I felt the final stroke cut in real deep, but still didn't cry from sheer bloody mindedness on my part. I began to feel faint, and as I was about to stand up, yet one more stroke caught me, completely by surprise.

I slumped over the desk, as I tried to find my feet and waited. Having lost count, I wondered if there was yet more to come.

"Stand up you miserable boy" Bailey shouted.

Slowly, I got to my feet pulling my pyjamas up, with me. I was unable to do the cord up, because of my trembling, fumbling hands not obeying my brains command, so I held them together instead.

I heard Bailey unlock the door, so I knew it was all over, at least until tomorrow. I don't really remember that long walk back, nor how I managed the four flights of stone stairs to my dorm.

Bob was waiting to receive me at my bed side, with my bed covers to my bed already peeled back in readiness. The arse of my pyjama trousers were already like blotting paper soaking up the blood from my bum.

He gently removed them from my body, although by this time I was long passed caring, as I had no feeling in my posterior. Bob lay me face down, and got into bed beside me, to keep the covers off my raw wounds, then burst into tears, which he was unable to hold back any longer. He lay on his side, holding my head to his chest, with one knee up high to keep the bed clothes off my sore backside. He continued to weep softly, but I knew, there would be no sleeping for me that night.

Sometime much later, the night watchman gave Bob some ointment to rub into my wounds. Bob gently massaged my bum, with the ointment into my open wounds, and started to sob again even louder. Perhaps it was just as well, I couldn't see my injuries, because it was obviously upsetting for Bob, who continued to cradle me like a baby, for the rest of the night.

In the morning as the feeling began to return to my bum, Bob applied a fresh coat of ointment, which we learnt had been supplied by the matron herself. There was no question that I would be unable to sit for several days to come.

At breakfast that morning, I was the only one standing up in the dining hall. Even Mr Walton made no attempt to enforce this minor infringement, one, of many rules within the dining room decorum.

Mr Bailey stepped up onto the stage and proceeded to lecture the entire school, on the evils of stealing valuable resources belonging to us all. After his very emotive lecture, I had the distinct impression that I really should have been hung for my crime. He called me up to the stage by name, so everybody knew what an evil bastard I was.

I walked upright, almost arrogantly, aware that some two thousand eyes were watching me. As I passed Sylvia's table, she winked and smiled at me. I then climbed the three steps onto the stage, where the headmaster made me stand on a chair, centre stage.

I could tell Fatty Arbuckle was not best pleased with my defiant attitude. Bailey handed me one of the nine very large green cooking apples, I had scrumped the night before. There was no bump at the front of his trousers now, I noticed.

He turned towards his captive audience and clearly stated "Ankorne, will stay on this stage until every one of these nine apples have gone. If any boy chooses to join this thief, they should also come onto this stage to join him!"

Without a word spoken, all the boys from my dormitory walked to the front, then climbed the stage to join me. I was near to tears, so overwhelmed with such a show of loyalty. Not one member of staff, including Mr Walton, made any attempt to prevent this rebellion. The headmaster was absolutely furious, his face got even redder than normal, before he stormed off in a fit of rage.

The matron came onto the stage, wielding a large knife, then cut up all nine apples into portions, which she handed to each boy, all forty of us, who then took it back to their respective table to eat. This exhibition was carried out in total silence, which affected me emotionally with more feeling, than Bailey's cane could ever do.

Bob told Mr Walton, that we would not be going to scouts on Tuesday as planned, as he didn't feel well and wanted to wait until the following week, when by that time, he knew, and hoped he would be feeling a lot better.

Both Walton and myself knew the real reason, for Bob not wanting to go that very first night, was because Bob wanted time for my wounds to heal. Mr Walton respected Bob's decision, and said he would relay Bob's message to Gina, the Scout Master.

About a week later, over which Bob diligently applied the ointment to my rump twice daily, Bob talked me into going to the pool, as he was worried about how withdrawn I had become of late. Until now I had said nothing about that dreadful night, when Bailey had abused me both mentally as well as physically.

We swam for over an hour, before sunning ourselves off in the heat, of what most people called an Indian Summer that year.

Bob asked me to turn over on to my front, while he scrutinised my bum.

"How many strokes did that bastard give you?" he asked.

"I'm not certain" I told Bob "but I think it was about seven."

"It's beginning to heal nicely," said Bob "in a week or two, your bum should be back to normal." Bob assured me.

I turned back onto my side to face Bob, then as I ran my finger tips through his pubic hair, which was once again, beginning to show a lot of new growth.

"You know Bob, in a few weeks your bush will also be back to normal." I said.

We both laughed out loud together.

"You don't know how good it is to hear you laugh again Paul" Bob stressed.

I explained to Bob in the smallest of detail, about how I felt when Bailey was leering at my cock, "I felt he was raping me," I told Bob. "But he never once touched me, with his hand."

"The filthy bastard" Bob said with great feeling, but we both knew, there was nothing to be done about it.

We ambled back to base with Bobby giving me extra hugs along the way.

CHAPTER NINETEEN
One Brick From The Wall

It was during a Wednesday lunch break, having eaten one of my favourite meals of sausage and mash potato, that I was outside the dayroom in the yard. I was casually leaning against the brick wall of the main building, perusing all the kids at play in front of me.

It was a typical Ashford scene with differing age groups of boys, absorbed in a variety of play activities. Absorbed in my own sexual fantasy, knowing I would be meeting my Girl Sylvia, this same Wednesday evening, which was my want.

My twelfth birthday was less than a month away, at Easter time. A loose brick, probably from war damage, from somewhere high up on the wall above me, dislodged itself, from the region of the third floor, and came hurtling down to meet me. Fortunately for me, it landed on my big toe of my left foot, and not my head.

I fell to the ground feeling a searing pain as if my toe had been severed from the rest of my foot inside my plimsole. My plimsole rapidly filled up with blood, as a couple of lads helped me into the office. Mr Sims, who was on duty at the time, promptly rang for Miss Richards the matron.

Mr Sims was more concerned with the blood I was spilling onto his office floor, than how I was feeling.

Being the big brave hero that he wasn't, he couldn't leave fast enough, once the matron arrived. She quickly cut the shoe away from my left foot, to inspect the extent of the damage. It wasn't a pretty sight, but showing all the care of a professional, she cleaned it up as best she could, and bandaged the horrible gash that went all the way down to the broken bone below.

The bandage helped to stem some of the flow of blood, but didn't prevent me from being violently sick, which left my throat like a burst water main, hitting the wall of the office more than eight feet away.

Meanwhile, the matron was on the phone to our infirmary ordering an ambulance.

The moment she put down the phone, it rang again, from somewhere out with the school. During this phone call, the matron gave me some very odd stares indeed as my throbbing toe swelled up to more than twice its normal size. The blood soaked bandage, had reduced the flow to a trickle. Miss Richards accompanied me in the ambulance, and I was taken directly to the operating theatre.

Under the bright theatre lights, I was given a general anaesthetic and as our own Mr Parker the surgeon leaned over me, I looked him in the eyes and said "Remember, it's my big toe, not my dick", then I went under, and out.

Later that evening, as I came too, Bob was sitting on my bed, holding my hand. Still feeling dozy from the effect of the anaesthetic, I heard a woman shout at Bob, to get back into bed at once. A few moments later the doctor leaned into my face, to tell me I was going to be just fine. Instant recognition, remembering him from previous years, I quickly lifted my bedclothes to check my dick. With a big sigh of relief, I let the bedclothes fall back into place.

"What do you think you're doing young man?" Said the Sister.

"I was just checking to see that the doctor hasn't stolen my foreskin." I replied.

The doctor smiled and told me my toe was broken and in time, would mend itself, but the toenail was a goner, before moving on to Bob in the next bed. I drifted back off to sleep. The next time I woke up, Bob was still sitting on my bed, also wearing a bandage on his big left toe.

"What the hell are you doing here?" I asked Bob.

"I don't know really" replied Bob "for some unexplained reason, I too was violently sick, so they sent me here."

I looked at Bob's face then at his big toe, and back again to his face.

"You're just a bloody fraud," I told him "you're just skiving off school," then I fell asleep again.

I hobbled about for a whole week, milking every bit of sympathy I could get, for all its worth. No housework was an added bonus, but alas, it was soon all over, and normal services were resumed.

Bob pointed out rather bluntly, a few inches more and the brick could have hit me on the head, which may have knocked some sense into me. This little pearl of wisdom from Bob, was delivered with a great sense of relief on his part, but gruesome none the less.

Our rooftop ventures, which we both performed over a good two years or more, began to fizzle out. We both found ourselves preoccupied with far more important things going on in our lives.

The scouts, Tuesdays and Thursdays and also weekends with other scouting activities, but Wednesday were always kept by for Sylvia and me. Dancing, swimming and film shows also ate into our time. With such a hectic social life, as well as Bob now going out with a new girl called Dolly, our rooftop vengeance with Hitler, died a natural death.

With this episode of our lives, now behind us, it came as a bit of a surprise when Mr Hammond called the two of us into his office It was even more of a surprise to learn through the grapevine, that the Matron had come across our disguises, on one of her annual spring clean outs.

Bob, in his wisdom found a final resting place for our garb, below the mattress of a boy called Johnny Nash, one of Mr Sims most important informers, no less.

The moment we entered the office, our garments of disguise were on top of the desk, plain to see.

"What do you know about this? Mr Hammond asked, pointing at our disguises with the end of a cane he was holding, looking from one to the other of us.

With the hallmark of a solid brass neck and a dead pan expression on his face, Bob asked "What is it sir?" all innocent like.

Bob would make a fine actor, I thought, he has the gall. I just stood there shaking my head to indicate to Mr Hammond, I didn't have a clue what he was talking about, either.

"Strange" said Mr Hammond "there hasn't been a single rooftop incident, since the school returned from summer camp."

Mr Hammond opened up one of our capes, then looking at me first to gauge the size, then looking at Bob.

"If there is one more rooftop occurrence, I shall come looking for both of you. Do I make myself very, very clear." Mr Hammond said.

We both looked at him without answering him, but Bob wore a face of how insulted and hurt he felt, for such outrageous accusations made against us.

Hammond made a mental note, of how aggrieved we were, and that he could think of such a thing then said "Right, the subject is now closed and these garments will be destroyed, now be off with the two of you."

As I glanced back at Hammond, as we both left the office, I thought I detected a wry smile upon his face.

Once clear of the office, Bob turned to me with one of his broad grins and said, "Well all things must come to an end, sometime!"

That Saturday morning as pre-arranged, my aunt came down to pick up Bob and myself from the Scouts hut in Staines. We were both busy cleaning an array of water craft, when my aunt found me caressing Gina's personal gig, lovingly.

Bob said to my aunt "I think Paul's in love," and we all laughed out loud, as Gina came over to greet my aunt.

My aunt was taking us both away for the weekend because it was my twelfth birthday. After arranging with Bob, to meet us in town, and having had a good chin wag with Gina, my aunt left them to go into Staines to do some shopping.

We went to the high street jewellers, where my aunt asked the owner of the shop, if she could possibly see a range of watches. As he brought back a tray of ladies watches, I thought my aunt was looking for a replacement watch for herself. She leaned into his ear and whispered something to him, before he quickly disappeared only to fetch another tray of watches, only this time, they were all gentlemen's watches.

"Take your pick," my aunt said to me. I studied the tray of watches in front of me, and eventually selected a fine specimen of a military black dial, which had large luminous hands and figures set into the face. I felt this style suited my character, and trying it on my wrist, my aunt agreed also, nodding her head with approval. The costly sum of three pound, ten shillings was handed over to the shopkeeper, which I thought was prohibitively expensive. After all in 1948, most people would be lucky to earn this kind of money for a month's full time employment.

As we left the shop, I refused to put the cuff of my jacket down, so I could flaunt my new wonderful time piece, I was so excited. When Bob joined us for lunch, he spotted my new watch instantly, admiring my choice. We both tucked into our food, but I was so excited, I couldn't manage to eat much.

On our journey to the New Forest, my aunt was also excited to show both Bob and I, our new home, which we had seen, under construction, and was now completely finished. My aunt had moved in many months before, and the decoration internally was now finished.

"I'm sure you're going to like it Paul," she must have told me a dozen times.

Once we reached the new house. I thought it was just fantastic, and my aunt positively glowed with pride, as she showed us all the latest innovations and gadgets built into the house. The house was nothing short of spectacular, as she asked us "What do you think of your new bedroom Paul?"

"I think it's just great" as Bob and I tested the springs in the very thick new mattress of the two new divan style beds. Each bedroom, had a lovely large bathroom en-suite, which were breathtaking to behold, with a fantastic shower arrangement of the latest kind, and so modern.

She showed us where everything was kept, and how to use all the equipment properly. As Bob and I went up top bed that night after supper, she warned me not to wear my new watch in bed, and she told me to get into a routine, winding it every morning. Bob went up ahead to run the bath, as he said he felt a little tired, but I suspected something else was on his mind.

When I followed some ten minutes later, I found Bob enjoying a soak, stretched out full length in the bath. He had obviously been playing with himself, judging by the size of his erection. I casually climbed in between his legs lying back against his chest, pretending I hadn't noticed.

"What's wrong Bob?" I asked.

"Nothing really" Bob replied "I just wonder sometimes if you realise how lucky you are, to have such a wonderful woman for your aunt"

"I think I do Bob, and I am very fond of her, but if I didn't have you Bob, I don't think life itself, would be worth having!"

Bob stayed very silent as he put his arms between my own arms around my chest, and pulled me back onto his own chest. We stayed interlocked in the bath for some time, as I felt his bishop, which had been prodding my back, deflate returning to normal.

As Bob got out of the bath to dry himself off, he leaned over to me, now lying back on my own in the bath, and kissed me on the forehead. I stayed in the bath for a further ten minutes before joining Bob in the bedroom.

"You know Paul," said Bob "I wish I could give you more than just friendship, if there was anyway I could give you any part of my physical being, I would" Bob said.

"I know," I told Bob "you have given me so much over the years."

The bedroom was too warm, and as my aunt knocked on the door, we both shouted for her to come in.

"It's awfully warm in here." I told my aunt.

She went over to the wall radiator on Bob's side of the bedroom, and turned it off explaining to us, because it was a new house, the builders advised her to keep the heat on for a while to dry out all the plasterwork. She kissed us both, for the night, and went into her own bedroom.

Bob turned down the bed clothes to cool down, as I joined him in his bed and I lay alongside him with my face on his chest. Like me he preferred to sleep in the nude. I studied his pubic hair and bishop, which was resting peacefully, at close quarters.

I noticed he was no longer a gangly youth, but rapidly turning into a young man. I moved down, and gently put his flaccid bishop into my mouth. I could feel it swell up inside me until it got so big, I could no longer retain it inside my mouth.

His length was about average, but the thickness was just too much to hold, within my mouth cavity.

I started to massage his bishop very slowly and very gently with my fingertips, that I had seen Bob do often to himself. I could see his balls fill up and started to pulsate wildly, as he got more and more aroused. After about twenty-five minutes, I knew he was ready to ejaculate, so I put the first two inches of his bishop back into my mouth, and moved my hand to the underside of his scrotum.

His body went very stiff as he ejaculated, and I drank him clean, swallowing all the time. I left him inside me, to make sure he had completely finished, and I could feel him returning to his normal self. I waited a little longer before I withdrew him.

We lay there together, as he put his hand down to check me out, but I had not been aroused.

"No Bob, I did this for you, now we both have a little of each other inside of us."

I kissed him goodnight and got back into my own bed, and went to sleep.

Unusually so, Bob was up first as he came into the bedroom carrying a tray of tea and biscuits.

After breakfast my aunt had a surprise for us both, as we headed off to Christchurch, which had a small private airport. My aunt had booked us both, a twenty minute flight in a light aircraft as a special birthday treat and she thought Bob would enjoy it with me. We both loved the sheer thrill of flying, especially as it was our very first flight ever.

We continued to thank my aunt all the way back to Ashford and we both talked about it for weeks later.

Once we got settled back to the cultural shock of being back inside this dump, we called Ashford, Pat kept on remarking about my new watch.

"I hope I can have one just like it one day," Pat remarked.

"I'm sure you will," I told him, remembering how wealthy the Turners were. I shouldn't think Pat would have to wait too long either.

That night at bedtime, Bob was still excited about our weekend at my aunt's new house.

You know Paul," Bob said, lying beside me on my bed "you really didn't have to drink me dry last night."

"I know I didn't have to, "I told Bob "and I didn't particularly want to either, but I did it because I had a need to take something from you internally, so it became a part of me" I said.

"No regrets?" asked Bob.

"None" I told Bob.

Next morning before school, but after breakfast, I was summoned to report to Fatty Arbuckle, the headmaster's office. As I walked down the long, flagstoned corridor to get to his office, I wished I had not eaten breakfast, as I was beginning to feel sick, with dread and repulsive fear.

My heart rate was climbing, as the scenes in his office after my failed scrumping adventure had gone terribly wrong, came flooding back to me. The sight of this man leering at the most intimate parts of my body, filled me with horror.

As I knocked on his office door, awaiting his command to enter, my legs started to get the shakes. As I entered, I deliberately left his door wide open, in the event of having to do a runner. Mr Bailey was at his most jovial, as if butter wouldn't melt. The matron was at his side. Could this be the same man I wondered, who not so long ago, studied my nudity whilst leering with almost pornographic intent.

The very same monster, who then removed long strips of my flesh from my buttocks, after thrashing me to within inches of my life, all for the sake of some rotten green cooking apples.

The same beast that gloated glaringly, at my most inner most sexual organs, that still filled me with violent disgust, and that still turned my stomach that made me very afraid.

Bailey's voice started to sound louder, as he brought me back to the here and now. The matron could tell there was something wrong, as she took me out of Bailey's office, into her own. Once inside her sanctuary, the matron asked me if I was feeling alright. I replied, it must have been something I ate for breakfast. I could see my explanation to her, made her somewhat more sceptical.

The matron told me in plain English. "You should be proud Paul, to have won a three year art scholarship to Wandsworth." She could tell I didn't understand what on earth she was on about.

"Do you remember the painting you gave to your aunt?"

"Yes" I replied.

"Well," the matron went on "your aunt entered it into an art competition in London, and it won first prize for your age group. That's why you have got this art scholarship, which runs from your thirteenth birthday until your sixteenth" she told me.

The penny dropped, and now I was over the moon, later when I told Bob all about it, he smiled at me saying what fantastic news it was, and reminded me I would soon be travelling up to London with him daily.

"I always knew" said Bob "you would end up with the elite, with me" he said smugly.

After we explored together my dread of seeing Bailey again, so soon after the thrashing he gave me, Bob jokingly reminded me, he hadn't forgotten either, as I clung onto him for three nights, sleeping in the same bed nursing, and massaging my bum with this ointment that matron supplied.

Somehow this confrontation with Bailey, and the deep discussion with Bob later, meant I could finally put all my fears behind me. I never stayed long enough in his office, before the matron rescued me, to find out how Bailey himself felt about my fortunate news of my art scholarship, and frankly I didn't care one way or the other.

As I went to bed that night, I floated off quickly into a dream world of my own, Dream boy, dream, I heard myself say as I drifted off.

Just as Bob and I were preparing to leave for our regular Tuesday night at the Scouts, Mr Walton handed me a brown paper package. I opened it very carefully, to discover a brand new naval hat, which had a beautiful blue silk head lining, with green and red pockets. Walton got great pleasure in explaining to me in detail that red was for port and green was for the starboard sides of the boat or ship.

This was a gift from himself, Walton explained, because my aunt was having great difficulty in finding one to fit my head size. No, I didn't have a big head, at least not physically, as it turned out, the opposite. My head was actually quite small.

When my aunt explained this to Mr Walton, he, in turn told her, he would try to obtain one for me through his naval connections. Because Bob was in the room, I refrained from hugging Mr Walton to save giving Walton a red face.

Walton often remarked I was ideal fodder material for anything nautical, and much later in my life he was proved right, in my passion for owning proper sailing yacht's.

Mr Walton's knowledge in all things nautical, to which I showed a great interest, as well as inclinations towards, was one of the reasons why he took an interest in me. Bob had his own ideas and harboured these thoughts for many years, but was never able to work out why, Walton showed more interest in me than any other boy in the school. When Bob made such remarks, I would fly off the handle, because I was never sure if Bob was joking or not.

Oh, that will be right, I would say to Bob, so explain to me why Walton has had my backside for thrashing, more than anyone else. As quick as a flash, Bob would say that's because he loves you. Anyway Bob added, Walton only belts you, when you deserve it, he pointed out to me. There was no arguing with that logic, so I didn't bother trying. I passed my investiture to full scoutshood with flying colours, much to everyone's surprise.

My expertise in the craft of knot tying and single handed sailing, in small dinghy's fairly impressed Gina.

When Bob suggested we skip out Tuesday night's scouting to make up a foursome with our girlfriends on a sexual date at the dove cott, I turned Bob down flat. I explained to Bob at length, I already saw Sylvia every Wednesday, and I was more than satisfied with my sex life as it was.

"However Bob," I told him "your oversexed libido may well care, for far more satisfaction."

Bob had never before seen me take such a hard line stance.

"Fair enough" said Bob" I suppose, I can see her an alternative night.

CHAPTER TWENTY
A Spurt of Growth

After less than a year in my new dorm, I felt both comfortable and settled. I was also feeling very content with my life, especially with all the exciting things happening outside Ashford's gates, in the big outdoors.

With all my scouting activities getting even more absorbing, demanding so much of my time, that stringent Ashford regulations would permit, I was now beginning to grow up even faster.

I was also getting more involved with Sylvia, and although only a year or so older than myself, was neither too demanding of my time, nor to radical with our sex lives, that we lovingly shared together.

Wednesday evening was always our night every week together, but occasionally we would also meet at weekends, as well. She was also physically more mature than myself, and we often had very deep discussions about a whole range of topics together. The more I wanted to perform full sexual intercourse with her, the more she was able to restrain my lustful intentions.

At scouts, I had recently been made a patrol leader, which gave me even more responsibilities to consider, as my thirteenth birthday rapidly approached. The very first of my teenage years.

Bob, pointed out to me once, that he thought my stature had grown a good two inches in the last year alone, and I was now taller or as tall, as any fourteen year old.

I was also well into, full weekends away with the rest of the other scouts, camping, canoeing, sailing and rock climbing. Mr Walton was given verbal reports by Gina, about my steady progress in all my scouting activities. Bob himself often made jibes, at what a goody good shoes, I had become.

Bob continued to take risks in seeing his latest girl friend Doris, or was it Dolly, who seemed more than able to meet Bob's over active sex drive. He never ever spoke of Margaret again, ever since she gave him crabs. According to Bob, Doris took his lustful desires into new realms.

"What exactly is that supposed to mean?" I asked Bob.

"She lets me fuck her all the way" said Bob "But its okay," He quickly explained "we always use a French Letter. No French Letter," said Bob "we just don't do it, I don't want a baby" added Bob.

Do you fancy making a foursome next Tuesday?" Bob asked.

"Not really" I explained, "I'm not into group sex, and I'll be seeing Sylvia anyway on Wednesday," I said. When I thought of the loving sexual play we shared between us, it has to be much better than some of the older lads sexual behaviour, I thought.

Bob was almost fifteen and never seemed happier, we both were. I remember my very first day travelling up to London with Bob, at my side as he went onto Battersea and me to Wandsworth Art College. I remember opening a long brown envelope that I was to hand in at school for my enrolment at Wandsworth, It was a copy of my birth certificate that simply read, Mother: Mary Elsie Ankorne, Father: Unknown, Date of Birth: 12th 4th 1936. I looked at it for a long time, then turned to Bob and said, "I'm a bastard!"

"So am I" Bob replied, but I knew he wasn't, "and half of all the boys at Ashford are, so what?" Bob asked.

He put his arm around me on the train, not caring who saw him, "You don't remember your mother anyway" said Bob.

"You're right Bob, I don't remember my mother, so not having a father, doesn't really matter" I told Bob.

"Does it really matter, if you have grown up parents?" asked Bob. "You have always had me, and you always will" Bob added. "Anyway" he continued, "you have a super aunt, which is more than I have."

I had spent my life as far back as my very first memories with Bob, always there for me, so who needs grown up parents anyway. Life was good just now, and I was determined to spend my first day at Art School, enjoying myself to the full. It was odd, finding myself in a grown up environment, where all the students talked only about art, and the different aspects of the love of art!

I was thrown in at the deep end and especially with a double period in the afternoon of Life Classes, where a very attractive, nude young girl model, posed as our art subject. A bit of a shocker for my first day at art school, but I loved it.

When I told Bob about my first day, as he sat beside me on the train returning to Ashford. Bob sat, completely gob smacked, thinking I was winding him up, but soon realised I wasn't

"I'm going to the wrong school" was all he could say.

I nudged him in the ribs and told Bob, he would not survive long at my school, as you would have to be able to draw with a pencil and not your dick!

"You don't think I could exercise or control my bishop do you?" Bob asked

"I know you too well" I reminded Bob "there is not an hour in the day when you don't think with the bishop between your legs, instead of your head." I said.

Bob put on an expression of being really hurt, but gave no reply. Over the first four terms at Wandsworth, we covered a very diverse range of subjects. Heraldry, Silk Screen Printing, Classical Architecture in Greek, Roman and Egyptian Graphics, Technical Drawing, interior design, gilding, as well as other subjects including Nude Life painting of both sexes

I was in my element and couldn't be happier, although I had a lot of catching up regarding the normal educational subjects, especially in both maths and English. That first full year was a tough one. My exam results were encouraging, being slightly better than I genuinely hoped for, but I was even more determined to do better in my second year results.

Why oh why, did my later years at Ashford suddenly take wings, with the weeks and months rattling by at break neck speed. With all my hobbies and outside interests filling so much of my time, I sometime found it difficult to keep track of all that I was involved in.

My constant thirst for more and more adult knowledge, and with a lot of support from my aunt, became insatiable.

My relationship with my only girlfriend Sylvia continued to flourish. On the other hand, Bob's conquest with so many different girlfriends, only five that he would admit to, was always a topic open for discussion. His great love of sexual experimentation was enough to boggle anybody's mind. Each different sexual method or variation was always met with great enthusiasm, which he use to rant on about.

"You know Bob, that Bishop of yours gets so much abuse, I'm only surprised it's not dropped off through wear and tear." I told him.

"It's just great," Bob would answer with a grin.

The more I, myself lusted after Sylvia to let me dip my wick, the more Sylvia would not permit such an act, without full protection. There were lots of boys at night time in the dormitories, calling more on Kenny's services, sometimes almost nightly.

Most of the older sexually active boys were willing to pay for his services, as a kind of male prostitute, to satisfy their appetites. I've no idea what the going rate for Kenny's services were, but I concluded with the paltry sum of pocket money we got at Ashford, they couldn't have been too expensive, as Kenny went for quantity, rather than quality. One thing was certain, Kenny had a healthier pocket money account than most boys.

When I look back to my primary years just before I was eight years old, witnessing such an act as buggery by two older lads on Kenny, in one session alone, filled me full of dread. Thankfully those nightmares I suffered at that time have long passed.

My awareness now, of certain homosexual practices, were only performed by a very small minority, and probably no more or less than that, which takes place in any, all boys residential establishment. Like our rooftop adventures, which had now stopped completely, the visits to our secret river pool became less frequent.

Our outside leisure interests became all absorbing for both Bob and myself, and as I also noticed with Bob, as he got older, even the interest with his bishop in bed, got less personal attention, from Bob.

In the early spring of 1950, just before my fourteenth birthday, Bob suggested most strongly, that we make a visit to our special oasis, that Bob preferred to call our pool in the River Ash.

I never once questioned Bob's motives, because my trust in Bob was always total. I naturally agreed with Bob, as I could tell that something out of the usual was occupying his troubled mind. My love for Bob, not sexual, and admiration for him, couldn't have been stronger, and had been built up, with great fondness for him over my life.

So on this beautiful sunny afternoon a few days before my fourteenth, we both headed off together, with Bob smuggling out two towels in case we wanted to swim. This time, I was first in, diving into the deep part of the pool with joyous nudity. I lay back soaking up the rays in a place, which was always very special to me.

All my wonderful memories of some of the most fantastic times of my childhood, belonged right here, in this pool of tranquillity. With Bob's help, I had come to terms with the biggest fears here, and I could recall my happiest moments in this very place.

Eventually, Bob joined me in the water and we swam leisurely for more than an hour, before we pulled our naked bodies onto the slabs. The rock slabs retained their warmth, generated by solar energy, from the sun.

Bob laid back in deep thought, restful with his eyes closed in silence. I studied his still slim body with ease. Bob was now quite tall, and once where he was skinny, his body now had more definition and shape. He was no longer that gangly five and a half year old, I clearly remember on my very first day that I came to Ashford. He was only a kick in the pants from his sixteenth birthday, but the changes in his body became even more apparent as I lay there looking at him.

He had filled out, with the thick black bushy hair around his penis was now substantial. Even his bishop, as Bob preferred to call it, was now fully much the penis of a man, both in girth and in length.

Even his facial features, had lost much of its boyishness. Physically Bob's body, had changed a great deal, but to me he would be my Bob, as I laid back myself and closed my eyes feeling at peace with the world. I was never more comfortable with my nakedness, or feeling of utter trust with Bobby at my side.

Bob suddenly started to sob, perceptively at first, but I could feel his sobbing body, through contact with my own.

I opened my eyes, turning my body towards him, then pulled him onto my chest before wrapping both my arms tightly around his body.

"Come on Bob" I said "please don't cry."

This didn't help, as Bob's sobbing cries got louder, and I could feel his warm tears running slowly down my chest. I hugged him even tighter, as I pleaded with him yet again, to stop crying as I watched his tears fill up the indentation of my belly button.

"What's the matter?" I demanded from Bob, thinking he was about to tell me something disastrous.

"Do you realise Paul," Bob sobbed "in only four months from now, I will have to leave Ashford for good."

With the realisation of what Bob had just uttered, was true, I looked at Bob's face just below my chin, and in turn I myself felt a welling up inside me. The tiny rivulets of Bob's tears had already filled my belly button to overflowing as I watched the overflow disperse into my pubic hair.

I gently whispered into Bob's ear, telling him all the wonderful things awaiting him on the outside of this dump, we had learned to call home, at Ashford.

"It's not this dump I will miss," sobbed Bob "it's you!"

"Well," I said trying to cheer him up "we'll see each other at Scouts, long after you shake the dirt from your shoes of this place" I told Bob. Also," I went on "I'll miss you just as much, especially knowing you're free on the outside" I added. "Anyway" I told Bob "you can always go to stay with your older sister."

Bob stopped sobbing as quickly as if turning off a tap.

"No" said Bob, "I will never stay one night under the same roof as that slapper," he said, with so much venom in his voice, I was afraid to ask him why. So I didn't.

"Anyway" said Bob "Gina, has offered me a room lodging, in his house."

This certainly was news to me.

"Well then" I said to Bob "why were you crying when you have landed on your feet. You couldn't get better digs." I told Bob.

A cloud at that moment covered the sun. Not a good omen I thought, so I jumped back into the water to swim over to the grass back to where our clothes were. I had almost finished drying myself off when I automatically started to towel Bob's body off, before I realised he was no longer wearing a plaster on his arm. I handed Bob his towel to finish himself off.

We stood there still naked, hugging and laughing at one another.

In that very moment in time, we both realised, that we had left our childhood behind, for good!

After we both got dressed, we ambled off with our arms across each other's shoulders, knowing our kinship of close friendship, we equally shared, would last for evermore.

CHAPTER TWENTY-ONE
The Rape of Swany

It was early summer of 1950, just after my fourteenth birthday, with less than five weeks to go before Bob would be leaving Ashford for good.

Bob was hoping for employment with a company of Architects, as a junior, but somehow Bob showed little enthusiasm. I also found it difficult to visualise Bob in this setting.

Meanwhile, Mr Walton informed Patrick and myself, that Pat would eventually move into Bob's bed, when the time came. Have I already been more than two years in this dormitory? It certainly didn't seem like it, I told myself.

Both my school work at Wandsworth, and my scouting activities were progressing well. I just loved everything about Scouting. Sylvia, my girlfriend, was fast approaching her fifteenth birthday, and I knew in a years time, she too, would leave Ashford. She was already developing into a young woman, with a sexual appetite to match, especially below her waistline.

So much so, I was now having difficulty in keeping up with her powerful sexual demands. I would always be thankful to her, for her gentle induction and sexual skill, she showed with my very first sexual encounter, with the opposite sex.

Meanwhile, Patrick my so called half brother, continued to make steady progress, with his own girlfriend, Maisy. He became a regular visitor, at Miss Lowman's house, in the village, who, like my aunt, adopted Maisy.

Miss Lowman grew fond of Pat, and was more than comfortable with their friendship. I couldn't help wondering, how long this would be the case, especially as Pat was showing more and more interest in his own libido.

Alas, I remembered, this interest eventually comes to all of us, sooner or later, so why should Pat be any different, I thought.

The last two weeks before Bob was due to leave, sped by so quickly, Bob's last weekend was soon upon us.

Bob suggested to me that Pat should be invited to our special pool, so he could share with me, once Bob had left. I personally, was not so keen, but reluctantly agreed, as all three of us frolicked around in the buff, enjoying ourselves.

Pat was over the moon, having been asked, but was unaware of the poignant meaning or significance of the occasion, while he romped around in his nudity state of joy.

Both Bob's and Pat's birthdays, fell in the month of August, which made their age gap four years apart. Knowing this, Bob's ultimate visit to a place which we had shared together, over so many years, now seemed, somehow strange with a third party present. The nostalgic bygone days with so much happiness, along with all the mixed emotions suffered while both of us, found ourselves, somehow, had a finality that just didn't feel comfortable.

Patrick was not attuned, into our vibes, playing and enjoying himself regardless.

That last Sunday evening, both of us went through the emotions of playing a final game of chess, but neither of us had our minds on the game in hand, each one of us, afraid to show our true feelings. I knew, that in less than twelve hours away, we would be split up, although I consoled myself with the knowledge that I would continue to see Bob, several times a week, at the Scouts in Staines.

After a very restless night, I went into my housework duties in a daze. Bob in his wisdom disappeared before breakfast, and on my route to London, I kept looking over my shoulder, hoping to get a glimpse of Bob, but knowing I would not.

It was a very wasted day, at art college that day, with Mr Gee, one of our classical art teachers, having to shake me several times back into reality. Besides teaching Greek-Roman and Egyptian art work, he was a virtuoso on the violin.

His own shape of head even looked like a violin, to which he played so expertly. On my return journey, by train to Ashford, I avoided my mates, by sitting in a carriage, on my own.

During the evening meal, which was daily set aside for all of us boys, known collectively as the 'Ashford Experiment', I chose to sit on my own at the end of the table. Unaware of what food I was putting into my mouth, if any at all, one of the older lads, started making snide remarks, about me behaving like a love sick puppy.

My temper, I felt hotting up within my body, into a rage, so I vacated my seat, then grabbed a boy called Saunders from out of his chair, and decked him. Standing over the rest of the group in an act of pure defiance, I glared at them. They wisely avoided eye contact with me, while Saunders squirmed on the floor, whimpering away. I slowly turned, and walked away.

The evening was still very young, but after a very quick shower, I went up to my dorm, feeling very depressed. In the centre of my pillow was a folded note simply marked Paul. I knew instantly, it was from Bob, well before I unfolded and read the note, which read, "I've left my chess set in your locker, as you need the practice, Ha Ha! All my love Bob. P.S. See you on Tuesday at the Scouts!"

I could hear some of the boys coming up the stairs, as my tears began to break over my cheeks. I quickly made my escape to a toilet cubicle, for urgent repairs and where I could also be alone.

I decided to go back down stairs, and as I wandered into the games room, Mr Walton collared me into a new game on the snooker table, he was keen to demonstrate. Secretly, I suspected, Walton was determined to pre-occupy my mind, away from my own troubles of woe.

This new game required a total of eight players and simply called Lives. Each player was given one ball apiece, and started each with a total of having three lives, each. The one exception was whoever was given the white ball, which started the game, had four lives. The balls in descending order of colour, was white, red, yellow, green, brown, blue, pink and black.

Starting with white chasing red, then each chasing the colour in front, in correct order, the aim was to pot the ball of your opponent. Every time you potted a colour in order, that boys colour lost a life. After having been potted three times, three lives, your ball was taken out of play. Once red had potted yellow three times, red then went onto green, then brown and so on.

The last ball standing was the winner. Simple, but very exciting to watch and play.

The beauty of the game was the involvement of eight players, instead of the standard two players, playing a game of billiards or snooker. There was always a group of boys, waiting for a table to become available. With a total of only six tables, this new game, which was fast and exciting, could involve forty eight players, instead of just twelve over all six table. The recreation of playing this game introduced to us by Mr Walton rapidly became an instant success. It certainly took my mind off my sorrowful state, as I went up to bed, feeling more buoyant.

On arrival upstairs, Pat was already settled into Bob's old bed, reading a comic book received in a parcel, sent to Pat by the Turner's, Pat's uncle and aunt, and relatives to my own Aunt Joan.

Sitting on Pat's bed was a little lad, called Swan, but liked to be called 'Swany'. A cheerful little guy, who was also enjoying a bag of sweets called mischiefs that the Turner's had sent in Pat's parcel. Swan was older than Pat by almost six months but had his final move up into the senior boys dorm delayed, because of his small body size. It was also obvious, that these two were very good friends, with Swan having the more dominant character.

Pat offered me a mischief from his bag, but not being a sweety fan, I declined his kind offer, so Swan grabbed it instead. Just before lights out, Swan returned to his bed with a comic provided by Pat, and I quickly fell asleep, pleased to be able to dream my own thoughts, of better times, and in my own space. Sometime in the very small hours, I was dramatically shaken from my slumber by Pat, who was leaning over me in a very agitated state.

With a sound of high urgency in his whispered voice, directly into my ear, I too was getting somewhat agitated. He was speaking so fast, I couldn't understand his gibberish, so I demanded he slow down, so that I could understand him more easily.

Pat, puffing out of breath, in his excited state, explained to me that two big boys from the cubicles at the other end of the dorm had taken his beloved Swany away. I looked across the dorm at Swan's bed, which was indeed empty, and judging by its dishevelled state, it had been vacated with some kind of fight.

I told Pat to stay put, as I went to see for myself. But I first went to Frank's bed to take a loan of his cricket bat, as I felt, I might well have a need for this useful weapon. Frank was, himself, in full snoring mode, but was also a real cricket nut. A bit of a boring aficionado, but harmless enough.

I uplifted his bat, which was always kept by his bedside locker, then headed off towards the only four cubicles within the dorm. I could hear the grunts and what sounded like muffled sobbing, as I approached the cubicle in question.

Before my eyes, I could see little boy Swan, spread eagled across the end of the bed frame, with his legs wide apart, and with his feet tied at the ankles to each of the beds iron legs, at least three feet apart. Swan's chest was face down onto the lower half of the bed mattress, with both arms outstretched and each wrist, firmly tied to the beds side rails.

I had no idea, how long these two animals, had Swan trussed in this sacrificial position. Both these oldest boys within the school were very powerfully built, with the lesser of the two, holding Swan's head, between his knees, while masturbating over and above Swan's back.

The bigger of the two, with his back to me, I recognised as a boy due to leave Ashford very soon, called Tom.

With Swan tethered in this way and only half the size of Tom's powerfully built body, Swan never stood any chance of resistance. Swan was motionless, and no doubt gagged, judging from his muffled tones.

Tom, had already forced himself into Swan, although he had his back to me, I could tell with the pronounced jerks of his buttocks, his penis was in deep.

I took careful aim with the full size cricket bat, with a backward long swing. The other boy, kneeling above Swan and facing me, did not see me, as he was far too engrossed in his own erection, which was nearing a climax, to even notice me.

With all my strength, I swung the bat at full speed, which struck, with a very loud slapping sound, as it sunk into his two buttocks or the cheeks of his arse.

So unexpected was this received, two things happened together. The kneeling boy out of sheer fright or terror ejaculated his spunk uncontrollably in great spurts, some of which, even splashed onto me. Simultaneously, Tom fell sprawling forward, as the cricket bat sunk painfully into his rear end, and was now desperately trying to disconnect or withdraw his own dick, which was stuck firmly inside Swan's anus.

He levered himself upright and in one movement extracted his enormous cock, from within Swan, who physically winced in agony. As Tom turned to face me, with his enormous, very thick hard on, which was throbbing like mad, I took another swipe downwards at his now ejaculating dick. The sound, when the flat of the bat, hit it's intended target, was like a bone splitting under impact, which doubled him over, and with his now hunched body, fled as best he could.

While he was fleeing, two very large red welts could be seen right across his rear end, where the face of the bat had left its mark. Pat peered around the cubicle corner, to check all was clear.

"You stay with Swany," I ordered Pat, "while I see if I can corner these naked animals."

Not a sign of them, but I suspected they were possibly hiding in the junior toilets or dormitories below.

Getting back to Swan as quickly as I could, I ungagged him, and also undid his bindings. Two pairs of long stocking socks were used to tether Swan, the kind we all wore at Ashford.

Even when Swan was free from all his bondage, he just lay there, motionless, in so much pain, sobbing his head off. Pat signalled for me to step outside the cubicle for a quite word, as he was concerned that Swany was bleeding from the back end.

I sent Pat off to find the night watchman, and also the matron, while I covered Swan up in a feeble attempt to save some of his dignity. Swan was shivering with traumatic shock, trembling and sobbing uncontrollably like an injured rabbit.

I fetched some extra blankets to cover him, and decided to climb in beside him, to give him some of my body heat. I put my arm over his back, talking to him in a soothing manner, desperate to stop him sobbing his little heart out.

It took all of twenty minutes for Pat to return, with both the matron and the night watchman. While Pat and the night watchman hovered a safe distance away, the matron asked me to hold Swan still, while she examined Swan's butt. The small bedside light put Swan's lower body into shadow, so withdrawing a pen torch from her uniform pocket, she uncovered us both, to examine this delicate part of Swan's anatomy, that had already bled onto the bed clothes. She gently wiped away the surplus blood from his wound, as I felt his little body convulse against her touch.

The sphincter muscle inside the anus had been ruptured, which didn't surprise me, when you saw the brutal girth of Tom's penis. Because no lubricant was used, the ruptured tear had been made considerably worse. The matron was instructing the night watchmen to ring our infirmary for an ambulance, and then to look and contain both boys in the dayroom office.

Pat was instructed to bring the ambulance men to us on arrival.

"You don't mind staying with Brian Swan, meanwhile?" the matron asked me.

I had seen many sex acts at Ashford in my years there, but I had never seen anything as beastly or brutal as this. There was an unwritten code, understood by most of the boys, in the twelve to sixteen years of age, group. This was well outside any code that I understood.

I have never before, seen the matron in such an emotional state, as she went away with the ambulance crew.

There was nothing more either Pat or myself could do, so we both headed back to our beds.

"Can I bunk in with you tonight Paul?" Pat asked.

How could I deny him, having just witnessed such brutal buggery on his mate Swany.

"Of course you can, if you must." I said to Pat, who fell asleep within minutes of climbing in beside me.

Before dropping off, Pat remembered to tell me, both boys were locked inside the day room office.

This wasn't sex, I reminded myself, this was buggery of the worst kind, much worse still I thought, this was rape.

CHAPTER TWENTY-TWO
Swany Makes Good

Remembering to put Franks cricket bat into its rightful place, I left Pat curled up in my bed, as I raced down the stairs for my early morning ablutions. Mr Walton lay in wait, and took me into his office, closing the office door firmly behind us.

I quickly looked about me, remembering the night before, as the office acted as a temporary prison. As if reading my mind, Mr Walton assured me, that these two louts would not be returning to Ashford, and had already been removed to a very secure environment.

"No Paul, I just want to thank you, for your valiant effort in rescuing Brian Swan" he said. "You're intervention was most timely, against such animals. I've been here, nigh on twenty years," Said Walton "and in all that time, there has never been a case of, of, of rape," he stuttered. "Well done" he said "and in a few days, you should visit Swan, in the infirmary, as the poor kid will need all the help in recovering from such a wicked ordeal."

I looked at Walton's solemn expression, as one who never ceases to astonish me.

"Now cut along, Paul," he murmured. So I completed my ablutions, deep in thought.

Just five days later, the matron came over to my tea table, and reminded me that Brian Swan was now ready for his first visit. "I would suggest you go after tea, as the sister in charge is expecting you."

With several comic books under my arm, and a bag full of mischief sweets in my pocket, I made my way down the drive to the infirmary. This place, held so many bad memories, and as I walked into the ward, I spotted the very doctor, Parker, who wanted to circumcise me, all those years ago. I lost my bottle, and turned on my heels, intent on doing a runner, only to be barred by Sister Goodman.

The sister whisked me into her cosy office, cooing like a dove on heat. Her large ample proportions were the talk of most little boys, with her melons of oversized breast, that looked as if they were more than prepared, to cross the winning tape first, and with a distinct advantage to her. A very tactile person, with arm movements always on the go, touching everybody she held conversations with.

"Brian," she oozed, with feminine silkiness "is doing fine, and I expect he will soon be back with you all, in about a week."

Sister made it sound as if Brian was on some exotic holiday, in a five star resort, pampered to excess. She took me by the shoulder and steered me into the ward, to ensure I did not lose my way.

I could see Swany, shaking his head to music he was listening to through headphones, from the local station. As soon as he spotted me, off came the headphones to be replaced by one of the most infectious grins, I've ever seen for a long time, followed by a wave of both arms, as if I had known him all my life.

A sign above his head, clearly stated 'Nil by Mouth', which I immediately thought, they were starving the little blighter. He looked so tiny, alone in a spotless bed, which were so much bigger than our dorm beds.

I asked him why they were not feeding him any food, which made him laugh out loud, as he lifted the covers, to reveal, he was fed liquids by tube, into his body. For the time being at least, they did not want solids to pass through, to give the sphincter a chance to heal.

Surprisingly, to what he had so recently suffered, he was in excellent spirits.

"You can sit up okay then?" I asked, as he then showed me his inflated ring inner tube, cushion below him.

I handed him the comic book, but when I produced the bag of mischief sweets, his eyes lit up, like a jukebox, putting them quickly below his bedclothes, out of sight.

The matron and sister rustled their way down the ward, like a pair of maiden battleships, on patrol in the North Sea.

With Swany blethering like an excited monkey, oblivious of these overbearing brace of womanhood, on a mission, approaching his bed, he calmly said "They're here to throw you out."

Indeed, I was firmly, but politely told to sling my hook, as they didn't want the patient overtired.

Swany, threw both his arms around my neck, hugging me and kissing me, whispering in my ear. "Please come back again." He sounded desperate for my answer.

"I will," I said "and I'll bring your mate Pat with me." He beamed his delight, waving me goodbye, until I was out of sight.

We both made several visits, until ten days later, he returned to the fold. Brian's recovery was wonderful, considering the physical damage inflicted. I wondered how long the mental scars would take to heal.

In mid July eighty boys were selected within the age group of twelve or over, for a two week exchange to Scotland. Walton was keen for me to go, if only to nurse maid Swan, who now saw me as the protector, he felt so strongly he needed.

Walton had already discussed the whole delicate sexual incident, explaining my timely intervention, to my aunt. So between them, my normal holiday with my aunt was put on hold. Having manipulated my summer break, it was felt the benefits to Swan, for this Scottish trip would help speed his recovery, in the process of trusting other boys interactions.

Patrick, who had been to Scotland with the Turner's, would also be on this expedition, who was, in fairness, Swan's best mate. This would mean Patrick would also be available to share the burden of responsibilities.

I didn't protest, but as Bob pointed out to me at the Scouts that week, I was a real sucker, taking on not one, but two lame ducks.

We, all eighty boys, went up by rail to Scotland on the Flying Scotsman train, which in itself was real treat. We arrived in Glasgow where we were transferred onto a fleet of super old coaches, called Bluebirds, and were whisked off to a place called Bellahouston. The school we used as our base was in an area considered by many, as fairly rough, but as most of us were from many rough areas of London, this was the least of our worries.

Our two weeks touring, by Bluebirds coaches, all over the Trossachs, Glencoe and the West Coast of Scotland, was a real eye opener. My love affair with Scotland was instantly set in stone, as I chose later on in my life, to make it my home.

Loch Lomond area was a particular favourite with everyone, as each day, with our packed lunches, set off for a delightful tour. The one small thing, that impressed me as unusual, was seeing the Scottish coppers, always patrolling in two's and three's, never on their own. This was because of the difference between Scottish and English criminal law, we were informed.

I lost my heart completely to Glencoe, with its dramatic mountain scenery and mountain tarns. This combination, I felt was unbeatable and vowed in later years to return for some superb climbing trips, which I did.

Alas, like all wonderful treats in life, especially those experiences, that have a strong impact, in influencing us, as individuals, they are but a fleeting moment in one's lifetime.

We soon re-settled back into Ashford's mundane routine, but all feeling much richer, for having had the Scottish experience. Patrick along with myself, both decided to introduce Swany to our secret pool. Like a duck to water, Swany was in his element. For some strange reason, Mr Sims, left me alone, and on several occasions, became almost human in his few dealings with me.

At the back end of that summer in 1950, I went to stay with my aunt for an extra long weekend, before starting back at Wandsworth, for the term running up to the Christmas break.

Meanwhile, I was saving my money like mad, towards owning my very first racing cycle. This was to be my last Christmas with my aunt's extended family at the family Manor house, in Guildford.

This historic pile would be sold off next Easter at about the same time as my fifteenth birthday, as this vast property of thirty-two bedrooms, was no longer required, with the family spread all over the world.

My aunt had always instilled in me, the value and virtues, of earning ones way in life. The real value of money, she said, could only be appreciated, if earned by the sweat of one's brow, she often said. I agreed with my aunt, as I saw no benefits or advantages, of easy come, and just as easy gone!

One particular story my aunt related to me more than once, was as a child, one of her older brothers, wrote to Queen Victoria, a good friend to the Leigh-Clare family, asking Aunt Victoria to send him ten shillings, because he had spent his allowance at prep school. Dear Aunt Victoria, in answer to his request, wrote back, telling him, certainly not! Or words to that effect.

My aunts brother, promptly sold Victoria's letter, for ten shillings, which caused a media scandal, especially among the Leigh-Clare family. My aunt reminded me of this tale of woe, every time I was flippant about money values.

Christmas went well, and she made me hand over all my savings, I had put aside for my bicycle. Before I returned to school, my aunt's brother, Harry, was made to take me, to pick up the new bicycle, I had been saving so hard for, with my aunt meeting the considerable shortfall.

My aunts explanation was, she felt I had acted so responsible over the Swan affair, I deserved some reward "and anyway" she calmly said, "That's your Christmas and next birthday present."

Needless to say, I was delighted to be riding my very first bike.

However a fortnight before my fifteenth birthday, Bob handed me a card with some money, along with a condom, in the envelope. I looked at him, full of surprise, as he explained that tomorrow, Wednesday, would be the last time, I would have my evening love session with Sylvia.

"I think," Bob said "Sylvia has a rather special fifteenth birthday present for you, and believe me Paul," Bob emphasised "you will be needing a French letter.

Wednesday evening started off well, with Sylvia, at her very best, as she undressed me slowly, very slowly, working her magic, with tender foreplay, lasting almost an hour. At the most critical moment, with my hard penis, dripping in anticipation, she very carefully rolled the sheath along my shaft. My erection had never been stiffer, or bigger, it felt so hard it hurt with a throbbing ache.

Sylvia's vaginal fluids were running freely, and by now we were both so excited, our whole bodies tingled with sexual tension. My now covered erection, stood almost vertically, swaying in pure lust and expectation. She took hold of my shaft, which was vibrating or trembling so much, I was in fear of pre-ejaculation. She inserted my dick, slowly into her love cavern, which was very warm. The entire length slipped in with ease, because of her internal, self lubricating glands.

Deeper and deeper, we both explored her love cavern, with sheer adjoined pleasure. Sylvia climaxed first, so I continued on solo, but slowly, making the enjoyment last as long as possible. I felt my ejaculated sperm, shoot into the slack end of the bag. We lay there, locked together as one union, with my dick deep inside her, neither of us moving, but savouring the joy between us, Twenty minutes later, I was still very hard, so we agreed to repeat the act all over again.

Almost two hours after we had started, we both said our long protracted goodbyes. The evening ended very emotionally, each in turn shedding many tears. I had seen Sylvia St. John, for the last time, she would be gone for ever, before the weekend. Another chapter in my life was over, but soon, I would need to turn the first page to a whole new chapter, as life itself, demands.

On Friday after a day in double art, I took the tube directly from Wandsworth to West Kensington; my aunt met me at the station outside. Here we took a taxi direct to the Turner's penthouse apartment where, unbeknown to me, a fifteenth birthday party had been secretly arranged..

Patrick met us at the door, beaming with pleasure at me, because we were the only two kids in among a dozen or more adults.

"How did you come up from Ashford?" I asked Pat.

"Bobby brought me." Pat replied.

"Great" I said, "so is he inside then?"

"No" Pat replied "but he's coming back later" he added.

The large spacious apartment of the Turner's was prepared at no expense spared, more, I suspected for an unnamed celebrity's benefit, than mine.

It transpired the honoured guest was Walt Disney with his latest lady friend. The Turner's had recently been offered a very lucrative offer in the States, working for the J. Arthur Rank organisation, who just happened to be working on a Disney project.

The whole do, which was very posh indeed, was simply a hook for Lydia Turner, to hang her mink coat on. I wasn't impressed, nor was Patrick, who was overjoyed that the Turner's were moving lock stock, over to America.

The party was very grown up affair, not at all ideal for us kids, although at seventeen, Bob could hardly be called a kid. I greeted Bob with exuberance, much to the Turner's displeasure, as she felt I was not doing enough sucking up to Mr Walt Disney, who quite frankly, did not impress me.

He was nice enough, and even gave me a hand drawn card, with several of his well known cartoon characters, as a birthday card come gift. Being at Art College, I had seen, better cartoon drawings, but I did appreciate his efforts.

My present from the Turners' was this so called party, which I knew, I could well do without. Like Pat, I too was pleased they were to settle in the States. With luck Lydia, who was very much a wannabe film star, might become famous.

Within a month after my fifteenth birthday, the Turner's had sold the penthouse, and moved permanently to New York, U.S.A.

"Good riddance" said Pat, who was normally very polite.

Back in Ashford, I found Swany had recovered from his ordeal well, and in fact, become a right little character.

Reminding myself of Bob's introduction to the wonderful game of chess, all those years ago, I felt the time was ripe to introduce both Pat and Swany to this fine game.

Both took to it well, but Swany's grasp of understanding, of this intricate and most challenging of board games, was meteoric. He took to playing the game as often as possible and beat me on several occasions. Pat was also a steady player, but no match for Swany.

In the summer of '51, Bob received his call up papers to do his national service. He announced to us all, at the weekly scout meeting in mid June. He was to undergo his basic training on the 1st August, 1951, and after he completed his training, there was even talk, that he could be posted abroad.

This was a blow, to all our scouting friends, and myself of course, because he was well liked by all, as well as being such value to the group. Working as a junior, in a firm of architects, Bob was not considered to be exempt from this service, whereby for two years you belonged to the armed forces.

Having escaped from one institution, Ashford, Bob was not at all keen on being forced into another, although Bob would have no difficulty in fitting in, so to speak.

My aunt was more than pleased with my second year exam results, although she still felt I should strive far more academically. I continued to see as much of Bob as possible, knowing full well, our time together was rapidly running out.

I remember one evening, sitting on the grassy bank overlooking the river, in front of the scout hut, with the radio blaring away through the huts open doorway. When the ballad of Shenandoah, wafted over the air, which I know to be one of Bob's very favourite tunes of all time. Bob was stretched out on the grass bank beside me with both his eyes closed and hands clasped behind his head.

The evocative sounds of Shenandoah's sweeping over us, stirring our emotions of memories and feelings I could see the tears forcing their way to the surface, squeezing their way through Bob's closed eyelids, and unashamedly flow onto his cheeks. We just lay there together, undisturbed, as nostalgia washed over both of us, of wonderful memories, we'd shared over the years.

"Come on Bob," I said gently "it's time to go home." Even if it wasn't to the same home, together.

On my return to Ashford, I was informed that Mr Walton had taken ill, hopefully, he would soon be back at work, in his rightful place, as he was only suffering from a bad bout of influenza.

Less than a week later, I was called into the office by Mr Hammond, who informed me that Mr Walton had passed away.

"What do you mean passed away?" I demanded from Hammond.

"I'm afraid" said Hammond, trying to pick his words carefully "our friend died last night" Hammond said in a whisper, close to tears.

"He can't be dead, he just can't be" I insisted "he was easily the fittest master in the school, it's impossible" I cried.

"The fact is," said Hammond "he is!"

The doctor, who was treating Walton for influenza, should have been treating him for malaria, which Walton caught while in the navy, more than twenty years previous, in the Far East.

"Bloody doctors!!" I said out loud, running outside to be alone.

CHAPTER TWENTY-THREE
My Final Year of Art

My year between fifteen and sixteen, started well enough, but as we neared the end of the present year of 1951, the trauma of events, were beginning to stack up against me.

Firstly Bob, with whom I had a closer relationship, than any other person in the world, had left Ashford for good, and now was on the very threshold of no longer being such an important part of my life, was about to leave for ever.

Now Mr Walton, who had thrashed me countless times over the years, but nevertheless, I held in great esteem, had also departed this world, unexpectedly. What other disaster, I wondered, was waiting for me, in the shadows.

I for one felt his death, deeply, and openly grieved his passing for more than long enough. I also felt a certain amount of bitterness and anger, as the people who had influenced my life so much, were one by one, deserting me. Or so I felt.

Leonard Jackson, Bobby, Sylvia and now Mr Walton, all had powerful effects on my growth and unfortunate years, I couldn't help wondering, who or what next could happen.

My final exams, especially on all of my art subjects went well, with far higher marks achieved, than I genuinely expected. My final practical piece, for Heraldry, was a six foot, by four foot Coat of Arms, which was worked on over the whole of my final year. The ultimate accolade of a 97% pass mark, and the full Coat of Arms, in glorious colour and gilding work of pure gold and silver was presented to the Royal Town of Staines. I was even persuaded to attend the opening presentation, where it was proudly installed above the main entrance of the Staines Council offices.

The other nine academic subjects were all passed, with two subjects just squeezing into a pass mark.

Needless to say, one was maths and the other English.

My aunt was so chuffed, she asked both Bobby and myself to our new house in the New Forest, for the weekend.

I asked Bob, who was still coming to scouts, if he could manage a weekend, while he was undergoing his basic training. He explained, it could not be this weekend, but the following was okay, as he had a forty eight hour pass, and yes, he would be delighted.

I let my aunt know, by phone, on my return to school, that evening. It was pointed out to me by Patrick, that his pal Swany had been skipping some of his evening showers.

"Why?" I asked Pat

"Have you not noticed?" Pat asked me.

"Notice what?" I replied.

"He won't take a shower unless you're in the shower room" Pat said.

"I hadn't notice, but this can't go on, so I had better have a talk, one to one, with Swan," I said.

I promised Swany, I would leave him my chess set, but only if he had a shower every night without fail. He readily agreed, but I warned him, miss just one and he could kiss the chess set goodbye. That did the trick, Pat was able to tell me, months down the line.

One early morning, I noticed Pat get out of bed with his pyjama trousers on, which itself was unusual. On closer inspection, I called him over, and could see a large damp patch, as if he had pissed himself through the night. Pat knew exactly what I was thinking, and hasten to prove to me, he had not gone back in years of being an energetic bed wetter.

He leaned over my bed, which I was still in and made me feel for myself.

"You've been wanking yourself off, you dirty little bastard" I grinned at him.

"No, no" he said "I've just had my first wet dream" he was at length to explain, looking somewhat embarrassed.

I signalled him closer, and gave him a hug, whispering in his ear, he had nothing to either be embarrassed or ashamed about. A smile returned to his face, as he dropped his pyjamas and quickly donned his shorts, before running down to his ablutions.

Bob turned up at Ashford on Friday night to pick me up in readiness for our weekend at my aunts, as arranged.

I was looking for Bob arriving in a car, I thought he had, when instead he came roaring up the drive and into the yard on a 500cc B.S.A. motor cycle. I nearly fell over with surprise and excitement.

"Whose bike is it?" I asked Bob, out of breath with awe.

"Mine" replied Bob "I bought it last week, from a mate in dire need of cash. Great isn't it?"

"Wonderful," I said "but it looks brand new" I queried.

"Well, it's almost new, being only three months old." Bob said. "Come on, jump on, don't let us keep that wonderful aunt of yours waiting."

We sped out of Ashford, like a bat out of hell, me clinging onto Bobby for dear life.

Once on the open road, he opened her up to a cruising speed at a steady 60 m.p.h. It was fantastic and, as I began to relax, at Bob's skilful handling, I really enjoyed myself. That trip made me determined, that one day, I too would own such a marvellous machine.

We made the village of Burley in the New Forest in good time. My aunt had already prepared a sumptuous tupper for us both, and admired Bob's new motorbike. I was absolutely thrilled, making Bob promised to give me a lift back to school, come Sunday.

"You've got it" was Bob's only reply. I, on the other hand couldn't stop speaking about his new bike. I had a great evening helping Bob cleaning and polishing his new toy, and my aunt suggested Bob keep it in the garage, alongside her car, as there was ample room. At bed time, Bob noticed I was all tensed up, as he illustrated, yet another skill he had obtained, since he left Ashford.

He gave me my first body rub, or massage, manipulating my neck and shoulder muscles, with such ease and dexterity. It certainly made me feel great, as well as fully relaxed, ready for sleep. On Saturday we all went into Ringwood in my aunt's car, to do some shopping and after lunch, Bob took me on his bike, to Christchurch for the afternoon. We had a great time.

Bob, was forced to return to barracks by tea time, and I elected to go with him, on his bike, as promised. We were back at Ashford in no time, with the weekend disappearing faster, than a light summer shower of rain.

Before Bob roared off into the yonder, he explained to me that the next and last time he woud see me, would be his last weekend in the country, as his regiment were off to Korea, before the end of November1951.

I waved him off, realising this was less than ten weeks time.

I learnt, in my absence, that Mr Hammond had been promoted to Senior Housemaster, which joyfully, for most of the boys, was treated with great jubilation, much to the disgust of Mr Sims. Pat told me, with mischievous joy on his face, and in his voice, that our friend Hitler the second, spent the whole weekend, with a face like thunder. Swany chipped in with his own penny's worth, saying that Sims was having difficulty farting, his face was so screwed up, Swany said with glee.

My aunt was now fully retired, and well established in her lovely new house. She was determined to sort out the garden, now she had all the time in the world, to devote herself to her yearnings.

Harry demanded increasingly more help, from my aunt, and having lost Bruno, his beloved dog, he got more and more depressed. In reality, my aunt got more involved in village life, helping with this and that, neglecting her garden so much, that the local stable of riding ponies, were encouraged to graze the grass, of most of the two acres. They were thankful for the use of the field, as it was so close, just on the corner to the entrance of Honey Lane.

She asked me, what my intentions were, once I left Ashford, as regards to employment. We debated well into the night, that weekend on my own, but in all honesty, I felt when the time came, my job prospects were bound in reality, within London.

She understood, but was just hoping, I would come to live with her in the New Forest, on a full-time basis. We both knew this was a non-starter.

We also both realised, that finding worthwhile work of an artistic nature, and in her neck of the woods, was nigh impossible. Nevertheless, my aunt informed me, she would do her utmost to try. "Anyway," I said to my aunt "in truth, I have more than six months, before I need to worry too much about that bridge to cross."

At fifteen and a half, heading at breakneck speed towards my sixteenth birthday, I was determined to make the most of the run up to Christmas, which would certainly be my last landmark at Ashford. I spent as much time as I was permitted to, with the scouts, camping, hiking and rock climbing, as well as all the water based activities, there for the taking.

Gina, the scout master, informed me he had organised a bit of a send off do, for Bob on 12th November, the last weekend before Bob's embarkation by troop ship abroad. I was more than welcome to the sole use of the Scout hut that final Saturday night, before Bob departed on Sunday. How could I not accept his generous offer, as Gina explained he would pick me up on Sunday, to run me back to Ashford.

Bob had telephoned the school to pick me up first thing after breakfast, that Saturday morning. As arranged, he roared into school on his bike and uplifted me. For some reason, the short trip to Staines was somewhat solemn, completed in silence, save for the beat of the engine between out thighs. Slowly, the strong feeling and awareness, that something was wrong, overshadowed the occasion.

The morning, with most of our scouting mates about us, cheered up Bob, with the knowledge that all his friends, made over many joyous years, were all there for him. He was very much liked and respected, and was known as a bit of a character, always joking and playing tricks on the unsuspected.

Today, however, it was as if Bob had recently received a personality bypass, his mood was so different, which didn't go unnoticed.

After a bean feast of a lunch, which I noticed Bob ate very little, the boys began to go home. By early afternoon, all our mates, after cleaning away all the debris from the celebrations, had gone.

Bob was sitting on his own, on the river bank, looking somewhat glum. I suggested we take a sail in a nearby sailing Cadet dinghy. Bob just sat without saying a word, so I bent the sails on the cadet dinghy in readiness.

"Come on Bob, you miserable sod, or I'll sail away without you!"

He got to his feet and climbed into the boat, as I cast off, setting and trimming the sails, heading for mid river. We were taking turn about, Bob enjoying himself as we worked our way beating to windward, upstream.

After helming for a while, Bob indicated he wanted to relinquish the tiller, so we changed our positions, within the boat. During this delicate manoeuvre, Bob fell over the side and I was several boat lengths away, speeding across the tidal stream, before I realised he had gone.

I let fly the mainsheet, putting the helm hard aport, as the boat spun a full 180°, so I was now facing Bob, in the tidal race, flapping around with difficulty. I re-trimmed the boom, pointing the boat at Bob's position in the water. The dinghy under full sail, pulling on a maximum broad reach, haring along at speed, in danger of running him down. With only seconds to spare, just feet away from my target, I spun the boat into the eye of the wind, let go of the tiller, heaving Bob into the boat by his armpits.

He lay floundering in the bottom of the boats floorboards, spluttering like a beached whale. Having had one hell of a fright myself, I helmed back to the slip, where I quickly beached the boat, lifting the dagger board in time, before we came to rest on the slip.

Bob was still spluttering away, having swallowed half the river. Having tethered the dinghy securely, I helped Bob into the hut. Not a word passed between us, as in our own ways, we were both recovering from what could easily have been disastrous. After settling Bob comfortably into a warm sleeping bag, I took his clothes outside to dry them off.

I went into the galley to make us both a steaming hot mug of sweet tea, which Bob took willingly enough, but still without speaking. He obviously needed time to recover, I thought, so I busied myself in the galley preparing us something hot to eat. I kindled a fire in the grate, then pulled Bob's sleeping bag, with Bob still inside it, in front of the fire.

I soon had a simple hot meal of sausages, bacon, eggs and beans in front of Bob, who wolfed it down hungrily, having eaten so little at lunch. After washing the dishes, I made us both another mug of tea, and settled beside Bob on top of a spare set of blankets.

I later spread Bob's still damp clothing in front of the roaring fire to dry. I felt the time was ripe to attempt some kind of conversation with Bob, who hadn't spoken for several hours.

"Were you trying to avoid embarkation, tomorrow?" I asked jokingly.

Bob gave me an unpleasant stare, but didn't answer, any reply.

"Look Bob," I said uncharitably "if you continue to give me the cold shoulder, I'm going home!"

I could see from Bob's expression, I hade verbally wounded him, and wished I had kept my big mouth shut, as I saw Bob fighting back the tears. I quickly put my arms about him, assuring him I was just chiding him, and had no intentions of leaving him on his own.

"You know Bob," I said "I could really do with one of your body rubs as my lower shoulders are hurting me, after hauling you out of the water." Surprisingly he agreed, which I felt might take his troubled mind, off himself.

I laid myself out on top of a large bath towel, in front of the fire. Bob got out of his kip, and then shut the curtains, before kneeling over my back, as I spread eagled my body face down. Bob started with the back of my neck, before tackling my shoulders, un-knotting my tensed up muscles.

Keeping his mind and hands occupied, seemed to be helping Bob also, as I felt his legs relax, astride me.

"Just carry on down my whole body," I said to Bob, wanting the magic through his hands, to last forever.

Bob skilfully got to work, expertly down the entire length of my body, all the way to the very soles of my feet. Some twenty minutes later, Bob smacked my bum lightly, to indicate he was finished. As he climbed to his feet, to go back to his sleeping bag, I turned over onto my back and waited. Thankfully, Bob took the hint and got back down, kneeling between my spread apart legs.

"Fantastic" I said, as he finished my front.

"Right" I said "your turn, but I warn you now, my hands are nowhere near as skilful as yours."

He lay face down, with some reluctance, as I did my best to emulate his methods. Bob gave me great encouragement, as well as verbal guidance. By the time I started on his front, my own abilities got better, and I found it enjoyable as well as therapeutic. I was impressed with Bob's knowledge of all the body's pressure points, and the different medical names for the complex muscle system. Bob every week had several hours at a Turkish bath establishment, where he acquired, over time, all his present skills, he told me. While I was away at the loo, as well as making a final mug of tea, Bob had been busy remaking the bed into a double.

He chatted away, almost being his true self, but I felt Bob was putting on a brave face, concealing something from me. After a while, the feeling became even more persistent, and I was determined to challenge him sometime during the evening.

We talked into the small hours, when we should have both been fast asleep. Then, Bob told me about a premonition he had recently, of being killed in Korea. I now realised Bob's anxiety. I fell silent, having no answer, or words to part.

As shocking a statement that Bob had just made, leaving me flabbergasted, I knew instinctively, that any words of comfort I attempted to give to Bob, would be false, and meaningless. There were times for words, but this was definitely not one of them.

I cradled Bob into my arms, transmitting as much love and understanding as my body was able to give, as we both eventually fell fast asleep.

A few hours later, I felt Bob disentangle himself from my arms, assuming he needed the toilet, as I drifted back off to sleep. Sometime later, he woke me up, handing me a mug of tea and a biscuit, as I noticed he was fully dressed in full army garb. As that Sunday morning ripened, we cleared everything away neatly, removing any evidence of our presence. Locking the scout hut firmly behind us, as Gina drove up in his car.

Bob gave me one last kiss, with a big hug, fired his bike into life, then roared away in a cloud of smoke. A few moments later, I climbed into Gina's car beside him, as in total silence we returned to Ashford.

I just knew I would never see Bob again.

CHAPTER TWENTY-FOUR
Good Riddance

It was a very quiet Christmas, that year end of 1951. I went home to my aunt for a couple of weeks, more to get away from Ashford, and to lick my wounds.

Patrick came up for the second week, as he felt somewhat deserted, now that the Turner's had moved over to the States. He was so impressed with the new house, seeing it for the very first time. My aunt was fond of Patrick, as she preferred to call him, and always made him feel very much at home. He had been invited to spend the first week of his holiday with Miss Lowman, so he could be near his girlfriend Maisy, who he had a genuine affection for.

At night time, once alone in my bedroom, he would ask me all kinds of sexual questions, to do with his relationship with his girl Maisy. I did my best to guide him, in his urges, which Pat led me to believe, were very strong in his regards to his girlfriend. Swany, Pat assured me, was doing well, but was looking forward to the two of us returning, after our holiday.

I spent long periods on my own, leaving Pat to his own devices, with my aunt, while I took long rides on my bicycle into the countryside. Being the middle of winter didn't dissuade me, as I often preferred my own company. Other times, we would spend time together, reading our own books, often swapping reads with each other.

To be truthful, I couldn't wait for the turn of the year, when I could return to Art College, to finish my last three months there, especially knowing all my exams were over. It would be a solid period of art, with no academic schooling to worry about. Three months of solid artistic pleasure, would, for me, be pure heaven.

With the Christmas holidays now over, I used Ashford as a base only, throwing myself into all my outside interests, with such vigour, I was like an animal possessed.

In early January 1952 I went back to Wandsworth Art College, attending almost every 'Life Study' class on offer. I built up a portfolio, containing so many nudes, of both sexes, it was almost embarrassing.

One day, in the first days of February, I was standing back admiring my latest artistic effort, of a young woman's body, which I had worked very hard on, when without warning, I collapsed in a bundle on the floor, in front of my easel.

I was rushed to the Middlesex Teaching Hospital, the very place of my birth, with a raging high temperature, and in a coma!

It was almost two weeks, before I realised how ill I was, and even where I was. I had vague recollections of being turned onto my side, being injected in my rear end, by ladies in uniform. Apparently, once I was in hospital with such a high temperature, the only other thing that was wrong with me was a highly inflamed sore throat, which according to the doctors, meant I had tonsillitis.

They operated within the hour of arriving, but the anaesthetic tube, tore the back of my throat, making matters very much worse. For almost four weeks, I was injected every six hours, twenty-four hours a day, with penicillin, the new wonder drug of the day.

My aunt spent days at my bedside, and was nodding off, when I first came out of my coma. She was so pleased to see me, but kept on remarking how much weight I had lost. Several days later, my aunt came to see me again, carrying a small package, about the size of a book.

My very first words spoken for more than two weeks, to my aunt, just tripped off my tongue.

"It's Bobby, my brother, isn't it?

"Yes my darling" she said, as I studied her worried brow. I whispered in her ear, "my brother Bobby is dead!"

"Yes" my aunt replied "I'm so sorry, my darling, I really am, so sorry," whereby I tried to squeeze her hand, then gently feeling exhausted, I fell asleep again.

After four weeks, I had been injected with so much penicillin, my butt resembled a pin cushion. Later, in my early twenties, a single injection of penicillin almost killed me, as my body was to become violently allergic to this so called wonder drug.

As I regained my strength and interest on what was going on about me, I looked at the package, left by my aunt, in my bedside locker. I began to wonder, if it was wise, to open the package and decided, meanwhile to leave it.

At the weekend, in walked my aunt with both Pat and Swany in tow. Swany was beaming ear to ear, but my aunt quickly prevented him from jumping on my bed, to hug me to death. I gave him a wry smile, but he had to be content, to sit by me, holding my hand, in his sweaty palm. I was still too weak to argue or feel embarrassed. My aunt explained she would be taking them both for a treat later, before returning them back to Ashford.

I spent a total of six weeks in hospital, before I was fully recovered, and they, then operated to remove my tonsils. I could be discharged, but the hospital doctors insisted on a period of convalescence. So my aunt took me home to the New Forest. She noticed my package still in my locker, still unopened. It's not that I didn't want to open it. I was afraid it would only serve to confirm what I already knew, about Bob.

Towards the end of the journey, my aunt pulled over in to a layby, handing me the package. There was a set of motorbike keys, Bob's watch and the compass I had given him for his last birthday. There was also a sealed envelope addressed to me, just marked Paul.

I slit open the envelope and read Bob's last words to me.

"Paul, I've left you my motorbike, but more importantly, I leave you my love, please take great care of yourself. All my love Bob. X X X"

I returned to Ashford at the end of March fully recovered. My aunt explained to me, that Gina the Scoutmaster had been looking after Bob's motorbike, but was bringing it over to my aunts house for safe keeping, and for when I was ready for it.

My aunt would ask a mechanic from the local garage, to come and prepare it for storage in my aunts' garage.

By Monday, I was back in Wandsworth for my final week of art. The week went too quickly, and given a choice, I would like to have stayed on a lot longer. All good things must come to an end, I could here Bob saying in my head, as he was prone to say, often enough.

It was good to be back amidst some of my mates in the dorm, and Swany had been sleeping in my bed, keeping it warm for me, so he said. He was so good at chess, he had recently become Ashford champion, beating all comers, including staff members, or at least those brave enough to face him.

Pat flashed his thickening bush of pubic hair, with great pride, as I thought, Maisy would soon have to fight off his amorous advances, or maybe not, I smiled to myself.

On Sunday morning after breakfast and well before church parade, I was called to Fatty Arbuckle, the headmaster's office. I duly reported to him, wondering what he wanted me for.

"Ah, come in Ankorne, but don't sit down" he said, all official like. He looked up from behind his desk "Do you know what day it is tomorrow?" he asked.

"Monday, Sir" I said as quick as a flash.

"That's right," said Fatty "but it's also your sixteenth birthday" he assured me.

"That's right" I smiled, thinking he might have a birthday present for me, although I didn't hold my breath in excited anticipation, I thought.

"You leave tomorrow," he calmly said, which really knocked the wind out of my sails.

"Leave Ashford?" I queried.

"That's right," he said with just a glint of glee in his voice, as I could tell he was enjoying the moment.

"Where will I go from here?

"Not my problem" came his snappy reply, the smarmy git.

"But I don't have any money or a job" I spluttered, feeling very vulnerable.

"That's not my problem either, you're no longer 'our' responsibility," he answered, just a bit too smugly.

I looked at him in complete astonishment, then turned on my heels, as he shouted after me, "First thing Monday" he said.

I wandered around aimlessly for more than an hour, before making my way for one last visit to our secret pool. I sat for hours on my own, looking into the water where so much of my growing up had been spent. After much crying, I realised it was no longer our pool, mine and Bob's, it was now Pat's and Swany's place. I would find no answers here. Where can I hide, and feel safe, I wondered, at least until bedtime. My last bedtime in Ashford, I thought. I decided to skip lunch, I couldn't have eaten anyway, I was too choked up in self pity.

By teatime, my stomach was beginning to complain, so I decided it was time to face the music.

What was I afraid of? I asked myself, for years I had been looking forward to shaking this dump from beneath my feet. I had more than enough skills, to find a place to live and get myself a suitable job, I told myself with confidence.

"Just you wait and see," I said out loud, for Fatty Arbuckle's benefit, knowing he was well out of earshot. With a false smile on my face, but a genuine spring in my step, I headed back in time for tea.

While I was taking my last shower, with Pat on one side and Swany on the other, I realised that neither knew yet, of my imminent departure. I decided for the time being at least, to delay telling them, until bedtime. I didn't want their tears adding to the flood water of the showers.

At bedtime, delaying as long as possible before lights out, I called them both over to my bedside.

Swany sat on my bed, his usual smiling carefree self, and Pat sat beside him.

"Well Swany," I started cheerfully enough, as I reached into my locker, and took out Bob's old chess set off the shelf. "This is for you, but you must take great care of it."

"Pat," I looked at with more seriousness in my voice, "you must take good care of Swany, because tomorrow I leave Ashford, for good."

Pat nodded with understanding, having lost his voice momentarily. Swany burst into a flood of tears, sobbing his wee heart out, so I put my arm around him, in an effort to console him.

"And Pat," I said "you must take Swany to my aunt in the New Forest, as I've arranged for you both to have a good weekend there, providing Swany behaves himself."

Swany stopped crying, turning his water works off instantly, like a tap. Now all I have to do is ring my aunt to lay on the weekend visit, which I'm sure I could do, I thought to myself.

"Swany" I said "you move into my bed tomorrow, okay!" I told him.

He nodded his approval, with great gusto.

"Now go to bed" I ordered them both, "I've got a very busy day tomorrow." I lied.

In the morning I timed my departure, to coincide with all the boys heading for breakfast, as I told myself, it was time to make my final move.

I had a quick word with the gate keeper, turning to look at Ashford, for the very last time

I walked through the gate, onto Woodthorpe Road, with a brown paper parcel, tucked under my arm, and a bag of mischief sweets in my pocket, which I forgot to give to Swany.

'Mischief in Long Trousers' is a sequel to 'A pocket full of mischief', by the same author, and is the second book of a trilogy.

In his second book, the opening scene starts on his sixteenth birthday when Paul is forced to leave Ashford residential school an orphanage run by the London County Council that housed a thousand children of both sexes.

In April 1952 having walked through the Institutes Lodge gates for the last time Paul finds himself utterly alone for the very first time in his young life.

Home-less, job-less, and penniless, after thirteen years in residential care, with no assistance whatsoever Paul is now expected to make his own way in the hard knock world of reality and out with the care of the London County Council (L.C.C.)

Leaving this place under dramatic and tragic circumstances, Paul's endeavours to carve a niche in society for himself, is both funny and adventurous in it's self.

Until his eighteenth birthday where once again Paul finds himself thrown into yet another regimental regime, simply known in the 1950's as National Service. The resentment that Paul feels for the loss of his freedom once more just to earn the "Queens Shilling" is understandable, but with an unquenchable thirst for adventure he is easily persuaded to sign on for three years, guaranteeing him excitement overseas on active service with the *RIFLE BRIGADE.* (An elite regiment of the British Army.)

Adventures, in Kenya and Malaya with the armed services, and helping to establish the first "Outward Bound" climbing school on Mount Kilamanjaro in Tanganyika, (East Africa) are just some of the madcap adventures that Paul enjoys undertaking.

The offer from a British Mountaineering expedition to the Himalayas was just to good to pass up, so Paul expends a great deal of energy in convincing the "Powers that be" to allow him to get demobbed in Singapore. Eventually the Army were more than happy to get rid of him and granted demob status in Singapore, as the only soldier in 1957 within the "Far Eastern Command" to be released.

With almost nine months in hand before joining the expedition in Nepal, Paul decided to walk overland from Singapore to India.

'Forbidden journey' two simple words, proved for Paul the hardest undertaking of his life.

This trek lasting almost a full year, should really be a book in it's own right. Needless to say with excitement in his heart, lots of determination stirring his hungry loins and with just the right amount of madness tingeing his young befuddled brain, Paul set about this journey with an overdose of enthusiasm and a large portion of ignorance.

The several near death experiences he encounters along the way are very graphic, pulling no punches which illustrates vividly just how stupid he was in daring to undertake such a punishing journey.

Through the length of Malaya (the easy bit), across Thailand (or Siam) and into Burma, where anywhere north of Mandalay was strictly forbidden and was over run by opium gangs and Dacoits* who ruled by the gun.

It was as if Paul had acquired a kind of death wish, at this stage in his young life (perhaps he had), the hard slog up through the Hukong Valley (otherwise known as the 'Valley of Death') and picking up several tropical diseases along the way, Paul somehow manages to struggle over the 13,000ft high Paunsaw Pass into Assam India.

On arrival at Nampong the first village in Assam, Paul is thrown into a deep hole in the ground by the headman in authority and also the chief of Police, who refused to believe Paul had come overland through Burma.

This second book ends shortly after his arrival in India, where the author now 22 years of age is desperate to find employment that will keep him in India, having decided he no longer had any desire to return to England.

His future success and exploits in this fantastic country is the subject of a third book to complete the trilogy.